The SYBEX Prompter Series

dBASE
INSTANT
REFERENCE

To Susan and the Egg, once again

The SYBEX Prompter Series

We've designed the SYBEX Prompter Series to meet the evolving needs of software users, who want essential information presented in an accessible format. Our best authors have distilled their expertise into compact *Instant Reference* books you can use to look up the precise use of any command—its syntax, available options, and operation. More than just summaries, these books also provide realistic examples and insights into effective usage drawn from our author's wealth of experience.

The SYBEX Prompter Series also includes these titles:

WordPerfect Instant Reference
Greg Harvey and Kay Yarborough Nelson

DOS Instant Reference
Greg Harvey and Kay Yarborough Nelson

Turbo BASIC Instant Reference
Douglas Hergert

Lotus 1-2-3 Instant Reference
Greg Harvey and Kay Yarborough Nelson

The SYBEX Prompter™ Series

dBASE®
INSTANT
REFERENCE

Alan Simpson

San Francisco • Paris • Düsseldorf • London

The SYBEX Prompter Series
Editor in Chief: Dr. Rudolph S. Langer
Managing Editor: Barbara Gordon
Series Editor: James A. Compton
Editor: Judy Ziajka

Screen printing in this book was produced with XenoFont from XenoSoft, Berkeley, CA.

Library of Congress Card Number: 87-63042
ISBN 0-89588-484-4
Manufactured in the United States of America
10 9 8 7 6 5 4 3 2 1

TABLE OF CONTENTS

Introduction   vii

Chapter 1: User-Assistance Commands   1

Chapter 2: Commands to Create and Use Database
           Files   11

Chapter 3: Commands to Add New Data   21

Chapter 4: Commands for Custom Screens   34

Chapter 5: Commands for Printing Data   64

Chapter 6: Commands for Editing and Deleting
           Records   83

Chapter 7: Commands for Sorting and Indexing   100

Chapter 8: Commands for Locating and Querying
           Data   113

Chapter 9: Commands for Performing Calculations   126

Chapter 10: Commands for Managing Files   135

Chapter 11: Commands for Managing Multiple
            Database Files   160

Chapter 12: Programming Commands   177

Chapter 13: Commands for Procedures and Param-
            eters   207

Chapter 14: Commands for Memory Variables   217

Chapter 15: Debugging Commands   231

Chapter 16: dBASE Functions   248

Chapter 17: SET Commands   342

Chapter 18: Event Processing and Error Trapping   413

Chapter 19: Commands for Networking   422

**Chapter 20: Commands for Running External Pro-
grams**   441

**Appendix A: Configuring and Starting dBASE III
PLUS**   450

Command Index   469

Function Index   471

Introduction

At last count, dBASE III PLUS consisted of 166 commands and 74 functions. Few of us, including the real power users, can remember the details of every command and function. This book was written to provide quick and easy access to all those little tidbits that are easily forgotten, and contains all the nitty-gritty details that we are likely to forget (or perhaps never knew) and some undocumented tricks and information about unexpected bugs as well.

This book is terse; it contains little chit-chat and hand-holding. Here we just stick to the facts. So, without any further ado, we'll pinpoint exactly the type of dBASE user this book is intended for.

Who Should Use This Book

This book is specifically designed for experienced, and perhaps frequent, users of dBASE, primarily dBASE III PLUS. It is not intended as a tutorial for beginning users or beginning programmers. Instead, this book is designed to provide quick access to specific information about particular dBASE commands, functions, and, to some extent, techniques.

If you are just learning dBASE or feel that you need tutorial support, you might want to read one of the many tutorials available on dBASE III PLUS. For example, my own *Understanding dBASE III PLUS* and *Understanding dBASE III*, both published by SYBEX, are specifically designed for dBASE beginners. My book *Advanced Techniques in dBASE III PLUS*, also published by SYBEX, provides training in dBASE III PLUS programming for those making the transition from one-command-at-a-time mode to command file use and custom applications development.

Versions of dBASE Addressed

The focus of this book is on dBASE III PLUS, which has largely supplanted dBASE III. However, most dBASE III PLUS commands are also available in dBASE III. To assist the hundreds of thousands of people still using dBASE III (and the programmers who maintain applications for them), this book notes which commands are available only in dBASE III PLUS. If a command operates differently in the older program, that fact is noted here, but it is not within the scope of this book to describe those differences at any usable level of detail. Consult your dBASE III PLUS documentation for information about version differences.

Within dBASE III PLUS, the few differences between version 1.0 and 1.1 are described in the appropriate entries' "Usage" sections.

How to Use This Book

The commands in this book are listed by topic, rather than in encyclopedic, A to Z order. This is so that you can quickly reference all the commands that relate to a particular task and thereby make some decisions about which approach to take. In addition, this structure may also inform you of alternative techniques that you were not aware of for performing some task.

There is, of course, a command index at the back of the book that will help you to locate a specific dBASE command or function.

In short then, when you want to know what commands are available to you to perform a given task, use the table of contents to look up the general category of commands you are interested in. When you already know which command you need but need some reminders about how to use the command properly, refer to the index at the back of the book for the page references for that command.

Acknowledgments

All books are a team project, and this one is certainly no exception. Much credit and thanks are due the following people:

To everyone at SYBEX who guided and supported me through this project, including Judy Ziajka, who edited the entire manuscript; and Jim Compton, series editor; John Kadyk and Maria Mart, word processing; Michelle Hoffman, graphics assistant; Cheryl Vega, typesetting; Ingrid Owen, design; Karin Lundstrom and Lucie Zivny, art and pasteup, and Winnie Kelly, proofreading.

To Mitchell E. Timin of Timin Engineering, Inc., for contributions to Chapter 20.

To Mick Keily for many contributions to Chapters 16 and 17.

To Bill, Cynthia, Tara, and Syrus Gladstone, our friends, family, and literary agents.

And to my wife Susan, who once again supported me through a long and demanding project while carrying a pretty demanding nine-month project of her own.

User-Assistance Commands

As you work with dBASE, you can get help directly on your screen in two ways: by using the ASSIST mode, which provides a menu for building dBASE commands, and by using HELP, which presents brief descriptions of dBASE commands. Both ASSIST and HELP are discussed in this chapter.

The ASSIST Command

Accessing the Assistant Menu

The ASSIST command calls up the dBASE Assistant menu, a menu-driven aid to building command lines.

SYNTAX

ASSIST

VERSION

dBASE III PLUS, dBASE III (with significant differences)

USAGE

The Assistant menu provides a top menu, as shown in Figure 1.1, of major database management functions. Pressing the ← and → keys moves across the top menu, displaying additional options in a pull-down menu (in Figure 1.1, the pull-down menu for the Set Up option is displayed).

The ↑ and ↓ keys move the highlight up and down through pull-down menu options. Pressing the Return key selects the currently highlighted menu option. Pressing ← erases a submenu and returns to the higher-level menu. Pressing F1 displays help information for the currently highlighted menu item.

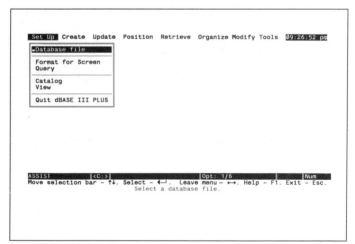

Figure 1.1: Assistant Menu

Many options are available only after a database file is opened with the Database File option under the Set Up menu. Those options that are available on the menu are displayed in brighter print.

As you select options from the Assistant menu, dBASE builds a *command line* above the status bar (in an area of the screen referred to as the *action line*). Table 1.1 lists all the Assistant menu options and the dBASE command that each option accesses. For more information about a particular item, look up the associated dBASE command in the index to this book.

To leave a pull-down menu and return to the higher-level menu, press the ← key. To leave the Assistant menu altogether and access the dBASE dot prompt, press the Esc key. If the status bar remains at the bottom of the screen and you wish to remove it, type the command **SET STATUS OFF** and press the Return key.

EXAMPLES

To open a database file from Assist mode, highlight the Database File option on the Set Up pull-down menu and press Return. The action line shows *Command: USE,* indicating that you've accessed the USE command. The screen presents a list of disk drive options (for example, *A:, B:, C:*). Highlight the letter representing the disk drive on which the database you want to access is located and then press Return. The action line displays the disk drive name with the command (for example, *USE C:*), and the screen displays a list of any existing database file names.

Using the ↑ and ↓ keys, highlight the name of the database file you wish to open and then press Return to select that file. The file name appears in the action line (for example, *USE C:MAIL*), and the screen displays the question *Is the file indexed [Y/N]*. If you answer **Y**, the screen displays a list of any existing index file names. You can select up to seven index files by highlighting the index file name and pressing Return. These too are added to the command line. For example, if you select an index file called Names.ndx, the command line reads *USE C:Mail INDEX NAMES.*

When you do not wish to select any more index files, press ← to return to the higher-level menu. The name of the currently selected database file appears near the center of the status bar.

ASSISTANT MENU OPTION	dBASE COMMAND	FUNCTION
Set Up		
Database file	USE	Opens an existing database file
Format for Screen	SET FORMAT	Opens a format file
Query	SET FILTER	Opens a query file
Catalog	SET CATALOG	Opens a catalog file
View	SET VIEW	Opens a view file
Quit dBASE III PLUS	QUIT	Exits dBASE back to DOS
Create		
Database file	CREATE	Creates a database file
Format file	MODIFY SCREEN	Creates a format file
View	MODIFY VIEW	Creates a view file
Query	MODIFY QUERY	Creates a query file
Report	MODIFY REPORT	Creates a report format
Label	MODIFY LABEL	Creates a label format
Update		
Append	APPEND	Adds records to a database
Edit	EDIT	Changes a database record
Display	DISPLAY	Displays the contents of a record

Table 1.1: Summary of Assistant Menu Options

ASSISTANT MENU OPTION	dBASE COMMAND	FUNCTION
Update (continued)		
Browse	BROWSE	Changes database records
Replace	REPLACE	Globally changes database records
Delete	DELETE	Deletes database records
Recall	RECALL	Un-deletes records marked for deletion
Pack	PACK	Permanently removes records marked for deletion
Position		
Seek	SEEK	Locates a record in an indexed file
Locate	LOCATE	Locates a record in a database file
Continue	CONTINUE	Repeats the last LOCATE operation
Skip	SKIP	Moves the record pointer forward or backward
Goto Record	GOTO	Moves the pointer to a particular record
Retrieve		
List	LIST	Displays database records
Display	DISPLAY	Displays records with pause for full screens

Table 1.1: Summary of Assistant Menu Options (continued)

ASSISTANT MENU OPTION	dBASE COMMAND	FUNCTION
Retrieve (continued)		
Report	REPORT FORM	Displays data using a predefined report format
Label	LABEL FORM	Displays data in predefined mailing label format
Sum	SUM	Adds values in a numeric field
Average	AVERAGE	Averages values in a numeric field
Count	COUNT	Counts the number of records
Organize		
Index	INDEX	Creates an index file
Sort	SORT	Creates a sorted database file
Copy	COPY	Copies a database file
Modify		
Database file	MODIFY STRUCTURE	Modifies a database file structure
Format file	MODIFY SCREEN	Modifies a format file
View	MODIFY VIEW	Modifies a view file
Query	MODIFY QUERY	Modifies a query file
Label	MODIFY LABEL	Modifies a label format

Table 1.1: Summary of Assistant Menu Options (continued)

ASSISTANT MENU OPTION	dBASE COMMAND	FUNCTION
Modify (continued)		
Report	MODIFY REPORT	Modifies a report format
Tools		
Set Drive	SET DEFAULT	Assigns a default disk drive
Copy File	COPY FILE	Copies any file
Directory	DIR	Displays file names
List Structure	LIST STRUCTURE	Displays database structure
Rename	RENAME	Renames a file
Erase	ERASE	Erases a file
Import	IMPORT	Converts PFS data to dBASE format
Export	EXPORT	Converts dBASE data to PFS format

Table 1.1: Summary of Assistant Menu Options (continued)

TIPS

The Assistant menu provides only limited access to the full capabilities of dBASE. However, it is a useful teaching tool if you watch the command lines that ASSIST builds as you select menu items.

The Config.db file determines whether or not the Assistant menu appears automatically when dBASE is first run from the DOS prompt.

SEE ALSO

HELP

The HELP Command
Displaying Help Screens

The HELP command displays the dBASE help screen for general help or for help with a particular command or function. The file named Help.dbs, which came with your dBASE package, must be on the same disk and directory as your dBASE.ovl file for help to be accessible from the dot prompt. For help to be accessible from the Assistant menu, the file named Assist.hlp must be on the same disk and drive as your dBASE.ovl file.

SYNTAX

HELP *[command/function]*

where *command/function* is the name of the command or function you want help with.

VERSION

dBASE III PLUS, dBASE III

USAGE

To access the dBASE help system main menu, press F1, or type the command **HELP** at the dot prompt and press Return. The help system main menu will appear on the screen, as shown in Figure 1.2. Use the ↑ and ↓ keys to highlight the topic you wish to explore and then press Return to select the topic. Optionally, move the highlight to the bottom of the screen (next to the *ENTER >* prompt), type the particular command or function you need help with, and press Return. Press F10 at any time to redisplay the help system main menu.

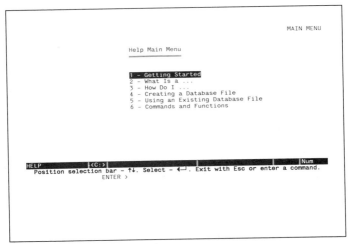

Figure 1.2: Help system main menu

For help with a particular command or function, type **HELP** followed by the name of the command or function you need help with directly at the dot prompt. (From the Assistant menu, highlight the menu option you need help with and then press F1).

Pressing PgUp displays the previous page in the help system. Pressing F10 displays the previous menu in the help system. Entering a new command after the bottom *ENTER >* displays the help screen for that command. To leave the help system and return to the dot prompt, press Esc.

If the SET HELP parameter is on, help is also available automatically whenever an error occurs. The dBASE program will display the prompt *Do you want some help? (y/n)*. Type **Y** to access the help system.

EXAMPLES

Entering the command **HELP REPORT** at the dot prompt displays the help screen shown in Figure 1.3. The syntax portion displays the general syntax of the command, with optional parameters displayed in brackets ([ ]). The description section displays a brief explanation of the command. Pressing Esc leaves the help screen and returns control to the dot prompt.

```
                                                                    REPORT
                                        REPORT
                                        ‾‾‾‾‾‾

      Syntax      :   REPORT FORM <report form file>/? [<scope>] [FOR <condition>]
                          [WHILE <condition>] [PLAIN] [HEADING <expC>]
                          [NOEJECT] [TO PRINT] [TO FILE <file>] [SUMMARY]
      Description :   Displays a tabular report file generated with
                      CREATE/MODIFY REPORT.
                      Use ? to display a list of available form files.




   HELP                    <C:>                                            Num
   Previous screen - PgUp. Previous menu - F1Ø. Exit with Esc or enter a command.
                           ENTER >
```

*Figure 1.3: Help screen displayed by the HELP REPORT
command*

Note that the option to use ? in lieu of a report format file name, as
shown in the help screen, works only when a catalog file is in effect
(see SET CATALOG).

TIPS

The SET HELP command determines whether help is automatically available when an error occurs. If the error was caused by a
misspelled command, the help system main menu appears, rather
than the help screen for the particular command.

SEE ALSO

ASSIST
SET HELP
ON ERROR

Commands to Create and Use Database Files

This chapter discusses the commands for creating and using database files: CREATE and USE. To most experienced dBASE users, these commands will undoubtedly be "old hat." However, these commands do provide some advanced options, such as the use of ALIAS with USE and the use of FROM with CREATE, that may be news to even experienced users.

For additional information about handling dBASE files, refer to the commands listed in the "See Also" sections accompanying the command descriptions that follow.

The CREATE Command

Creating a New Database File

The CREATE command allows you to define a structure for a new database file.

SYNTAX

CREATE *file name* [**FROM** *structure extended file*]

where *file name* is the name of the new database file to create. The FROM option uses a special *structure-extended file* created with the COPY STRUCTURE EXTENDED command, as discussed under the COPY command in Chapter 10, "Commands for Managing Files."

VERSION

dBASE III PLUS, dBASE III

USAGE

From the Assistant menu, you can access the CREATE command by highlighting Create on the top menu and selecting the Database File option from the pull-down menu. When you select this option, you'll be asked to designate the disk drive for the new file (for example, B: or C:) and a name for the new database file. If you use the CREATE command from the dot prompt to create the database file, the new database is created on the currently logged drive and directory unless otherwise specified. The dBASE program adds the extension .dbf to the name of the file you provide.

The USE command, which opens existing database files, also assumes the .dbf extension.

A database file name can be up to eight characters long (excluding the extension). Never use the letters A through J alone as database file names, as dBASE will confuse these with the SELECT A through SELECT J commands. The file names Abcdefgh.dbf and AA.dbf are both valid, but the file name A.dbf is not.

Each database field name can be up to 10 characters long. Field names must begin with a letter and should not be the same as any command or even a valid abbreviation of a command. (Technically, dBASE *allows* field names that are the same as a command, but it will sometimes handle them incorrectly, causing your program to behave unpredictably.) The only punctuation allowed in field names is the underscore (_) character. Examples of valid and invalid field names are shown in Table 2.1.

Each field must be assigned one of the five data types (character, numeric, date, logical, or memo) by typing the initial letter of the data type. Date, logical, and memo fields are assigned widths automatically. You must assign widths to the other data types. You must also assign a number of decimal places to the numeric data type.

CREATE displays error messages and instructions for managing the cursor at the bottom of the screen. In addition, pressing the F1 key toggles a help menu on and off. The cursor cannot be scrolled beyond an incompletely or improperly defined field.

Up to 128 fields can be entered into a database structure, with a maximum combined width of 4,000 characters.

Use the PgUp and PgDn keys to scroll from page to page of field names. The Ctrl-N keys allow you to insert a new field at the currently highlighted position. The Ctrl-U keys delete the field at the currently highlighted position. Table 2.2 lists all the control keys used with the CREATE command.

VALID FIELD NAME	INVALID FIELD NAME
FirstName	1stName (begins with a number)
Last_Name	Last Name (contains a space)
Restaurant	Rest (name of a scope condition)
F_Other	Record (name of a scope condition)
Is_Ready	Is:Ready (colon not acceptable punctuation)

Table 2.1: Examples of Valid and Invalid Field Names

KEY	ALTERNATE	EFFECT
Return		Finishes data entry in one field and moves cursor to next field
F1		Toggles help menu on and off
Num Lock		Toggles numbers/arrow keys on numeric keypad
→	Ctrl-D	Moves cursor right one character
←	Ctrl-S	Moves cursor left one character
Ctrl-→	Ctrl-B	Pans to the right
Ctrl-←	Ctrl-Z	Pans to the left
Home	Ctrl-A	Moves cursor to previous word, start of field, or previous field, depending on cursor's current position
End	Ctrl-F	Moves cursor to next word, end of field, or start of next field, depending on cursor's current position
PgUp	Ctrl-R	Scrolls to previous page, if any
PgDn	Ctrl-C	Scrolls to next page, if any
↑	Ctrl-E	Moves cursor to previous field
↓	Ctrl-X	Moves cursor to next field
Ins	Ctrl-V	Toggles insert mode on/off
Del	Ctrl-G	Deletes character at cursor

Table 2.2: Control Keys Used with the CREATE Command

KEY	ALTERNATE	EFFECT
Backspace		Moves cursor to left, erasing character
Ctrl-T		Deletes word to right
Ctrl-Y		Deletes all characters to right
Ctrl-U		Deletes field
Esc	Ctrl-Q	Aborts current structure and exits CREATE/MODIFY STRUCTURE mode
Ctrl-End	Ctrl-W	Saves current structure and exits CREATE/MODIFY STRUCTURE mode

Table 2.2: Control Keys Used with the CREATE Command (continued)

Typing ^**W** or ^**End** saves the current database structure and presents the prompt *Press ENTER to confirm. Any other key to resume.* Pressing the Return key saves the current structure. Pressing any other keys moves the highlight back into the screen for defining the database structure.

When you save the database structure, the screen presents the prompt *Input data records now? (y/n).* Typing **Y** moves you directly to the APPEND mode for entering new records. Typing **N** returns you to the dot prompt.

The CREATE FROM command copies a structure-extended file back to a standard database structure. (See the COPY command in Chapter 10, "Commands for Managing Files," for a definition and example of a structure-extended file.)

EXAMPLES

The following command lets you define a new database file named MyData.dbf on the currently logged disk drive and directory.

CREATE MyData.dbf

Figure 2.1 shows a sample database structure created for the MyData database. In this example, all data types are represented: character, numeric, logical, date, and memo. Note that the numeric data type includes a specification for the number of decimal places (two in this example).

TIPS

If you use the COPY STRUCTURE EXTENDED and CREATE FROM commands together in a command file, you can give your users the same power to modify a database structure that they get with the MODIFY STRUCTURE command, while maintaining more program control over the user's changes than you can with MODIFY STRUCTURE.

SEE ALSO

MODIFY STRUCTURE
DISPLAY STRUCTURE
COPY
APPEND

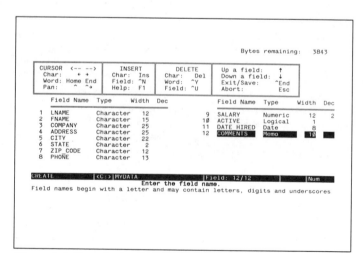

Figure 2.1: Sample database structure on the CREATE screen

The USE Command

Opening an Existing File

The USE command opens an existing database file and can also activate any existing index files and assign an alias name for use as a pointer when multiple database files are in use.

SYNTAX

USE *file name [***INDEX** *index files][***ALIAS** *alias name]*

where *file name* is the name of an existing database file. The optional INDEX *index files* command can include up to seven index files that have been created previously with the INDEX ON command. The optional ALIAS *alias name* command can provide a name that can be used as a pointer when you use multiple databases simultaneously. If you've intentionally assigned a file-name extension other than .dbf to a database, you must specify the extension in the USE command, as in **USE Customer.dat**.

VERSION

dBASE III PLUS, dBASE III

USAGE

The USE command alone (with no file name) closes the database in the currently selected work area. If the database opened by the USE command contains a memo field, the .dbt file containing the memo field is opened automatically by the USE command. If the .dbt file has been erased or corrupted, the following error message appears: *.DBT file cannot be opened.* To rectify the problem, you'll need to either locate the missing .DBF file or use the MODIFY COMMAND editor to create a new, empty file with the appropriate file name and the .DBT extension.

USE with Variables

If the name of the database you want to open is stored in a memory variable, the variable name must be treated as a macro. For example, the following commands store the file name MyFile in a variable named SomeFile. The USE command attempts to open MyFile.dbf (rather than SomeFile.dbf) because of the macro substitution (&).

```
SomeFile = "MyFile"
USE &SomeFile
```

USE with the INDEX Command

Any index files that are listed to the right of the INDEX portion of the USE command are automatically updated whenever any command adds, changes, deletes, or packs data. By default, the first-listed index file is the controlling (or *master*) index file, which determines the sort order for displays and the fields that can be located with the FIND and SEEK commands. (The SET ORDER command, however, can specify any index file in the list as the controlling index file.)

If no index files are specified in the USE command, the record pointer automatically points to the first record in the database when the database is opened. If one or more index files are listed in the INDEX portion of the command, the pointer will point to the first (top) record in the controlling index file.

USE with the ALIAS Command

The optional ALIAS command specifies a name to be used with a work-area pointer when multiple database files are in use simultaneously. In the following example, the file named Customer is opened with the alias Lookup. The LIST command uses this alias to display the LName and FName fields from the Customer database.

```
SELECT A
USE Charges
SELECT B
```

```
USE Customer INDEX Customer ALIAS Lookup
SELECT A
SET RELATION TO CustNo INTO Lookup
LIST CustNo,Lookup->FName,Lookup->LName,Part_No
```

Note also that the alias is used directly in the SET RELATION command. The alias can be used as the name of the file or the work area. For example, the command SELECT Lookup is equivalent to the command SELECT B in the preceding example.

USE with Catalogs

If a data catalog has been created and opened, the command USE ? displays the names of all database files in the catalog, along with any index files that were created while the catalog was in effect. USE *file name* also adds a new file name to an open catalog if the file name was not already defined for the catalog.

EXAMPLES

The following command opens a database named Members and two index files named Names.ndx and Zips.ndx.

USE Members INDEX Names,Zips

In this example, Names is the controlling index and will determine both the sort order in which records are displayed and the fields that can be accessed with the SEEK and FIND commands. However, both the Names and Zips index files will be updated whenever any data is added to, changed in, or deleted from the database.

TIPS

To see which database, index files, and aliases are in use at any given moment, use the DISPLAY STATUS command. To close all open databases, use the CLOSE DATABASES command. To close all active index files, use the CLOSE INDEX command.

SEE ALSO

SELECT
INDEX
REINDEX
CLOSE
SET INDEX
SET ORDER
SET CATALOG

3

Commands to Add New Data

There are basically two techniques for adding data to a dBASE database. One is to type new information, record by record, onto the screen. The APPEND and INSERT commands, discussed in this chapter, let you add new data in this fashion.

Both the APPEND and INSERT commands automatically present simple screens for entering data. If you are interested in developing fancier custom screens for data entry, see the MODIFY SCREEN, SET FORMAT, and @...SAY...GET commands in Chapter 4 "Commands for Custom Screens."

A second way to add new data to a database is to copy data from one file onto the bottom of another file. The APPEND FROM and IMPORT commands provide these capabilities. APPEND FROM can be used for appending data from one dBASE database to the bottom of another or for importing data from spreadsheets and ASCII files into dBASE databases. IMPORT imports data from a PFS:FILE database into a dBASE III PLUS database.

The APPEND Command

Adding New Records to a Database

APPEND allows new records to be added to the bottom of the database currently in use.

SYNTAX

APPEND

VERSION

dBASE III PLUS, dBASE III

USAGE

The APPEND command initiates full-screen data entry mode for adding new records to a database. Use the command keys shown in Table 3.1 to control the screen and cursor. These work both for the simple screen that APPEND shows automatically and for a fancier screen that you design yourself with the MODIFY SCREEN command.

APPEND can add data only to a single database file. If several database files are open and related, APPEND adds data only to the currently selected file.

Any currently active index files are automatically updated and resorted. Any inactive index files are not updated and will need to be rebuilt using the INDEX ON or REINDEX command.

The master index file, if any, controls the order in which PgUp and PgDn scroll through records. If there is no active index file, scrolling takes place in sequential record number order.

Some newly added records are stored in a buffer before being written to disk. A CLOSE DATABASES, CLOSE ALL, USE, or QUIT command transfers all new records from the buffer to the database file.

KEY	ALTERNATE	EFFECT
Return		Finishes data entry in one field and moves cursor to next field
F1		Toggles help menu on/off (if no format file is in use)
Num Lock		Toggles number/arrow keys on numeric keypad
→	Ctrl-D	Moves cursor right one character
←	Ctrl-S	Moves cursor left one character
Home	Ctrl-A	Moves cursor to previous word, start of field, or previous field, depending on cursor's current position
End	Ctrl-F	Moves cursor to next word, end of field, or start of next field, depending on cursor's current position
PgUp	Ctrl-R	Scrolls to previous page or record, if any
PgDn	Ctrl-C	Scrolls to next page or record, if any; otherwise, exits EDIT mode
↑	Ctrl-E	Moves cursor to previous field
↓	Ctrl-X	Moves cursor to next field
Ins	Ctrl-V	Toggles insert mode on/off
Del	Ctrl-G	Deletes character at cursor
Backspace		Moves cursor to left, erasing existing character
Ctrl-T		Deletes word to right
Ctrl-Y		Deletes all characters to right

Table 3.1: Command Keys Used with the APPEND Command

Key	Alternate	Effect
Ctrl-U		Marks record for deletion
Esc	Ctrl-Q	Aborts last entry and exits EDIT mode (if a memo field is being entered, aborts current entry and returns to EDIT screen)
Ctrl-End	Ctrl-W	Saves entry and exits EDIT mode
Ctrl-PgDn	Ctrl-Home	Edits a memo field
Ctrl-PgUp	Ctrl-End	Saves a memo field and returns to EDIT screen (when entering a memo field)

Table 3.1: Command Keys Used with the APPEND Command (continued)

If the SET CARRY option is ON, all data entered into a record is automatically carried over to the next newly added record.

The APPEND command is accessible from the Assistant menu by highlighting the Update option on the top menu and selecting Append from the pull-down menu.

EXAMPLES

The following commands open the Mail database and MailScr format file and allow you to add new records using the screen defined in the format file. The CLOSE FORMAT command returns the screen to its default state.

```
USE Mail
SET FORMAT TO MailScr
APPEND
CLOSE FORMAT
```

SEE ALSO

APPEND BLANK   BROWSE
APPEND FROM   READ
INSERT   CLOSE FORMAT
SET FORMAT

The **APPEND BLANK** Command
Adding a Blank Record to a Database

The APPEND BLANK command adds a blank record to the bottom of the database currently in use.

SYNTAX

APPEND BLANK

VERSION

dBASE III PLUS, dBASE III

USAGE

APPEND BLANK adds a single blank record to a database that can be filled in using a READ command with a custom screen. If a format file is open, the READ command will use the screen defined in that file.

The newly added blank record is always the current record until some action is taken to move the record pointer. Any active index files are immediately updated, just as with the APPEND command.

EXAMPLES

In the following commands, the Mail database and MailScr format files are opened, a blank record is added to the database, and the READ command allows data to be entered into the new blank record.

USE Mail
SET FORMAT TO MailScr
APPEND BLANK
READ
CLOSE FORMAT

TIPS

APPEND BLANK and READ are generally used for customized data-entry programs that allow a user to add only one record at a time. Such programs can provide sophisticated data validation constraints that limit the user to entering data that meets certain requirements.

SEE ALSO

APPEND   BROWSE
APPEND FROM   READ
INSERT   CLOSE FORMAT
SET FORMAT

The APPEND FROM Command
Adding Records from Another Database

APPEND FROM appends database records from an external file to the currently selected database file.

SYNTAX

APPEND FROM *file name [***FOR** *condition] [***TYPE** *file type]*

where *file name* is the name of the file to append records from, *condition* is any valid query criterion, and *file type* defines the format of the foreign file.

VERSION

dBASE III PLUS, dBASE III (DBF, SDF, and DELIMITED files only)

USAGE

When data are appended from one dBASE database to another, only data with identical field names in both databases are appended to the currently active database. If the width of a field in the active database is less than the width of the database being read, any character data will be truncated to fit the new width. Large numbers that do not fit into the currently active database are replaced with asterisks.

The current disk drive and directory are assumed, unless otherwise specified in the *file name* parameter of the APPEND FROM command. The extension .dbf is assumed in the file name being read, unless otherwise specified in the *file name* parameter. If the database from which you are reading does not have a file name extension, place a period at the end of the file name in the APPEND FROM command.

If SET DELETED is off, records marked for deletion are read into the current database but are *not* marked for deletion in the current database. If SET DELETED is on, records marked for deletion are not read into the active database file at all.

The FOR expression works only with fields that exist in both database files.

The TYPE expression defines the structure of a non-dBASE data file and allows you to import data from foreign software systems into an existing dBASE database. To import ASCII text files, first open a dBASE database (with USE or CREATE) with a structure that matches the structure of the file being imported. Then issue the

APPEND FROM command with the appropriate TYPE option for the data being imported.

If the ASCII file being imported is in SDF (structured data format), the fields will be the same width in each record (i.e., the data will be in a tabular format). Each record will be terminated with a carriage return and line feed, and dates will be stored in yyyymmdd format. The APPEND FROM *file name* TYPE SDF command can import such a database into a dBASE database with a similar structure.

When you import an SDF file into a dBASE database, the field widths in the dBASE file must *exactly* match the field widths of the file to be imported, and the order of the fields in the dBASE database must match the order of the fields in the file being imported. Otherwise, data may be scattered across fields.

The TYPE DELIMITED option with the APPEND FROM command allows you to import ASCII files stored in delimited format. In delimited format, individual fields are separated by a comma (or other delimiter), and each record terminates with a carriage return and line feed. In some cases, character strings are enclosed in quotation marks. The APPEND FROM *file name* DELIMITED command could be used to read this database into an existing database with a similar structure.

When importing a delimited file into dBASE, the order of the fields in the dBASE database must match the order of the fields in the file being imported.

If the file being imported is delimited with some character other than the comma, you may specify that delimiter in the command. For example, to import an ASCII file with fields delimited with semicolons, use the APPEND FROM *file name* DELIMITED WITH ; command. To import a file with fields separated by a single blank space, use the APPEND FROM *file name* DELIMITED WITH BLANK command.

When using the APPEND FROM command with a TYPE SDF or DELIMITED option, dBASE assumes that the foreign file has the extension .txt unless you specify otherwise. If the file to be imported has no extension, use the DOS or dBASE RENAME command to add the extension .txt before importing it.

If the ASCII file being imported has dates stored in yyyymmdd format (for example, if it stores 19871231 for 12/31/87), APPEND FROM will properly import dates into a field of the date data type.

If the ASCII file dates are not stored in yyyymmdd format, you can import the dates into a character field and then use the REPLACE ALL command to convert the imported dates to the dBASE date data type.

The TYPE option also allows you to import data from VisiCalc, Multiplan, and Lotus 1-2-3 spreadsheet files. Table 3.2 summarizes the TYPE options for various spreadsheet packages and assumed file-name extensions. If the spreadsheet file to be imported has a file-name extension other than that listed in the table, you must specify that extension in the command. If the file to be imported has no extension, use a period at the end of the file name.

When you import spreadsheet files, dBASE expects the data to be in columns and rows that can be converted to fields and records. If you attempt to import a spreadsheet file whose data is not stored in even columns and rows, the format of the imported data will be unpredictable.

EXAMPLES

The following commands append records from the OrdTemp.dbf database into the currently open Orders.dbf database. However, records that are marked for deletion in OrdTemp and records that have no entry in the PartNo field are *not* appended. (Both Orders and OrdTemp have a character field named PartNo.) After appending, all records are removed from the OrdTemp database with the

TYPE OPTION	FILE-NAME EXTENSION	SPREADSHEET PACKAGE
DIF	.dif	Data Interchange Format used in Visicalc and some other spreadsheets
SYLK	none	Multiplan spreadsheet and Multiplan add-on packages
WKS	.wks/.wk1	Lotus 1-2-3

Table 3.2: TYPE Options for Importing Spreadsheet Data

ZAP command, so a future APPEND FROM command does not read these records again.

```
USE Orders
SET DELETED ON
*------ Append records from OrdTemp.dbf
APPEND FROM OrdTemp FOR PartNo # " "
*------ Empty the OrdTemp database.
USE OrdTemp
SET SAFETY OFF
ZAP
```

The following commands open a database file named Master.dbf and read in records from an ASCII text file named Master.txt. In this example, the file to be imported is stored in SDF format.

```
USE Master
APPEND FROM Master.txt TYPE SDF
```

TIPS

You can store newly entered records in a temporary database file and then use APPEND FROM to read these records into the actual database. This method is often preferred in networking environments or in situations in which data needs to be verified after initial entry before being processed in the final database.

SEE ALSO

APPEND
IMPORT
COPY

The IMPORT Command
Importing a PFS:FILE Database

IMPORT copies a PFS:FILE database to dBASE III PLUS format.

SYNTAX

IMPORT FROM *file name* **TYPE PFS**

where *file name* is the name of the PFS:FILE file to import.

VERSION

dBASE III PLUS only

USAGE

The IMPORT command automatically creates three dBASE files from the single imported file: a database (.dbf) file, a format (.fmt) file, and a view (.vue) file. Each of these dBASE files has the same name as the imported file, with the appropriate dBASE extension added.

Because PFS:FILE file names have no extension, you do not use an extension in the IMPORT command. (Of course, if you've purposely added an extension to a PFS file name, that extension must be used in the IMPORT command.)

You can access the IMPORT command from the Assistant menu by highlighting Tools on the top menu and selecting Import from the pull-down menu.

EXAMPLES

The following command imports a PFS:FILE database (and screen) named MailList.

IMPORT FROM MailList TYPE PFS

TIPS

As soon as a PFS:FILE database is imported, it is open and ready for use. The DISPLAY STATUS command shows the files that are automatically opened by the IMPORT command.

SEE ALSO

EXPORT
APPEND FROM

The INSERT Command

Inserting Records into a Database

The INSERT command inserts a record into a particular position in the database.

SYNTAX

INSERT /BLANK/ /BEFORE/

VERSION
---

dBASE III PLUS, dBASE III

USAGE

INSERT is identical to APPEND, except that it places the new record immediately after the current record, rather than at the bottom of the database.

INSERT allows data to be entered into only a single record, unless the inserted record is entered at the bottom of the file. In this case, INSERT allows multiple records to be added, just as APPEND does.

The optional BEFORE clause inserts the new record at the current pointer position. The INSERT BLANK command inserts a blank record into the database but does not activate full-screen mode for entering data. A REPLACE command or a READ command with a custom screen will allow you to enter data into the newly inserted record.

The SET CARRY and SET FORMAT commands work with INSERT in the same way as they do with APPEND. Command keys used in APPEND work similarly in INSERT. INSERT automatically updates all currently active index files. Any custom screen activated by SET FORMAT will be used by INSERT.

The INSERT command is not accessible from the Assistant menu.

EXAMPLES

The following commands insert a record into the appropriate alphabetical position for the last name Miller (assuming that the Mail database is already sorted on the LName field, and LName contains last names). Data can then be entered through the MailScr format file.

```
USE Mail
SET FORMAT TO MailScr
LOCATE FOR LName > = "Miller"
INSERT BEFORE
CLOSE FORMAT
```

TIPS

In dBASE III PLUS version 1.0, INSERT causes the bottom record in the database file to disappear—a bug that should certainly be avoided.

SEE ALSO

APPEND
APPEND BLANK
INDEX

Commands for Custom Screens

When you issue the dBASE APPEND, EDIT, or INSERT command without a custom screen (or *form*) in use, dBASE draws a very basic form for entering and editing data. This basic form only lists field names down the left side of the screen, with a prompt to the right of each field name.

For more sophisticated applications, such simplified screens are rarely sufficient. Instead, you'll want to create forms that are visually appealing, easy to use, and efficient for entering and editing data. These custom forms usually include prompts that are more descriptive than the field names alone. They may also employ a variety of enhancements, including color, boxes, data checking, and validation. This chapter discusses the commands used for creating and using custom forms.

The @...SAY...GET... PICTURE...RANGE Command
Displaying and Entering Data

The @ command positions the cursor at a location on the screen, displays a prompt, and allows data entry into a field or memory variable. The optional PICTURE statement provides data verification, transformation, or a template. The RANGE statement limits numeric or date entries to a particular range of values.

SYNTAX

*@ row,col [***SAY** *message] [***GET** *variable]*
   *[***PICTURE** *template] [***RANGE** *value,value]*
   *[***CLEAR***] [***TO***]*

where *row* is the row number and *col* is the column number for the screen or printer. The optional *message* can be a literal, variable, field, or combination of elements concatenated with the plus (+) sign. The *variable* can be a database field or memory variable. The *template* must consist of valid picture functions and template characters. The *value* parameters are dates or numbers. The optional CLEAR clause is used to clear a portion of the screen, and the optional TO clause is used to draw lines or boxes.

VERSION

dBASE III PLUS, dBASE III

USAGE

Each component of the @ command is discussed separately in the following sections.

Note that the @...SAY...GET command is used only in format files and command files and hence cannot be created directly through the Assistant menu. However, the MODIFY SCREEN command, discussed later in this chapter, is accessible through the Assistant menu and can be used to "draw" format files on the screen.

@ *row,col*

The first component of the @ command, @, positions the cursor (or printer head) at the row and column position specified by *row* and *col*. The *row* and *col* parameters can be numbers, variables, fields, expressions, or functions that evaluate to numbers.

On the standard 24-row × 80-column monitor, the row value must be between 0 and 23. The column value must be between 0 and 79. The functions ROW( ) and COL( ) return the current position of the cursor on the screen. These functions can be used for relative addressing. If the command @ *row,col* is used with nothing else following it, all characters to the right of *col* in the specified *row* are erased from the screen.

When the command SET DEVICE TO PRINT is issued, the output from @...SAY commands is routed to the printer. (The GET portion of the command is never displayed on the printer.) When sending text to the printer, the maximum *row* and *col* coordinates are each 255.

The PROW( ) and PCOL( ) functions are the printer equivalents of the screen's ROW( ) and COL( ) functions and can be used in the same manner for calculating relative rows and addresses. Note, however, that attempting to print data above the current line causes the printer to eject to the next page before printing the new line.

SAY

The optional SAY portion of the @ command displays any text or the contents of any database field or memory variable (though not memo fields). The PICTURE template can be used with the SAY command to format the displayed text. Literal text must be enclosed in quotation marks, as follows:

@ 2,40 SAY "This is printed literally"

SAY can display information from the currently open database as well as from related databases.

Only the plus sign (+) concatenator is allowed in SAY commands to join literals and variables. For example, the Up memory variable in the following example contains the character string for displaying an up arrow. The @ command below it displays the up arrow in midsentence.

Up = CHR(24)
@ 20,1 SAY "Press " + Up + " to make corrections."

Optionally, a macro can be embedded directly in the SAY command, as follows:

Up = CHR(24)
@ 20,1 SAY "Press &Up to make corrections."

If the data to be concatenated is not of character data, it must be converted to character data.

GET

The optional GET component of the @ command displays the contents of an existing field or memory variable in a template that matches the size and data type of the field or variable. When a READ, APPEND, EDIT, INSERT, or CHANGE command is issued, the user can change the contents of the field or variable displayed in the GET command.

Note that unlike the SAY command, the GET command can be used to read data into a memo field. However, data can be read into a memo field only when the GET command appears in a format file that is opened with the SET FORMAT command.

Unlike the STORE command (and assignment operator), GET cannot create a new variable from scratch. If the field or variable that GET is attempting to display does not exist in memory or in the currently selected database, the error message *Variable not found* appears on the screen. If you use GET to read in a variable, you must predefine the variable.

With a view (.vue) file in effect, the GET command can read in values for the nonselected database during editing. However, trying to get data for two separate databases simultaneously can be very tricky and should be avoided.

Unlike data entered into a memory variable in an ACCEPT command, any data entered into a memory variable through GET retains its original size. For example, if in response to the commands

```
AnyName = SPACE(15)
ACCEPT "Enter name " TO AnyName
```

you enter **Albert,** the AnyName variable simply contains Albert. However, if in response to the commands

```
AnyName = SPACE(15)
@ 2,2 SAY "Enter name " GET AnyName
READ
```

you enter **Albert,** the variable AnyName actually contains Albert plus 9 spaces, because GET retains the original length of 15 characters. This subtle difference can cause confusion in application programs, particularly in memory variables used with the SEEK command. To remove the trailing blanks from the memory variable when using SEEK, use the TRIM( ) function, as follows:

```
AnyName = SPACE(15)
@ 2,2 SAY "Enter name " GET AnyName
READ
SEEK TRIM(AnyName)
```

PICTURE

The optional PICTURE component of the @ command translates data from one format to another, rejects invalid entries, and adds template characters to data. Picture templates must be enclosed in quotation marks unless they are previously defined in a memory variable.

A PICTURE clause can contain a picture function, a picture template, or both. If both are used, their specifications must be separated by a space. Picture functions affect the entire SAY display or GET entry. Picture functions are summarized in Table 4.1.

Picture templates apply to all characters in data displayed by SAY and GET. Picture template characters are summarized in Table 4.2.

RANGE

The optional RANGE component of the @ command specifies an acceptable range of numbers or dates for an entry. The lowest acceptable value is listed first, followed by a comma and then the highest acceptable value. If you enter any value outside the acceptable range, dBASE beeps and displays an error message, along with the lowest and highest acceptable values, near the top of the screen. To try again, press the space bar.

CLEAR

The optional CLEAR command is used only with @ *row,col* to clear the screen from the specified coordinates down. The @ *row,col* command used alone clears the current line from the *col* position to the right.

TO

The optional TO component of the @ command is used for drawing boxes. For example, the command

@ 1,2 TO 5,79

draws a single-bar box on the screen, starting at row 1, column 2, and ending at row 5, column 79.

The addition of the word DOUBLE draws a double-bar box, as in the following example.

@ 1,2 TO 5,79 DOUBLE

FUNCTION	DATA TYPES	EFFECT IN SAY	EFFECT IN GET
@(	N	Displays negative number in parentheses	None
@B	N	Left-justifies a number	Left-justifies a number in display
@C	N	Displays CR (credit) after positive number	None
@X	N	Displays DB (debit) after negative number	None
@Z	N	Displays a zero as a blank space	Displays a zero as a blank space
@D	C,N,D	Displays date in U.S. MM/DD/YY format	Displays date in U.S. MM/DD/YY format, though date is stored on file in SET DATE format
@E	C,N,D	Displays date in European DD/MM/YY format	Displays date in European DD/MM/YY format, though date is stored on file in SET DATE format

FUNCTION	DATA TYPES	EFFECT IN SAY	EFFECT IN GET
@A	C	None	Permits only alphabetic characters to be entered
@!	C	Displays all letters in uppercase	Converts all letters to uppercase
@R	C	Inserts template characters into displayed data	Displays template characters in highlight, but does not store them in file
@S<*n*>	C	Displays the left <*n*> characters of the data	Creates a highlight that is <*n*> spaces wide; if data are longer than <*n*> spaces wide, user can scroll with arrow keys

Table 4.1: Picture Functions Used with the PICTURE Clause

TEMPLATE CHARACTER	DATA TYPES	EFFECT IN SAY	EFFECT IN GET
A	C	None	Accepts only an alphabetic character
X	C	None	Accepts any character
!	C	Displays the letter in uppercase	Converts the letter to uppercase
L	L,C	None	Accepts only upper-case or lowercase T, F, Y, or N
Y	L,C	Converts .T. to Y and .F. to N	Accepts only Y or N and converts lowercase to uppercase
9	C,N,N	None	Accepts only a number
#	C,N	None	Accepts a number, space, decimal point, plus sign, or minus sign
$	N	Displays leading $ in front of number if space permits	Fills highlight with leading dollar signs

TEMPLATE CHARACTER	DATA TYPES	EFFECT IN SAY	EFFECT IN GET
*	N	Displays asterisk in place of leading zeros	Displays asterisk in place of leading zeros
,	N	Displays comma if digits are present on both sides	Displays comma if digits are present on both sides
Other		Any other characters are added as template characters	Any other characters are added as template characters

Table 4.2: Picture Template Characters Used with the PICTURE Clause

The CLEAR command can also be used in the @...TO command. For example, the command

@ 1,2 CLEAR TO 5,79

erases the box drawn from coordinates 1,2 to 5,79, as well as the contents of the box.

EXAMPLES

The command file DemoGet.prg demonstrates several aspects of the @...SAY command. Enter it with MODIFY COMMAND and use the DO command to run it. Press the → key a few times to watch the scrolling of the @S function. Refer to the original program to see the effects of other pictures and commands. After you run the entire DemoGet program, your screen should look like Figure 4.1.

```
*********************************** DemoGet.prg.
*---------- Demonstrate various @ command lines.
*---------- Set up color, if available.
CLEAR              && Clear the screen.
SET TALK OFF

*--------- Set up a few memory variables.
SSN = "123456789"
PosNumb = 12345.67
NegNumb = -98765.432
Logical = .T.
Today = DATE()
Right = CHR(26)
Left = CHR(27)
Text1 = "Press &Right to scroll this line."

*-------- Demonstrate @S picture function.
@ 1,1 TO 3,79 DOUBLE
@ 2,5 SAY "Sample screen with @...SAY...GET commands"
@ 5,5 GET Text1 PICTURE "@S17"
@ 19,1 TO 23,79 DOUBLE
@ 20,5 SAY "Test &Right and &Left arrow keys"
@ 21,5 SAY "Then press Return."
READ

*-------- Demonstrate Y picture template.
@ 7,5 SAY "Yes or No? " GET Logical PICTURE "Y"
@ 20,2 CLEAR TO 22,78
@ 20,5 SAY "The next field will accept only"
@ 21,5 SAY "A Y or an N.  Try it"
READ
```

```
*--------- Demonstrate miscellaneous templates.
a 9,5 SAY SSN PICTURE "aR 999-99-9999"
a 11,5 SAY PosNumb PICTURE "a( $99,999.99"
a 13,5 SAY NegNumb PICTURE "aX $99,999"
a 15,5 SAY "European date today is: "
a 15,29 SAY Today PICTURE "aE"

*--------- Rearrange boxes.
a 20,2 CLEAR TO 22,78
a 20,10 TO 22,68
a 21,11 SAY REPLICATE(CHR(176),57)
a 21,35 SAY "All done!"
```

TIPS

If a picture template is used with a number containing a decimal point, be sure to place the decimal point within the template.

Picture templates with character strings less than two characters long do not always work properly.

You can set the number of simultaneously active PICTURE, RANGE, and GET commands through the BUCKET and GETS commands within the Config.db file.

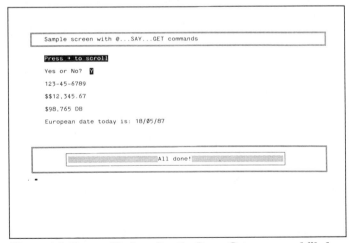

Figure 4.1: Screen display after the DemoGet command file has been run

SEE ALSO

MODIFY SCREEN   EDIT
SET FORMAT   CHANGE
CLEAR GETS   INSERT
READ   SET DELIMITERS
?   SET INTENSITY
TEXT...ENDTEXT   SET COLOR
APPEND   SET DEVICE

The CLEAR GETS Command

Releasing Previous GET Commands

CLEAR GETS releases GET commands from future access with the READ command and initializes the number of used GET commands to zero.

SYNTAX

CLEAR GETS

VERSION

dBASE III PLUS, dBASE III

USAGE

This command prevents any previously issued GET commands from being accessed by the next READ command. The number of active GET commands is limited by the amount of memory and the GETS setting in the Config.db file. (The default value is 128.) To

avoid running out of memory for GET commands, you can issue the
CLEAR GETS command where convenient in your programs.

In some applications, you might want to display all the fields of a
record but allow the user to change only some fields. In such a situation, first issue the @...GET command for the fields that you *do not*
want the user to edit and then issue a CLEAR GETS command.
Next, issue the @...GET command for the fields you *do* want the
user to edit and then issue the READ command.

EXAMPLES

Assume that all of the GET commands in the following routine are
sending data straight to a database file (no memory variables are used).
All fields will be displayed on the screen, but the operator can change
only the Cust_Name and Cust_Add fields. Figure 4.2 shows how the
screen looks after running this program.

```
****************************** ClearGet.prg
*-- Command file demonstrates a practical
*-- use for the CLEAR GETS command.

CLEAR
@  1,  0  TO  3, 50
@ 11,  0  TO 17, 50    DOUBLE

*------ Set up "uneditable" fields.
@  2,  1  SAY "Customer Number"
@  2, 17  GET  CustNo
@  5,  1  SAY "**** Only Name and Address below may be edited ****"
@ 12,  5  SAY "Starting Balance"
@ 12, 22  GET  Start_Bal
@ 14,  6  SAY "Current Charges"
@ 14, 22  GET  Curr_Bal  PICTURE "999999999.99"
@ 16,  6  SAY "Current Payment"
@ 16, 22  GET  Curr_Pay
CLEAR GETS              && Release from read access.

*------ Now set up "editable" fields.
@  7,  1  SAY "Customer Name"
@  7, 18  GET  Cust_Name
@  9,  1  SAY "Customer Address"
@  9, 18  GET  Cust_Add
READ              && Read values for editable fields.
```

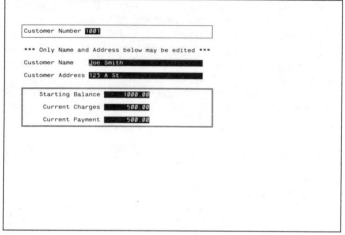

Figure 4.2: Screen produced by the Clearget.dbf routine

SEE ALSO

READ
@...SAY...GET
CLEAR

The MODIFY SCREEN Command

Activating the Screen Painter

The MODIFY SCREEN command activates the menu-driven screen painter for drawing custom data-entry forms.

SYNTAX ═══════════════

MODIFY SCREEN *file name*

where *file name* is the valid DOS file name for the screen (.scr) file and the generated format (.fmt) file. The command CREATE SCREEN is equivalent to the command MODIFY SCREEN.

VERSION ═══════════════

dBASE III PLUS only

USAGE ═══════════════

MODIFY SCREEN brings up the dBASE screen painter, which allows you to develop a custom form for any database (.dbf) file. When you save your work, dBASE automatically creates a format (.fmt) file that can be used with the SET FORMAT command to define a custom form for use with APPEND, EDIT, CHANGE, INSERT, and READ.

To access the dBASE screen painter from the dot prompt, type

MODIFY SCREEN *file name*

where *file name* is a valid DOS file name with no extension (that is, eight letters with no spaces or punctuation). The dBASE program will add the extension .scr to the screen file and the extension .fmt to the format file that the screen painter generates.

To access the screen painter from the Assistant menu, first highlight either the Create option (to create a new format file) or the Modify option (to change an existing format file); then select Format File from the pull-down menu. You will be prompted for a disk drive and file name in the usual manner.

Once loaded, the screen painter displays a menu of options at the top of the screen, a status bar at the bottom of the screen, and a blank area on which you can compose your custom form. The options are Set Up, Modify, Options, and Exit.

Each menu option has a pull-down menu associated with it. To move across the main menu, press the ← and → keys. To highlight options within a pull-down menu, use the ↑ and ↓ keys. To select an option in a pull-down menu, move the highlight to that option and press the Return key.

Selecting the Database for the Form

The first step in creating a custom form is to select the database file for the form. (The database should already exist.) To do so, highlight the Select Database File option on the Set Up menu and press Return. The dBASE program will display a list of your database (.dbf) file names. Move the highlight to the name of the database file that the form will serve and press Return. The file names will disappear, and the highlight bar will return to the first pull-down menu.

You can also select the appropriate database file with the USE command before entering the screen painter.

Loading Fields for the Form

Selecting the fields you want displayed is the second step in creating a new form. Select the Load Fields option from the Set Up menu. This brings up a list of fields in the currently selected database. You can use the ↑ and ↓ keys to highlight field names and the Return key to select them for display. A triangle will appear next to each field that you select. (To deselect a field, highlight it and press Return again.) You need not include all field names on your form.

After selecting the fields you want to include on your form, press the ← or → key to leave the Field Names submenu. The field names you selected will appear on the screen, with highlights showing the size and default templates for each field immediately to the right of each field name.

The Screen Painter Blackboard

The portion of the screen in which the fields appear is called the *screen painter blackboard*. The blackboard is where you compose your form. Note that the lower-right corner always displays the current cursor position. Each page or screenful of a form should begin at row 1 or lower on the screen (not row 0) and should not extend beyond row 24. To access the menu at the top of the screen at any time, press F10; to return to the blackboard, press F10 again.

Table 4.3 lists the keys you can use to write, erase, and move items on the blackboard.

Inserting Lines, Text, and Fields   To insert text into a form, first make sure the cursor is *not* in a field highlight. Then turn on insert mode by pressing the Ins key. (*Ins* appears in the status bar.) Once insert mode is on, pressing Return inserts a new line at the current cursor position. Moreover, any letters that you type will be inserted at the current cursor position, and all characters to the right of the cursor will move to the right. To type over existing text, turn insert mode off before typing.

To insert new fields onto the form, first move the cursor to where you want the new field to appear. Then press F10 to bring back the menu and highlight the Set Up option. From the Set Up menu, select Load Fields. Highlight the field you wish to add and then press Return to select it. Press ← or → to leave the submenu and F10 to return to the blackboard. The newly selected field and its highlight will appear at the cursor position.

Deleting Lines, Text, and Fields   To delete an entire line from a form, position the cursor on that line and type Ctrl-Y. To delete only the text (such as a field name), place the cursor to the left of the text to be deleted. Then press Del, Ctrl-G, or Backspace to delete individual characters, or Ctrl-T to delete entire words. To erase text without repositioning anything on the line, turn insert mode off and press the space bar repeatedly over the existing text.

To delete a field from the form, move the cursor inside the field highlight and type Ctrl-U. The dBASE program will ask whether you want to delete the field from the database as well. Doing so permanently deletes all the data in that field; enter **N** to delete the field from the form but not the associated database.

Moving Field Highlights   To move a field highlight, first place the cursor inside that highlight; then press Return. The navigation line at the bottom of the screen will give you some basic instructions

KEY	ALTERNATE	EFFECTS
F10		Switches between menu and blackboard
←		Moves cursor left one character
→		Moves cursor right one character
↑		Moves cursor up one line
↓		Moves cursor down one line
Ins	Ctrl-V	If cursor is not in a field highlight, turns insert mode on and off; otherwise, extends the length of the field highlight
Ctrl-N		Inserts a blank line at the cursor position
End	Ctrl-F	Moves cursor to beginning of next word
Home	Ctrl-A	Moves cursor to beginning of current or previous word
Return	Ctrl-M	If insert mode is on, inserts a new line; otherwise, just moves down a line (also used for moving field highlights and boxes)
Del	Ctrl-G	Deletes character over cursor, or decreases the size of a field highlight if the cursor is inside a field highlight
Backspace		Deletes the character to the left of cursor

Table 4.3: Control Keys Used on the Screen Painter Blackboard

KEY	ALTERNATE	EFFECTS
Ctrl-T		Deletes the word to the right of cursor
Ctrl-Y		Deletes an entire line
Ctrl-U		Deletes a field highlight or box at the current cursor position
PgDn	Ctrl-C	Scrolls down 18 lines on screen
PgUp	Ctrl-R	Scrolls up 18 lines on screen

Table 4.3: Control Keys Used on the Screen Painter Blackboard (continued)

about moving the field. Use the arrow keys to move the cursor to the new field position and then press Return to complete the move operation. (If you change your mind before pressing Return, you can press Esc to cancel the move operation.)

Changing Field Widths   To change the size of a highlight on the form, first place the cursor inside the field highlight. To widen the highlight, press the Ins key until the highlight is the desired length. To narrow the highlight, press the Del key repeatedly.

Adding Boxes and Lines to Forms   You can add single- and double-bar boxes and lines to custom forms by pressing F10 and highlighting the Options pull-down menu. Highlight either the Double-bar or Single-bar option and press Return. The navigation line at the bottom of the screen will give you instructions for drawing the box.

To delete a box that has already been drawn, move the cursor to any place on the box and type Ctrl-U. The entire box or line will disappear. To expand or shrink a box, move the cursor to a corner of the box and press Return; use the arrow keys to resize the box and then press Return.

Changing Entry Characteristics The Modify option from the main Screen Painter menu offers several options for altering the characteristics of fields on the form. Before using this option, move the cursor to a specific field highlight on the form. Then press F10 and → to display the Modify pull-down menu which displays the current characteristics for that field. The Source, Content, Type, Width, and Decimal options define the database, field name, data type, and size of the currently highlighted field. Any changes made here will affect the database structure, so you should avoid these options.

In some situations, you'll want to display a field but not allow it to be edited. The Action option on the Modify menu determines whether a field can be edited. If this option reads Edit/GET, the field can be edited on the custom form. If it reads Display/SAY, the field will be displayed but cannot be edited. Highlighting the option and pressing Return toggles between the Display and Edit modes. The Picture Function, Picture Template, and Range options add data transformation, templates, and verification to your custom form.

The Picture Function option allows you to select from among the options listed in Table 4.4 (only the options relevant to the data type of the currently selected field will be displayed). For a more complete discussion and examples of picture functions, see the @...SAY...GET command.

To select a picture function, type the appropriate letter (or letters) in the box presented at the bottom of the screen and press Return. You can combine two or more picture functions. The picture function that you specify here will automatically be incorporated into the format file that the screen painter generates.

The Picture Template option allows to you specify a character-for-character template for a field (rather than an overall template for the field). This can be used in conjunction with a previously defined picture function. The options for defining a picture template are summarized in Table 4.5.

A common example of a picture template is (999)999-9999 for phone numbers. With this template the user can type only numeric characters (because of the "9" template), and dBASE automatically puts in the parentheses and hyphen.

As with the picture functions, you can type your template directly into the box provided on the screen painter blackboard. Press

OPTION	EFFECT
!	Converts all alphabetic characters in the field to uppercase
A	Allows only letters (A–Z and a–z) to be entered into the field; any previously entered nonalphabetic characters are hidden if displayed by a SAY command
R	Used in combination with a template to ensure that data are always *displayed* within a predefined template but *stored* on disk without the extra template characters; for example, a phone number is *displayed* as (123)555-1919 but compactly *stored* on disk as 1235551919
D	Displays date in American mm/dd/yy format
E	Displays date in European dd/mm/yy format
S	Allows horizontal scrolling on a wide character field
B	Left-justifies a number
Z	Displays a blank instead of a zero value

Table 4.4: Picture Function Options Available from the Screen Painter

Return after entering the template. The template is automatically incorporated into the format file that the screen painter eventually generates.

The Range option lets you define a range of acceptable values for a numeric or date field. (Range is not a valid selection if the field currently highlighted on the blackboard is not of the date or numeric data type.) When you select the Range option, the screen presents two options:

Lower Limit:
Upper Limit:

First highlight Lower Limit to specify the smallest number or earliest date that can be entered into the field; then press Return to enter

OPTION	EFFECT
A	Allows only letters (uppercase and lowercase) to be entered into a field
X	Allows any character, including letters, numbers, and punctuation, to be entered into a field
#	Allows only numbers, spaces, plus (+), and minus (−) signs to be entered into the field
!	Converts any letter entered into the field to uppercase
N	Allows both letters and numbers to be entered into a field
9	Allows only numbers to be entered into a field
.	Specifies the exact position of the decimal point in a number
,	Displays commas in thousands places if number is large enough
L	Allows only logical data to be entered into a field (uppercase or lowercase T, F, Y, or N)
Y	Allows a Y or N to be entered into a field
Other	Inserts any other character automatically into the user's entry (unless the R function is used)

Table 4.5: Picture Template Options Available from the Screen Painter

a value. Next highlight Upper Limit to specify the highest number or latest date that can be entered into the field and press Return to enter a value. Press the ← or → key to leave the submenu when you are done.

The range options you select are automatically incorporated into the format file the screen painter creates.

Saving a Text-File Image of the Form   To save a text-file image of the form that can be displayed on the printer, select the Generate a Text File Image option from the top of the Options menu. The generated file will have the same name as the screen file, but with the extension .txt.

Saving the Form

When you've finished designing your form, press F10 to select the top menu and then move the highlight to the Exit menu. Now select the Save option to save your work (or Abandon if you want to abandon changes made during the most recent session). Selecting Save saves the screen painter file (with the extension .scr), the format file that has been created automatically (with the extension .fmt), and the text-image file if you requested one (with the extension .txt).

The screen painter always opens a file with the name provided in the MODIFY SCREEN command and the extension .scr. This file is required for future modifications of the custom form. If this file is erased, there is no way to convert the .fmt file back into a form usable by the MODIFY SCREEN command.

Note that any changes made directly in the .fmt file will not affect the .scr file. Furthermore, any changes made in the custom form through the MODIFY SCREEN command will overwrite any previous changes made directly in the format (.fmt) file. (The screen painter always completely overwrites the existing .fmt file.)

Multiple-Page Screens

A single format file generated with the screen painter may contain up to 32 pages or screenfuls of prompts. This allows you to create a single continuous form for databases with a large number of fields. To keep track of which page you are on while creating or modifying a custom form, just check the *Pg* prompt on the status bar.

Once you've saved your multiple-page form, you can treat it as you would any custom form. Use the SET FORMAT TO command, along with the name of the file (for example, enter **SET FORMAT TO Taxes**). The APPEND, EDIT, INSERT,

CHANGE, and READ commands will use the custom form as usual. The only difference in control-key commands is that PgUp and PgDn will scroll from page to page before they scroll from record to record.

The screen painter simply inserts a READ command between each page. Should you ever decide to develop your own multiple-page format files without the aid of the screen painter, remember to place a READ command between each screenful of data-entry fields.

Screens for Multiple Files

The screen painter can create forms for multiple files linked together in a view (.vue) file. Before issuing the MODIFY SCREEN command, make sure that the .vue file has already been created and that SET FIELDS TO has been used to define the fields for the view. Then use SET VIEW TO to open the view file and SET FIELDS ON to activate the previous SET FIELDS TO command. From this point on, the screen painter will treat the view file as a single database file. However, the options on the Modify menu that would normally alter the database structure will have no effect on databases in the view file.

EXAMPLES

The commands

USE Customer
MODIFY SCREEN CustScrn

open a database file named Customer.dbf and allow you to create a format file named CustScrn.fmt. The screen painter will also create its own working file named CustScrn.scr.

SEE ALSO

SET FORMAT
CLOSE FORMAT
READ

@...SAY...GET...PICTURE...RANGE
APPEND
EDIT
INSERT
CHANGE

The READ Command

Activating GET Commands

The READ command activates the GET commands displayed on the screen so that you enter or edit data.

SYNTAX

READ *[SAVE]*

VERSION

dBASE III PLUS, dBASE III

USAGE

READ is used to enter or edit memory variables or fields in a single database record. Often, READ is used in conjunction with APPEND BLANK to append a single record to a database file. READ can be used either with an open format file or in a command file containing GET commands. READ is also used to separate individual pages within a format file.

The READ command allows the user to move the cursor about freely to edit the data displayed on the screen. The cursor-control keys used with other full-screen operations also operate when the READ command is issued and active GET commands are on the screen.

Only the GET commands displayed on the screen since the last CLEAR, CLEAR GETS, CLEAR ALL, or READ command are activated by READ. After the user cycles through all the GET commands on the screen, they are cleared from further access. Unlike READ, the optional READ SAVE command does not automatically clear the GET commands that were just cycled through. Therefore, if you use READ SAVE instead of READ to edit a database record, the next READ SAVE or READ command accesses the same fields.

Note that the number of GET commands per READ command is limited. The default limit is 128 GET commands per READ, though this value can be changed to any value from 35 to 1023 through the Config.db GETS setting. The CLEAR GETS command also frees GET space between READ SAVE commands. Use the CLOSE FORMAT command to close a format file after data entry or editing to prevent the format file from reappearing when it is not needed.

EXAMPLES

The following commands add a blank record to the currently open database file, open a format file named AScreen.fmt, and let the user enter new values into the blank record through the format file.

```
APPEND BLANK
SET FORMAT TO AScreen
READ
CLOSE FORMAT
```

The following small sample command file creates a few memory variables and displays them on the screen with some prompts. The READ SAVE command allows you to enter or change values, and then the READ command allows you to do so again. The second READ command can access the same GET commands, because the previous READ SAVE command did not clear the GET statements.

```
********** Test the READ SAVE and READ commands.
*----- Create memory variables.
Name = SPACE(20)
DATE = DATE()
TIME = TIME()
AMOUNT = 0

CLEAR
*---- Display prompts and "gets".
a 2,1 SAY "Name " GET Name
a 4,1 SAY "Date " GET Date
a 6,1 SAY "Time " GET Time
a 8,1 SAY "Amount " GET Amount PICTURE "999.99"
*---- Read once, then again.
READ SAVE
READ
*---- Show results.
DISPLAY MEMORY
```

SEE ALSO

@...SAY...GET	INSERT
CLEAR GETS	CHANGE
APPEND	SET FORMAT
EDIT	MODIFY SCREEN

The SET FORMAT Command

Opening a Format File

The SET FORMAT command opens a format (.fmt) file for use with
APPEND, EDIT, READ, INSERT, and CHANGE commands.

SYNTAX

SET FORMAT TO *file name*

where *file name* is the name of an existing format file created with
either the screen painter or any text editor.

VERSIONS

dBASE III PLUS, dBASE III

USAGE

SET FORMAT opens an existing format file, reading only the @...SAY...GET...PICTURE...RANGE and READ commands in the file. It ignores any other commands within the format file.

Once a format file is opened, all ensuing APPEND, EDIT, READ, CHANGE, and INSERT commands use the format specified in the format file rather than the simpler default screens these commands usually generate. Once opened, a format file stays in effect until either a CLOSE FORMAT or different SET FORMAT command is issued.

If the format file consists of several pages (screens), the PgUp and PgDn keys scroll through pages before they scroll through records in the database. Note that each page in a format file must be separated by a READ command. Furthermore, multiple-page forms work only in format files opened with the SET FORMAT command.

EXAMPLES

Assuming that you've already created a format file named MailScrn.fmt (using the MODIFY SCREEN command or a text editor), the following commands open the Mail database and the MailScrn format file and use the format file to add new records to the Mail database.

```
USE Mail
SET FORMAT TO MailScr
APPEND
CLOSE FORMAT
```

SEE ALSO

CLOSE   EDIT
MODIFY SCREEN   INSERT
@...SAY...GET   CHANGE
READ   SET DEVICE
APPEND   SET DELIMITERS

5

Commands for Printing Data

This chapter presents the basic commands for displaying dBASE data, including the MODIFY LABEL, LABEL FORM, MODIFY REPORT, and REPORT FORM commands for printing formatted reports and mailing labels. Also discussed are the ? and EJECT commands, which are often used within programs to display database data. The TEXT...ENDTEXT command is generally used to display information on the screen from within programs, but can also be used to display information on the printer.

Other dBASE commands display data, but these have additional or specialized functions. These include the @...SAY command discussed in Chapter 4, "Commands for Custom Screens," and the LIST and DISPLAY commands discussed in Chapter 10, "Commands for Managing Files."

The ? and ?? Commands

Displaying Fields, Variables, and Results

The ? and ?? commands display a field, a memory variable, or the results of an operation at the dot prompt or from a command file. They are not accessible from the Assistant menu.

SYNTAX

> **?** *expression*

or

> **??** *expression*

where *expression* is any valid field name, existing memory variable, or calculation.

VERSION

dBASE III PLUS, dBASE III

USAGE

A single ? command always prints its data at the start of a new line. The ? command alone (with no expression) prints a blank line.

The ?? command prints its data at the current cursor position (or print-head position of the printer).

EXAMPLES

The command

> **? EOF( )**

displays .T. if the currently active database is at the end of the file. The command

> **? 27 ^ (1/3)**

displays 3, the cube root of 27.

TIPS

Avoid using ?? to display memo fields. An anomaly in dBASE allows only the first memo field to be printed correctly with ??.

SEE ALSO

@...SAY
TEXT...ENDTEXT
DO WHILE...ENDDO
SET PRINT
SET ALTERNATE

The EJECT Command

Ejecting the Current Page from the Printer

EJECT causes the printer to eject the current page.

SYNTAX

EJECT

VERSION

dBASE III PLUS, dBASE III

USAGE

The EJECT command is used primarily to force the printer to eject the last printed page, thereby ensuring that no text is stuck in the printer buffer until the next page is printed.

An EJECT command generates an error if the printer is not currently connected and on line. In some cases you may need to reboot the computer, potentially causing a loss of data.

The EJECT command is not accessible from the Assistant menu.

TIPS

Many laser printers will not print a page until the page is entirely filled or a form-feed character is sent. Be sure to follow all printed reports with an EJECT command when using a laser printer.

SEE ALSO

?
SET PRINT
SET DEVICE

The LABEL FORM Command
Printing Labels

LABEL FORM prints mailing labels in the format specified in a file created by the MODIFY LABEL command.

SYNTAX

LABEL FORM *file name* **[SAMPLE]** *[scope]* **[WHILE** *condition]* **[FOR** *condition]* **[TO PRINT]** **[TO FILE** *text file name]* where *file name* is the name of the associated label file, and *scope* is an optional scoping parameter. The *condition* option is any valid query expression, and *text file name* is the name of the disk file on which the labels are to be stored.

VERSION

dBASE III PLUS, dBASE III

USAGE

LABEL FORM prints mailing labels from the database currently in use, using the format specified in the label (.lbl) file created by the MODIFY LABEL command.

The optional WHILE and FOR commands specify records to be printed. The TO PRINT option sends the labels to the printer. If SAMPLE is used with TO PRINT, dummy labels are printed to help align the labels in the printer.

The TO FILE option sends mailing labels to a disk file. The disk file is assigned the extension .txt unless another is provided in the command line.

To access the LABEL FORM command from the Assistant menu, first be sure that the appropriate database file is open. Then highlight Retrieve on the top menu and select Label from the pull-down menu. Select the appropriate disk drive and file name in the usual manner.

EXAMPLES

The commands

USE MailList
LABEL FORM ThreeUp SAMPLE TO PRINT

display all records from the MailList database using the format specified in the ThreeUp.lbl label file. Labels are sent to the printer, and you are given the opportunity to print several dummy labels to help align the labels in the printer.

SEE ALSO

MODIFY LABEL

The MODIFY LABEL Command
Formatting Labels

MODIFY LABEL provides an interactive, menu-driven technique for formatting mailing labels.

SYNTAX

MODIFY LABEL *file name*

or

CREATE LABEL *file name*

where *file name* is any valid DOS file name. If no extension is provided, dBASE adds the extension .lbl to the file name. CREATE LABEL is generally used to create a new mailing label format, and MODIFY LABEL is used to edit an existing label format.

VERSION

dBASE III PLUS, dBASE III (with a different format)

USAGE

The MODIFY LABEL command presents three pull-down menus for creating and editing mailing label formats: Options, Contents, and Exit. The arrow keys move the highlight to the various menu and submenu options, and the Return key selects the currently highlighted option. The F1 key toggles the cursor manipulation help screen on and off.

To design a mailing label format from the Assistant menu, first be sure the appropriate database file is open and then highlight either CREATE (to create a new label format) or MODIFY (to modify an existing format) on the top menu. Select Label from the pull-down menu and select the disk drive and file name in the usual manner.

The Options Menu

The Options menu offers several predefined label sizes to choose from, as well as individual size specifications.

The Predefined size option lets you choose from the following sizes by repeatedly pressing the Return key.

Width	Height	Number of Labels Across
$3\frac{1}{2}$ in	$\frac{15}{16}$ in	1
$3\frac{1}{2}$ in	$\frac{15}{16}$ in	2
$3\frac{1}{2}$ in	$\frac{15}{16}$ in	3
4 in	$1\frac{7}{16}$ in	1
$3\frac{2}{10}$ in	$1\frac{1}{12}$ in	3 (Cheshire labels)

Selecting one of these options automatically adjusts all settings in the lower menu items.

The acceptable settings for the remaining menu items are shown in Table 5.1. Note, however, that the total width of all labels across the page cannot exceed 250 characters.

The Contents Menu

Use the Contents menu to specify the contents of each line of the mailing label. To define a label line, move the highlight to that line and press Return. Then, to see a list of available field names, press

MENU OPTION	ACCEPTABLE RANGE
Label width	1–120 characters
Label height	1–16 characters
Left margin	0–256 characters
Lines between labels	0–16 lines
Spaces between labels	0–120 characters
Labels across	0–15 labels

Table 5.1: Acceptable Setting Ranges for Mailing Labels

F10. You can select a field from the submenu of field names by high-lighting the name and pressing Return.

Several fields can be combined on a single line. If a comma is used to join two fields, a space is inserted between those fields. If a plus sign is used to join two fields, no space is inserted.

To delete a line from the label format, highlight the line and press Ctrl-U. To insert a new line above an existing line, highlight the line and press Ctrl-N. Pressing Ctrl-Y deletes all characters to the right of the cursor on the selected line.

The Exit Menu

Select Exit when you've finished laying out your label format or when you wish to return to the dot prompt. The Save option saves all current changes made in the mailing label format and stores them in the .lbl file. The Abandon option abandons current changes and retains any settings in the previous .lbl file (if one exists).

EXAMPLES

The command

MODIFY LABEL ThreeCol

allows you to create a mailing label format file named ThreeCol.lbl.

Figure 5.1 shows a sample mailing label format defined on the screen. The database fields Mr_Mrs, FName, MI, and LName will be displayed on the top line of each label, separated by a single blank space. On the fourth line, the city, state, and zip code will be displayed in the format Palm Springs, CA 91234.

TIPS

Blank lines in the label format, or lines that would otherwise print an empty field, are squeezed out of the label. To force a label to print blank lines, place a nonprinting character, such as CHR(2), on the label line.

SEE ALSO

LABEL FORM
MODIFY REPORT

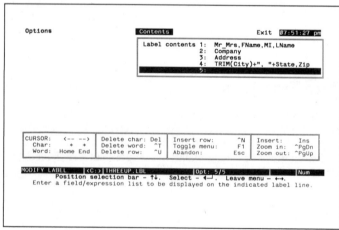

Figure 5.1: Sample label format displayed on the screen

The MODIFY REPORT Command

Designing a Report Format

MODIFY REPORT calls up the dBASE III PLUS report generator for designing report formats. The CREATE REPORT command is equivalent to the MODIFY REPORT command.

SYNTAX

MODIFY REPORT *file name*

or

CREATE REPORT *file name*

where *file name* is any valid DOS file name. The dBASE program automatically adds the extension .frm to the report format file name if none is specified in this command.

VERSION

dBASE III PLUS only (in dBASE III, use REPORT FORM)

USAGE

MODIFY REPORT activates a full-screen, menu-driven report generator that lets you format reports that can be printed with the REPORT FORM command. When you enter the command, the dBASE report generator screen appears. Its menu options, discussed in the following sections, are Options, Groups, Columns, Locate, and Exit. The help information in the box at the bottom of the screen can be toggled on and off with the F1 key. As you develop your report format, this box will be replaced with a preview of the printed report.

To design a report format from the Assistant menu, first be sure that the appropriate database file is open; then highlight either CREATE (to create a new report format) or MODIFY (to modify an existing format) on the top menu. Select Report from the pull-down menu and select the disk drive and file name in the usual manner.

The Options Menu

The Options menu provides options for formatting the margins, headings, and other aesthetic aspects of the report. These options are summarized in the following paragraphs.

Title   The Title option allows you to enter up to four lines of text as a report heading. After entering a heading, press Ctrl-End to return to the menu.

Page Width   The Page Width option determines the number of characters to be printed across a page. The default value is 80, but you can change it to any value from 1 to 500. The width of the printed report will be the total page width minus the sum of the left and right margins, as set in the two margin options.

Left Margin   The Left Margin setting determines the number of blank spaces between the left edge of the paper and the first printed column.

Right Margin   The Right Margin setting determines the number of columns between the right edge of the page and the character in the rightmost column.

Number of Lines per Page   The Number of Lines per Page option determines the number of lines that will be printed before the paper is ejected and a new page is started. Any value between 1 and 500 is acceptable.

Double Space Report The Double Space Report option places a blank line between each printed record if the option is set to Yes. Otherwise, the report is single-spaced.

Page Eject before Printing If the Page Eject before Printing option is set to Yes, REPORT FORM ejects the page currently in the printer before printing the report. If this option is set to No, the report starts printing at the current printer-head position.

Page Eject after Printing If the Page Eject after Printing option is set to Yes, the last page is ejected from the printer after the report is printed. If it is set to No, the printer head stays at the current page position after the report is printed. On laser printers, this option should be set to Yes. To combine several smaller reports on a single page, set this option to No.

Plain Page If the Plain Page option is set to No, the report heading, page number, and date are printed on every page of the report. If it is set to Yes, the report heading is printed *only* on the first page of the report, and the page number and date are completely suppressed.

The Groups Menu

The Groups menu allows you to group items of information in a report; it is typically used to print subtotals. Remember that a database must be sorted or indexed on the subtotaled field (or fields).

Group on Expression The Group on Expression option lets you group items in a report and optionally display subtotals for each group. For this setting to work correctly, the database must be indexed or sorted on the same expression.

Group Heading The Group Heading option places a title at the top of each group of items in the report. The value that identifies the group will be displayed automatically at the top of each group. Any text that you enter here will be printed to the left of that value.

Summary Report Only   If the Summary Report Only option is set to No, the report displays all details (records) from the database. If the setting is changed to Yes, only subtotals and totals are displayed in the report.

Page Eject after Group   If the Page Eject after Group option is set to Yes, each subtotal group will start on a new page. If it is set to No, each page can contain two or more subtotal groups.

Sub-group on Expression   The Sub-group on Expression option lets you define a secondary level of grouping and subtotals. The database must be sorted (or indexed) on both the primary and secondary grouping expressions.

Sub-group Heading   The Sub-group Heading option allows you to define a heading for a subgroup in the same manner that you create a heading for a primary group.

The Columns Menu

The Columns menu lets you define the contents of each report column. A column can contain a field from the current database file or a related one. It can also contain an expression including calculations or any valid dBASE function.

Contents   The Contents option lets you specify the contents of each column in the report. Pressing F10 displays all fields from the currently selected database, which can be selected by highlighting and pressing Return. To enter an expression or field from a related database, type the field name directly.

To scroll from one column definition to another, use the PgUp and PgDn keys. To delete the current column from the report format, type Ctrl-U. To insert a new column before the current column, type Ctrl-N.

Heading   To display a column heading at the top of each column, select the Heading option. You can enter up to four lines of text for each heading. After typing your heading, press Ctrl-End to return to the Columns menu.

Width   The Width option determines the width of the column (though dBASE adds an additional space between each column). A suggested width is automatically calculated by the width of the field or the width of the heading, whichever is larger. You can change this setting by selecting the Width option and entering a new value.

Decimal Places   The Decimal Places option specifies the number of decimal places displayed for numeric values. The suggested size equals the size specified in the database file structure. If you set a lower size, the number will be rounded.

Total this Column   The Total this Column option determines whether totals will be displayed for numeric columns. If this option is set to Yes, the column is totaled at the bottom of every total and subtotal group. If it is set to No, the number is not totaled.

The Locate Menu

The Locate menu displays a list of all currently defined columns. To quickly bring one of these columns to the Columns menu, move the highlight to the column and press Return.

Any blank column that appears in this display should be removed. Blank columns cause the report to display the error message *Syntax error in field expression*. To delete a blank column, move the highlight to it on the Locate menu. Select that column by pressing Return and then press Ctrl-U when the blank column appears on the Columns menu. Select Exit and Save to save the change.

The Exit Menu

The Exit menu provides two options for leaving the report generator and returning to the dot prompt.

Save   The Save option saves the current report definition in a file with the extension .frm. Any previous report definition with the same name is completely overwritten.

Abandon The Abandon option abandons the current report format. If an existing format was being modified, the current changes are abandoned and the original format remains intact.

EXAMPLES

The commands

USE OrdData
MODIFY REPORT Orders

allow you to edit a report format file named Orders.frm or create a new one if a file with that name does not already exist. The report format will use fields from the OrdData database.

Displaying Data from Other Databases

If more than one database is open and the databases have been related using the SET RELATION command, you can display data from the unselected databases by including the alias in front of the field name.

SEE ALSO

REPORT FORM
SET RELATION
TRANSFORM
IIF
ROUND
DO WHILE...ENDDO

The REPORT FORM Command

Printing a Formatted Report

REPORT FORM prints data using the format specified with the MODIFY REPORT or CREATE REPORT command. You can send the display to the screen, the printer, or an ASCII file.

SYNTAX

REPORT FORM *file name [scope]* **[WHILE** *condition]* **[FOR** *condition]* **[PLAIN]** *[HEADING expression]* **[NOEJECT]** **[TO PRINT]** *[TO FILE text file name]* **[SUMMARY]**

where *file name* is the name of the report (.frm) format file, and *scope* is any scope parameter. The *condition* parameters are any valid search criterion, *expression* is any valid character string expression, and *text file name* is the name of an ASCII text file in which the printed report is to be stored.

VERSION

dBASE III PLUS, dBASE III

USAGE

The PLAIN option suppresses the display of the date and page number on all report pages and limits the heading display to the first page of the report.

The HEADING option specifies an additional title to be displayed on the same line as the page number on the report. If the heading is literal text, it should be enclosed in quotation marks, as follows:

REPORT FORM AnyFile HEADING "This is the heading"

The heading can also be a variable or expression.

The NOEJECT option combined with the TO PRINT option causes the report to begin printing at the current page position in the printer rather than at the top of the next page.

The TO PRINT option sends output to the printer. The TO FILE option sends output to a file with the file name you specify. If you do not specify an extension for the output file name, the .txt extension is added automatically. The file output includes form-feed characters for automatic pagination. Hence, even a print spooler will properly paginate the text file.

The SUMMARY option suppresses the display of detail lines (individual records), displaying only the subtotals and totals specified in the report format.

If two or more databases were used and related to create the report format, the databases must be open and related in the same manner to print the report. If the correct files are open but the wrong one is selected, the error message *Syntax error in field expression* will appear (other errors might also cause this same message to be displayed).

If the report displays groups or subtotals, the database must be sorted or indexed on the grouping fields for the report to be accurate.

To access the REPORT FORM command from the Assistant menu, first be sure that the appropriate database file is open. Then highlight Retrieve on the top menu and select Report from the pull-down menu. Select the appropriate disk drive and file name in the usual manner.

EXAMPLES

The commands

> **USE Customer INDEX LName**
> **REPORT FORM CustList TO PRINT**

print data from the Customer.dbf database using the report format defined in CustList.frm. Assuming that LName.ndx is an index file of last names, the report is printed in alphabetical order by last name.

TIPS

An anomaly occurs when the page width and left margin differ by exactly 256, causing dBASE to skip printing the page title. If your titles disappear on the printed report, check for this situation.

SEE ALSO

MODIFY REPORT

The TEXT and ENDTEXT Commands
Marking Text for Display

The TEXT and ENDTEXT commands can be used to mark any block of text in a command file for display on the screen or printer.

SYNTAX

TEXT
text to be displayed
ENDTEXT

where *text to be displayed* is any amount of text to be displayed on the screen or printer.

VERSION

dBASE III PLUS, dBASE III

USAGE

To display a large body of text without using a series of @ or ? commands, enclose the text between a pair of TEXT and ENDTEXT commands.

Note that dBASE makes no attempt to process any commands, functions, expressions, or macros between the TEXT and END-TEXT commands. All text is displayed *exactly* as written in the program.

If SET PRINT is on, all text between the TEXT and END-TEXT commands is channeled to the printer. If a SET ALTERNATE file is active, all text is channeled to the text file.

TEXT and ENDTEXT are used only in command files. These commands cannot be accessed from the Assistant menu.

EXAMPLES

The following set of commands presents a menu of options to the user. The menu between the TEXT and ENDTEXT commands is displayed on the screen exactly as shown in the program. The routine beneath the ENDTEXT command asks the user to select a menu option and then stores the user's selection in a variable named Choice.

```
TEXT
                        Main Menu
                1. Add new records
                2. Edit existing data
                3. Print reports
                4. Exit
ENDTEXT
Choice = 0
a 20,2 SAY "Enter choice " GET Choice PICTURE "aZ 9"
READ
```

SEE ALSO

? and ??
@...SAY

6

Commands for Editing and Deleting Records

Data in databases needs to be maintained in a variety of ways. Addresses occasionally need to be changed in mailing lists, inactive customers in customer files must occasionally be deleted, prices in inventory files need to be updated from time to time. All of these tasks involve *editing* (changing) and deleting data.

The dBASE program offers many techniques for editing and deleting database data. With the use of *scope* options and the FOR and WHILE query options, you can easily pinpoint the exact record (or records) to change or delete.

The BROWSE Command

Displaying and Editing Records

BROWSE displays a full-screen, spreadsheet-like display of database records for editing.

SYNTAX

> **BROWSE** *[FIELDS field names]* *[**LOCK** columns]*
> *[**WIDTH** characters]* *[**FREEZE** field name]*
> *[**NOFOLLOW**]* *[**NOAPPEND**]* *[**NOMENU**]*

where the optional *field names* are the names of fields to include in the display, in the order in which you want them to appear. The optional *columns* are the number of fields on the left side of the screen that will not scroll as you pan to the right, *characters* is a number representing the maximum width of all columns, and *field name* limits editing to a single field. The FIELDS, LOCK, WIDTH, FREEZE, NOFOLLOW, NOAPPEND, and NOMENU options are outlined in Table 6.1.

VERSION

dBASE III PLUS, dBASE III (NOMENU, WIDTH, NOAPPEND options: dBASE III PLUS only)

USAGE

BROWSE provides a spreadsheet-like interface for editing data. It displays up to 17 records at once, with as many fields as will fit

COMMAND LINE OPTION	EFFECT
FIELDS	Specifies the names and order of fields to display on the BROWSE screen; each field name must be separated by a comma.
LOCK	Specifies the number of columns to be locked into place on the BROWSE screen; when the user pans to the right, locked columns remain in place on the screen.
FREEZE	Specifies the name of the only field that can be edited, even though all other fields are displayed.
NOFOLLOW	Normally, if a database file is indexed when the BROWSE command is issued, changing an indexed field automatically re-sorts the database and the BROWSE screen, moving the highlight to the new record position. However, if NOFOLLOW is issued in the BROWSE command, the highlight stays in the same general position after the screen is re-sorted, rather than following the record to its new position on the screen.
NOMENU	Prevents the user from accessing the menu bar with the F10 key.
WIDTH	Specifies the largest width for any field; any fields that are narrower than the specified width can be scrolled with the ←, →, Home, and End keys on the BROWSE screen.
NOAPPEND	Prevents the user from adding records to the database through the BROWSE screen.

Table 6.1: Command Line Options for BROWSE

across the screen. Command keys for editing and scrolling are virtually identical to those used with the EDIT command (shown later in this chapter in Table 6.3). In addition, Ctrl-← and Ctrl-→ pan the display of fields horizontally across the screen. The F10 key toggles the BROWSE menu bar on and off.

You can scroll the highlight past the last record displayed to add new records.

Any active index files are updated automatically by BROWSE. Furthermore, changing any data in an indexed field immediately re-sorts the BROWSE screen. If the NOFOLLOW option is used in the command line, however, the highlight will not follow the edited record to its new position.

The menu at the top of the BROWSE screen, displayed by pressing F10, presents several options, summarized in Table 6.2.

The BROWSE command can be accessed from the Assistant menu by highlighting Update on the top menu and selecting Browse from the pull-down menu.

EXAMPLES

The following command displays the LName, FName, CustNo, and Amount fields (in that order) from the database currently in use. Only the Amount field can be edited, and new records cannot be added to the database file.

BROWSE FIELDS LName, FName, CustNo, Amount ;
FREEZE Amount NOAPPEND

SEE ALSO

EDIT
READ

MENU OPTION	EFFECT
Top	Moves the highlight to the first record in the database file or the first record in the current index order
Bottom	Moves the highlight to the last record in the database file or last record in the current index order
Lock	Lets you specify the number of columns at the left side of the screen to lock into place; panning with Ctrl-← and Ctrl-→ scrolls through unlocked columns only
Record No.	Lets you specify a record number to move the highlight to
Freeze	Lets you enter the name of a single field in which to edit data; all other columns only display data
Find	Allows you to enter a value to search for in the indexed field; this option appears only if the database is indexed when the BROWSE command is issued

Table 6.2: Top-Menu Options in BROWSE Mode

The CHANGE Command

Displaying and Editing a Record

CHANGE is identical to EDIT; see the EDIT command later in this chapter.

The DELETE Command
Marking Records for Deletion

DELETE marks a record or group of records for deletion.

SYNTAX

DELETE scope [**WHILE** condition] [**FOR** condition]

where *scope* is one of the scope commands (RECORD, ALL, NEXT, REST) and *condition* is any valid query criterion.

VERSION

dBASE III PLUS, dBASE III

USAGE

DELETE affects only the currently selected database file, even if multiple related database files are in use. Records marked for deletion can be hidden from access with the SET DELETED ON command or removed permanently with the PACK command. Such records can be undeleted with the RECALL command. The DELETED( ) function is true (.T.) when the record pointer is at a record that is marked for deletion.

The LIST and DISPLAY commands display an asterisk to the left of records that are marked for deletion. The APPEND, EDIT, CHANGE, and BROWSE commands display Del for records that are marked for deletion, either at the top of the screen or on the status bar if SET STATUS in on.

If the record pointer is at the end of the file (EOF( )) when DELETE is executed, the command has no effect.

Global deletions are allowed with the scope and FOR/WHILE options.

The DELETE command can be accessed from the Assistant menu by highlighting Update on the top menu and selecting Delete on the pull-down menu.

EXAMPLES

The following commands attempt to find the database record with 1002 in the indexed field. If the appropriate record is found, it is marked for deletion.

```
USE Master INDEX Master
FindIt = 1002
SEEK FindIt
DELETE
```

SEE ALSO

DELETED( )
PACK
RECALL
SET DELETED
EDIT
BROWSE
ZAP
APPEND FROM

The EDIT Command

Displaying and Editing a Record

EDIT presents a full-screen display of data in a record and allows you to make changes or mark the record for deletion.

SYNTAX ===================

EDIT *[scope]* *[***FIELDS** *field names]* *[***WHILE** *condition]*
*[***FOR** *condition]*

where *scope* is one of the dBASE scope options, the optional *field names* are the names of fields to display (if a format file is not in use), and *condition* is any valid query criterion.

VERSION ===================

dBASE III PLUS, dBASE III

USAGE ===================

EDIT displays the contents of a single record on the screen and allows you to change the contents of any field. If a format file is not activated with a SET FORMAT command, EDIT will create a simple screen for editing data. The cursor-control keys that EDIT supports are similar to those used by the APPEND command. They are presented in Table 6.3.

Only the RECORD scope clause can be used in dBASE III.
If multiple related database files are open, EDIT displays data from the currently selected database, unless a format file with – > aliases specifies fields from the related database file.

If a format file is not in use, pressing the F1 key toggles a help menu on and off.

Any active index files are automatically updated when data are changed on the EDIT screen. Any inactive index files will need to be updated with the REINDEX or INDEX ON command when editing is complete.

Typing Ctrl-U while a record is displayed by the EDIT command acts as a toggle for deleting and undeleting records. EDIT will access and display records that are already marked for deletion only if the SET DELETED OFF parameter is in effect. Records marked for deletion are displayed with the *Del* indicator in the status bar or at the top of the screen.

KEY	ALTERNATE	EFFECT
Return		Finishes data entry in one field and moves cursor to next field
F1		Toggles help menu on and off (if no format file is in use)
NumLock		Toggles between numbers and arrow keys on numeric keypad
→	Ctrl-D	Moves cursor right one character
←	Ctrl-S	Moves cursor left one character
Home	Ctrl-A	Moves cursor to previous word, start of field, or previous field, depending on cursor's current position
End	Ctrl-F	Moves cursor to next word, end of field, or start of next field, depending on cursor's current position
PgUp	Ctrl-R	Scrolls to previous page or record, if any
PgDn	Ctrl-C	Scrolls to next page or record, if any; otherwise, exits EDIT mode
↑	Ctrl-E	Moves cursor to previous field
↓	Ctrl-X	Moves cursor to next field
Ins	Ctrl-V	Toggles insert mode on and off
Del	Ctrl-G	Deletes character at cursor position
Backspace		Moves cursor to left, erasing character
Ctrl-T		Deletes word to right

Table 6.3: Command Keys Used with the EDIT and CHANGE Commands

Key	Alternate	Effect
Ctrl-Y		Deletes all characters to right
Ctrl-U		Marks record for deletion
Esc	Ctrl-Q	Aborts last entry and exits EDIT mode (if a memo field is being entered, aborts current entry and returns to EDIT screen)
Ctrl-End	Ctrl-W	Saves entry and exits EDIT mode
Ctrl-PgDn	Ctrl-Home	Edits a memo field
Ctrl-PgUp	Ctrl-End	Saves a memo field and returns to EDIT screen

Table 6.3: Command Keys Used with the EDIT and CHANGE
Commands (continued)

To access EDIT from the Assistant menu, highlight the Update option on the top menu and select Edit from the pull-down menu. The record at the present record-pointer position will appear in Edit mode.

EXAMPLES

The command

EDIT RECORD 22

edits record number 22 in the database currently in use.

SEE ALSO

BROWSE
READ
SET FORMAT

The PACK Command

Permanently Deleting Database Records

PACK permanently removes records that have been marked for deletion from the database.

SYNTAX

PACK

VERSION

dBASE III PLUS, dBASE III

USAGE

The PACK command removes records that were marked for deletion, compresses the remaining records into the space the deleted records occupied, and reclaims the disk space occupied by the deleted records.

Only active index files are properly updated during a PACK command. Inactive index files will need to be rebuilt using the REINDEX or INDEX ON command.

PACK affects only the currently selected database file. Any related database files in use are unaffected by the PACK command.

To access PACK from the Assistant menu, highlight Update on the top menu and select Pack from the pull-down menu.

EXAMPLES

The commands

USE Charges INDEX CustNo, Dates
SET TALK ON

```
PACK
SET TALK OFF
```

permanently remove all records marked for deletion from the Charges database, display progress information, and automatically update the CustNo and Dates index files.

SEE ALSO

DELETE	ZAP
RECALL	DISKSPACE( )

The RECALL Command

Reinstating a Record Marked for Deletion

RECALL reinstates a record that has been marked for deletion.

SYNTAX

RECALL *[scope]* **[WHILE** *condition]* **[FOR** *condition]*

where *scope* is a dBASE scope command such as RECORD, ALL, NEXT, or REST, and *condition* is any valid query criterion.

VERSION

dBASE III PLUS, dBASE III

USAGE

To recall a single record, position the pointer at that record and issue the RECALL command. Optionally, use the RECALL RECORD command to specify a particular record (for example, the command RECALL RECORD 5 reinstates record 5).

To recall several records, use the scope or FOR/WHILE command. Note that RECALL ALL has no effect if the SET DELETED parameter is specified as ON. For safety, specify the SET DELETED command as OFF before issuing a RECALL command.

Even if multiple related database files are in use, RECALL affects only the currently selected database file.

The RECALL command can be accessed from the Assistant menu by highlighting Update on the top menu and selecting Recall on the pull-down menu.

EXAMPLES

The following command reinstates records marked for deletion that have February 1987 dates in the Exp_Date field and .T. in the field named Renewed.

```
RECALL ALL FOR MONTH(Exp_Date) = 2 .AND. ;
            YEAR(Exp_Date) = 1987 .AND. ;
            Renewed
```

(Exp_Date is assumed to be date data and Renewed to be logical data.)

TIPS

Use the DISPLAY ALL FOR DELETED( ) and RECALL commands to double-check deleted records before packing a database.

SEE ALSO

DELETED( )
DELETE
SET DELETED
PACK

The REPLACE Command
Placing New Data in a Field

REPLACE places new data into a database field.

SYNTAX

REPLACE *scope field name* **WITH** *data*
  [,field name **WITH** *data...]*
  *[***WHILE** *condition]* *[***FOR** *condition]*

where *scope* is a scope command (RECORD, ALL, NEXT, REST),
field name is the name of the field receiving the new data, *data* is the
new data being placed into the field, and *condition* is any valid query
criterion.

VERSION

dBASE III PLUS, dBASE III

USAGE

To place a literal data item or data stored in a memory variable directly
into a database field, use REPLACE without a scope or query condition. For global replacements, use a scope or query condition.

The data types on both sides of the WITH command must be the
same. Use the functions to convert data types, if necessary.

If an index file is active and you attempt to perform a global
replacement operation on one of the key fields in the index file, the
records will be re-sorted immediately after each individual field
replacement. Most likely, this will result in only some of the records
being replaced. For this reason, it is best not to perform global

REPLACE operations on indexed fields. Instead, perform the replacements without the index file active; then use the SET INDEX and REINDEX commands to activate and update the index files.

A single REPLACE command can update several fields at once, as long as the total command line width does not exceed 254 characters. Including several WITH statements in a single REPLACE command is much faster than using multiple REPLACE commands to perform the same task.

To build a REPLACE command from the Assistant menu, open the appropriate database file, highlight Update on the top menu, and select Replace from the pull-down menu.

EXAMPLES

The following commands increase the Unit_Price field by 10 percent for all part numbers that begin with the letter A in a database file named Master.dbf.

```
USE Master
REPLACE ALL Unit_Price WITH Unit_Price * 1.10 ;
    FOR Part_No = "A"
```

The example below shows a single REPLACE command that replaces the values in three different fields named PartNo, Rec_Date, and Vend_Code. Note that each WITH expression is separated by a comma. The command is broken into several lines, using the usual semicolon character, to make the line more readable.

```
REPLACE PartNo WITH M->PartNo, ;
    Rec_Date WITH DATE( ), ;
    Vend_Code WITH M->VendCode
```

SEE ALSO

APPEND BLANK
EDIT
READ

The ZAP Command

Permanently Deleting All Database Records

ZAP permanently removes *all* records from an active database file but leaves the database structure intact.

SYNTAX

ZAP

VERSION

dBASE III PLUS, dBASE III

USAGE

ZAP has the same effect as the commands

DELETE ALL
PACK

but it is much faster. All records are irretrievably deleted from the database file currently in use. The disk space previously occupied by the records is reclaimed. Any active index files are emptied automatically. If SET SAFETY is on, dBASE asks for permission before removing all records from the database. If SET SAFETY is off, all records are deleted immediately.

The ZAP command is not accessible from the Assistant menu.

EXAMPLES

In the following example, all records from the Charges database are appended to the bottom of the database file named History; then

ZAP removes all records from the Charges database. The SET SAFETY OFF command prevents dBASE from asking permission before zapping all records in the Charges database.

SET SAFETY OFF
USE History
APPEND FROM Charges
USE Charges
ZAP

SEE ALSO

DELETE
PACK
SET SAFETY

Commands for
Sorting and Indexing

In database management, the term *sorting* means to put the records in a database into some meaningful order, such as alphabetically by name, chronologically by date, or numerically by some amount.

The dBASE program offers two commands for sorting a database: SORT, which operates relatively slowly, and INDEX, which offers a more advanced and far faster technique. Both commands are discussed in this chapter.

The INDEX Command
Creating an Index File

INDEX creates an index file for rapid sorting and searching.

INDEX ON *field expression* **TO** *file name* **[UNIQUE]**

where *field expression* specifies the indexing key and *file name* is the name of the index file to build.

dBASE III PLUS, dBASE III

An INDEX file is conceptually similar to the index in a book. The index file contains the indexed fields, in sorted order, and the record numbers—just as a book index contains topics in sorted order and page numbers. When you display records with an index file active, dBASE uses the order specified in the index file. In the database file, however, each record retains its original record number.

The INDEX ON command creates a new index file with the name specified to the right of the TO command. The dBASE program supplies the default extension .ndx. To access the INDEX ON command from the Assistant menu, first open the relevant database file with the Database File option on the Set Up menu. Then highlight Organize and select Index. When the prompt *Enter an index key expression:* appears, you can type the expression directly or press F10 to select from a list of field names.

The *key* (or the field to be indexed) can be a single field or any combination of fields, as long as the combined width does not exceed

100 characters and the expression evaluates to a single data type. You cannot index on memo fields, nor can you index directly on logical fields.

The INDEX ON command only creates index files; it does not maintain them. To maintain index files, make sure that all index files are active whenever you add, edit, or delete data. To activate existing index files, use either the INDEX option in the USE command or the SET INDEX command.

Up to seven index files can be opened simultaneously. The first index file is the master, or controlling, index file. It is this index file that determines the sort order of the data being displayed, and it is also the only index file in which a SEEK or FIND command will operate.

Failure to include an index file in a USE or SET INDEX command will cause the missing index file to be corrupted when records are added, changed, or deleted. Once corrupted, the index file must be rebuilt with either the INDEX ON or REINDEX commands.

To index a database by a character expression, you should convert all letters to uppercase (in the index file only) so that upper- and lowercase distinctions do not affect the sort order. Use the UPPER function to do so.

If you want to display an entire database file in reverse order, you can index on the negative value of the record number.

The UNIQUE option deletes duplicate records from the index file. The effect of the UNIQUE option is identical to that of the SET UNIQUE command.

Indexing on Character Fields

When indexing a database on a character expression, you can convert all letters to uppercase (in the index file only) so that upper- and lowercase distinctions do not affect the sort order. Use the UPPER function to do so. The following example creates an index file named NameOrd by combining the last and first name and converting them to uppercase.

INDEX ON UPPER(LName + FName) TO NameOrd

To use a SEEK or FIND command with this index file, the value being searched for must be in uppercase, as in the following examples:

FIND SMITH

LookFor = "Smith"
SEEK UPPER(LookFor)

Indexing Numeric Fields

If a file is to be indexed on a single numeric field, there is no need to convert the numeric data to another data type. For example, in the following command, CustNo is assumed to be numeric.

INDEX ON CustNo TO CustNumb

If, however, you wish to combine numeric fields or combine numeric data with character data, the numbers must be converted to character strings. In the example that follows, both ProdNo and Unit_Price are numeric fields, but because they are combined in the indexing expression, both must be converted to character strings.

INDEX ON STR(ProdNo,4) + STR(Unit_Price,9,2) TO AnyFile

If you did not convert the fields above to character strings, dBASE would still accept the expression. However, rather than sorting items into part number order and then by unit price within part number, the index file would contain the sum of the part number and unit price fields on each record (that is, ProdNo + Unit_Price).

To combine a numeric field with a field of another data type, convert the number to a character string using the STR function. The following command line sorts records by last and first names, and then by total sale within each name.

INDEX ON UPPER(LName + FName) + STR(Tot_Sale,9,2) ;
TO AnyFile

Indexing Date Fields

If a date is the only field in an index file, there is no need to convert it. For example, the command

INDEX ON Hire_Date TO AnyFile

will properly place the dates on a database file into chronological order, even if dates outside the twentieth century have been entered with the SET CENTURY parameter on.

To combine multiple dates or combine dates with other data types in the indexing expression, you'll need to use the DTOC (date-to-character) function to convert the date data to character data. Doing so directly, however, has one major negative effect: It sorts the dates by months, and by years within months. Hence, January 1987 will be listed before February 1986.

There are two ways around this problem. The first is to use the SET DATE ANSI command to change the date format from mm/dd/yy to yy.mm.dd. In the following commands, the data will be sorted in proper date order, with names alphabetized within identical dates.

SET DATE ANSI
INDEX ON DTOC(Hire_Date) + UPPER(LName) TO AnyFile

To look up a date in this index file with the SEEK or FIND command, you must perform the same conversion. The following example shows a routine in a command file that uses SEEK to find a date stored in a variable named Search. The routine assumes that the database was indexed after a SET DATE ANSI command was issued to convert the date to yy.mm.dd format, and the date was also converted to the character data type.

```
*-- Initialize date as eight characters.
MDate = SPACE(8)
*-- Ask for date in mm/dd/yy format.
SET DATE AMERICAN
a 10,10 SAY "Enter date to search for ";
        GET MDate PICTURE "99/99/99"
READ
*--- Convert date to ANSI format for search.
Search = CTOD(MDate)
SET DATE ANSI
*---- Seek character string of ANSI date.
SEEK DTOC(Search)
```

The routine involves several steps, because the date to search for is first encountered as a plain character string in familiar mm/dd/yy format. Then the CTOD function and SET DATE ANSI command convert that string to the date data type in the ANSI format. However, because the index file contains the character equivalent of the ANSI date, the SEEK DTOC(Search) command also converts its ANSI format date to character data.

Incidentally, to convert the preceding routine to one capable of handling four-digit centuries, be sure to use the SET CENTURY ON command before creating the index file. Then change the command Date = SPACE(8) to MDate = SPACE(10), and change the PICTURE "99/99/99" command to PICTURE "99/99/9999".

The second way to sort dates that must be converted to character strings is to use the STR, YEAR, DAY, and MONTH functions to rearrange the date. The following commands create an index file with the dates properly sorted and names alphabetized within identical dates.

```
SET DATE AMERICAN
INDEX ON STR(YEAR(Hire_Date),4) + ;
    STR(MONTH(Hire_Date),2) + ;
    STR(DAY(Hire_Date),2) + ;
    UPPER(LName) TO AnyFile
```

The date is stored in the index file in the format "19870131," where the date is January 31, 1987.

To SEEK or FIND an item in this index file, the data being searched for must be in the same format as the date in the index file. The following sample command file shows a routine that lets you enter a date in mm/dd/yyyy format. The routine then converts the date to yyyymmdd format for the search.

```
*-- Initialize date as eight characters.
MDate = SPACE(8)
*-- Ask for date in mm/dd/yyyy format.
Listing 7.2 continued:

SET DATE AMERICAN
@ 10,10 SAY "Enter date to search for ";
        GET MDate PICTURE "99/99/9999"
```

```
READ
*--- Convert to Date data type.
AmDate = CTOD(MDate)
*--- Convert to yyyymmdd Character string.
Search = STR(YEAR(AmDate),4)+ ;
         STR(MONTH(AmDate),2)+ ;
         STR(DAY(AmDate),2)
SEEK Search
```

Indexing Logical Fields

Technically speaking, you cannot index directly on a logical field. However, you can use the IIF function to convert the logical data type to the character data type in the index file, as follows:

INDEX ON IIF(Paid_Yet),"YES","NO ") TO AnyFile

This assumes that the Paid_Yet field is the logical data type, and it results in an index file in which the .F. values in the Paid_Yet field will appear before the .T. values. Note that the "NO " value is padded with an extra space to keep the index key of uniform width.

To process only records with .T. in the Paid_Yet field, you could use an algorithm in a command file like the following:

FIND YES
DO WHILE Paid_Yet
   command
   SKIP
ENDDO

To display all records with .F. in the Paid_Yet field, you could use the following routine.

FIND NO
LIST WHILE .NOT. Paid_Yet

To combine a logical field with other data types using the IIF function, be sure all expressions result in character strings. For example, to index on the logical field Paid_Yet and the character field LName, enter a command like the one following:

INDEX ON IIF(Paid_Yet,"YES","NO ") + UPPER(LName) ;
   TO AnyFile

Again, a search string with the FIND or SEEK command must match this format to be successful, as in the following routine.

```
MPaid = .F.
MLName = "Jones"
Search = IIF(MPaid,"YES","NO ") + UPPER(MLName)
SEEK Search
```

Descending Index Order

Unlike SORT, INDEX does not offer a simple toggle for descending sort orders, but you can index on a negative or inverse expression to achieve the same result. For example, to achieve a descending sort based on a numeric Salary field, place a minus sign in front of the field name, as in the following command.

INDEX ON – Salary TO AnyFile

In the AnyFile index file, records will be displayed in descending salary order.

If you want to combine the numeric field with another type of field, you can use an inverse, rather than a negative, number when converting the number to a character string. In the next example, each salary is subtracted from a large number, converted to character data, and then linked to the LName field in the index key.

INDEX ON STR(9999999 – Salary) + UPPER(LName) ; TO AnyFile

The result is an index sorted in descending salary order, with last names listed alphabetically within each identical salary.

To index in descending order by date, subtract the date from a large date such as 12/31/1999. The following command presents an example using a date field named Hire_Date.

INDEX ON CTOD("12/31/1999") – Hire_Date TO AnyFile

If you need to combine the date with another field, place the entire expression inside an STR function, as shown in the following command.

**INDEX ON STR(CTOD("12/31/1999") – Hire_Date + ;
UPPER(LName) TO AnyFile**

As usual, you'll need to make sure that a SEEK or FIND expression performs the same conversion. For example, to locate the first record with the date January 1, 1986, in the Date_Hired field, you need to use the expression

SEEK STR(CTOD("12/31/1999") – CTOD("01/01/1986"))

There is no simple way to index a character field in descending order. The best you can do is index on the negative ASCII code value, as follows:

INDEX ON – ASC(LName) TO Names

Unfortunately, the – ASC(LName) expression operates only on the first letter of the name. Therefore, even though all the Zs will be listed before the Ys, the names beginning with a Z might not be in proper alphabetical order (for example, Zastro might be listed after Zygoat).

If for some reason you want to display an entire database file in reverse order (from last record to first), you can index on the negative value of the record number, as follows:

INDEX ON – RECNO( ) TO Backward

EXAMPLES

The command

**USE Charges
INDEX ON PartNo TO ChrgNx1
INDEX ON Date_Sold TO ChrgNx2**

creates two index files named ChrgNx1 and ChrgNx2. The first contains the PartNo field, and the second contains the Date_Sold field.

The following command opens the Charges database and activates the ChrgNx1 and ChrgNx2 index files.

USE Charges INDEX ChrgNx1,ChrgNx2

Any command that displays records will display them in PartNo order. Any command that modifies the database will automatically update both the ChrgNx1 and ChrgNx2 index files.

TIPS

The DISPLAY STATUS command displays all currently active index files as well as their key expressions.

Never use TRIM( ), LTRIM( ), or RTRIM( ) in an index key expression; doing so produces key expressions of varying widths, which disrupts the sort order.

Be sure to study the SEEK and FIND commands for tips on searching index files.

SEE ALSO

USE
REINDEX
FIND
SEEK
SET INDEX
SET ORDER

The REINDEX Command
Rebuilding Corrupted Index Files

REINDEX rebuilds corrupted index files.

SYNTAX

REINDEX

VERSION

dBASE III PLUS, dBASE III

USAGE

Index files that are not active when records on a database are added, changed, or deleted will become corrupted and unreliable. To rebuild the index files, open the database file and all index files and issue a REINDEX command.

REINDEX is not accessible from the Assistant menu.

EXAMPLES

The following commands rebuild the corrupted NameOrd and ZipOrder index files for the Mail database.

USE Mail INDEX NameOrd, ZipOrder
REINDEX

SEE ALSO

INDEX

The SORT Command
Copying Records in Sequence

SORT copies records from the current database to a new database in a specified sort order.

SYNTAX

SORT *scope* **TO** *[file name]* **ON** *field* *[/***A***] [/***C***] [/***D***]*
*[, additional fields... [/***A***] [/***C***] [***D***]]*
*[***WHILE*** condition] [***FOR*** condition]*

where *scope* is a valid scope option such as NEXT or REST, *file name* is the name of the file to store the sorted records in, *field* is the name of the primary sort field, *additional fields* are optional fields separated with commas, and *condition* is any valid query criterion.

VERSION

dBASE III PLUS, dBASE III

USAGE

Up to 10 fields can be included in the sort operation. Fields should be listed from left to right in order of importance.

Records must be sorted to a separate, unopened database file with the SORT command. A database file cannot be sorted to itself. The newly created database will have the .dbf extension unless you provide another one.

If SET SAFETY is on and you attempt to sort to an existing database file, dBASE will ask for permission to overwrite the existing file. If SET SAFETY is off, dBASE will automatically overwrite any existing files.

The /A, /C, and /D options can be used with each field name. The /A option specifies ascending order (small to large), and the /D option specifies descending order (large to small). If no order is specified, ascending order is used. The /C toggle ignores upper- and lowercase distinctions. Two options can be combined for a single field, as in the LName field in this example.

SORT ON LName/AC, Amount/D TO NewFile

Here we have a sort order with names from the LName field in ascending order (ignoring case distinctions) and from the numeric Amount field in descending order.

SORT does not support memo fields or logical fields. Similarly, substrings and other expressions are not allowed with field names.

To access the SORT command from the Assistant menu, open the database file using the Database file option on the Set Up menu. Then highlight Organize and select Sort from the pull-down menu.

The SORT command cannot reliably sort databases with more than 32,000 records.

EXAMPLES

The following commands create a database file named DateOrd that contains records with the year 1987 in the Hire_Date field.

USE Mail
SORT ON Hire_Date/D, LName/AC, FName/AC TO DateOrd ;
FOR YEAR(Hire_Date) = 1987

The records in DateOrd.dbf are listed in descending order by date (from December 31, 1987, to January 1, 1987), with names listed in ascending alphabetical order within each date. Upper- and lower-case distinctions are ignored.

SEE ALSO

INDEX

Commands for Locating and Querying Data

The dBASE program offers many techniques for searching, or *querying*, a database, including the LOCATE, FIND, SEEK, MODIFY QUERY, and SET FILTER commands. In addition, commands such as REPORT FORM, LABEL FORM, LIST, DISPLAY, DELETE, RECALL, REPLACE, and EDIT support the FOR, WHILE, and various scope options.

This chapter discusses commands for locating a particular record or a group of records that match some search criterion. To find a particular record, you'll use the LOCATE and CONTINUE commands (if the file is not indexed) or the FIND and SEEK commands (if the field you are searching is indexed). To hide records that do not meet some search criterion, a combination of the MODIFY QUERY and SET FILTER commands is a good choice.

The CONTINUE Command

Resuming a Search Operation

CONTINUE resumes a search operation that was initiated by a LOCATE command, beginning at the next record in the database.

SYNTAX

CONTINUE

VERSION

dBASE III PLUS, dBASE III

USAGE

The CONTINUE command searches the remaining records in the database (or those specified in the scope condition of the LOCATE command) for the next record matching the search criterion. If no record is found, the EOF( ) function is set to .T. and the FOUND( ) function is set to .F.

CONTINUE will find records that are marked for deletion only if the SET DELETED command is off. CONTINUE will not find records hidden by a SET FILTER or MODIFY QUERY condition.

To access the CONTINUE command from the Assistant menu, highlight Position on the top menu and select Continue from the pull-down menu.

EXAMPLES

The following command-file routine displays all records with Smith in the LName field.

```
LOCATE FOR LName = "Smith"
DO WHILE .NOT. EOF( )
    ? TRIM(FName),LName
```

```
    ? Hire_Date
    ?
    CONTINUE
ENDDO
```

SEE ALSO

LOCATE
FIND
· SEEK

The FIND Command

Finding a Value in an Index File

FIND quickly finds a value in an index file and sets the record pointer to that record.

SYNTAX

FIND *literal*

where *literal* is the value to look for in the index file; *literal* may not be a function or an expression containing operators.

VERSION

dBASE III PLUS, dBASE III

USAGE

FIND locates an item in the master index file for the current database. By default, the first-listed index file in the USE or SET INDEX command is the master index file. However, the SET

ORDER command can make any of several index files the master index file.

If the FIND command is successful, the record pointer will be at the first record that matches the value being searched for. If FIND is not successful, the pointer moves to the end-of-file position, the FOUND( ) function is set to .F., and the EOF( ) function is set to .T. (until some other command moves the record pointer). If the SET TALK parameter is on, an unsuccessful search operation displays the message *No Find*.

If SET EXACT is set to off, only the leftmost characters need to match for the search to be successful. If SET EXACT is on, only a character-for-character match will be successful.

FIND will locate a record marked for deletion only if the SET DELETED parameter is set to off. FIND will not find a record hidden by a SET FILTER or MODIFY QUERY condition.

If the index file contains several keys, the field widths and formats of both the data being searched for and the key expression of the index file must match exactly. FIND cannot locate characters embedded within the index expression.

The FIND command is not accessible from the Assistant menu, but the similar SEEK command is.

When FIND is used in a command file, a macro is required if the value to be searched for is stored in a memory variable; for example:

```
LookFor = "SMITH"
FIND &LookFor
```

EXAMPLES

Given that the DateOrd index file was created using the command

INDEX ON STR(CustNo,4) + DTOC(Date_Sold) TO DateOrd

and DateOrd is the master index file, as shown in the command

USE Charges INDEX DateOrd,Name

the command

FIND 1001

searches for a record with customer number 1001.

SEE ALSO

SEEK   SET ORDER
INDEX   SET EXACT
SET INDEX

The LOCATE Command
Finding a Record Matching a Search Criterion

LOCATE finds the first record in a database file that matches a
search criterion.

SYNTAX

LOCATE *scope [***FOR*** condition] [***WHILE*** condition]*

where *scope* specifies the range of records and *condition* is any valid
search criterion.

VERSION

dBASE III PLUS, dBASE III

USAGE

LOCATE searches the disk file directly rather than an index file, so
it can be used with any fields or combination of fields. LOCATE
supports all dBASE functions and operators.

If LOCATE fails to find a matching record, the EOF( ) function is
set to .T. and the FOUND( ) function is set to .F. If the SET TALK

parameter is on and LOCATE fails to find a matching record, the screen will display the message *End of LOCATE scope*.

LOCATE will find records marked for deletion only if the SET DELETED command is off. LOCATE will not find records hidden by a SET FILTER or MODIFY QUERY condition.

If SET EXACT is off, only the leftmost characters need to match for the search operation to be successful. If SET EXACT is on, only a character-for-character match will be successful.

The LOCATE command can be accessed from the Assistant menu by highlighting Position on the top menu and selecting Locate on the pull-down menu.

The CONTINUE command can be used with LOCATE to find the next record that matches the search condition.

EXAMPLES

The command

```
LOCATE FOR UPPER(LName) = "SMITH" .AND. ;
    Amount > 1000
```

will locate the first record in the database that has Smith in the LName field and an amount greater than 1000 in the Amount field.

TIPS

For faster searches, use the FIND or SEEK command with an active index file.

SEE ALSO

CONTINUE
FIND
SEEK
INDEX

The MODIFY QUERY and CREATE QUERY Commands
Specifying Search Criteria

MODIFY QUERY and CREATE QUERY both present full-screen menus that allow you to specify searching criteria in an interactive, menu-driven fashion.

SYNTAX

MODIFY QUERY *file name*

or

CREATE QUERY *file name*

where *file name* is the name of the query file to which dBASE adds the .qry extension.

VERSION

dBASE III PLUS only

USAGE

Both the CREATE QUERY and the MODIFY QUERY commands call up the Set Filter, Nest, Display, and Exit menus. The arrow keys move the highlight across the top menu and up and down within the pull-down menus. Pressing Return while a pull-down menu option is highlighted selects that option. Pressing ← returns you to a higher-level menu, where applicable. As you select menu items, instructions for using that option appear at the bottom of the screen.

Up to seven expressions for searching the database can be defined in the Set Filter menu. These can be joined with .AND., .OR., and

.NOT. operators. They can also be grouped with parentheses using the Nest menu.

After the query form is filled in, selecting Save saves the query form for future use and also automatically initiates the filter condition defined in the query form. The SET FILTER TO command, with no additional parameters, deactivates the filter condition.

The SET FILTER TO FILE *file name* command activates a previously defined query file without displaying the MODIFY QUERY form. The file name in this example must be the name of an existing and valid query form file. (The dBASE program assumes the .qry file-name extension.)

The menu options on the MODIFY QUERY menu options are summarized in the following sections.

The Set Filter Menu

The Set Filter menu lets you define the filter condition and must be used before either the Nest or Display menu options are accessed. The Field Name option displays a submenu of field names in the currently selected database file.

The Operator option displays a list of dBASE operators and a brief description of each. These vary, depending on the data type of the current field.

The Constant/Expression option lets you enter a value to search for. If the data type of the field being searched for is numeric, just type the number to search for and press Return. If the data type of the field being searched for is character, the expression must be enclosed in quotation marks or brackets. For example, to locate Smith, you must enter **"Smith"**, with the quotation marks, as the constant or expression.

If the data type of the field being searched for is date, a CTOD function is necessary—that is, **CTOD("12/31/87")**. If the data type of the field being searched for is logical, you need not enter a constant or expression. Instead, the Operator option will provide you with your only two options: Is true and Is false. Memo fields cannot not be queried in any way in dBASE III PLUS.

If you wish the constant or expression to be the name of another field in the database, first select Constant/Expression and then press

F10 to view the field names submenu. Highlight the appropriate field name and press Return.

The Connect option links the current field with the next field to be entered using a logical operator such as .AND. or .OR. A logical operator must be entered before moving to the next field.

The Line Number option lets you move to any existing condition in the Set Filter menu. To move to a new line, highlight the Line Number option, press Return, type the appropriate line number, and press Return again.

The Nest Menu

The Nest menu lets you place parentheses around any existing lines. This allows you to be more specific about the meaning of a search criterion. For example, the condition

LName = "Jones" .AND. State = "CA" .OR. State = "NY"

is somewhat ambiguous. However, with the addition of parentheses, as follows, the condition clearly specifies "Jones in either CA or NY."

LName = "Jones" .AND. (State = "CA" .OR. State = "NY")

The Start option places a left parenthesis at the left of the line you specify. The End option places a right parenthesis at the right of the line you specify. The Remove option lets you remove any pair of parentheses by specifying their start and end positions.

The Display Menu

The Display option lets you perform a quick test of the filter condition defined on the Set Filter menu. Selecting this option displays the first record in the database file (if any) that matches the condition. Pressing PgUp and PgDn scrolls through additional records that match the criterion.

The Exit Menu

To exit from the MODIFY QUERY form, you must select the Exit menu. The Save option saves the query form in a file with the .qry extension. This option also activates the filter criterion immediately. The Abandon option exits the query form without saving or activating the filter condition.

To access the query form from the Assistant menu, first open the database file of interest using the Database file option on the Set up menu. Then highlight the Create option (to create a new query) or the Modify option (to change an existing query) and select Query from the pull-down menu.

To activate an existing query from the Assistant menu, highlight the Set up menu option and select Query from the pull-down menu. Enter the name of the query to activate.

The Assistant menu offers no command for deactivating a query. Instead, you must press Esc to leave the Assistant menu, type **SET FILTER TO** at the dot prompt, and press Return. To return to the Assistant menu, type **ASSIST** and press Return.

EXAMPLES

The commands

USE Mail
MODIFY QUERY State

call up the MODIFY QUERY screen for the Mail.dbf database. If a query file named State.qry already exists, its contents are displayed on the screen. If State.qry does not already exist, a new, blank query form is created and displayed.

TIPS

If the record pointer is at a record that does not match the filter criteria when the Query condition is saved, the results may be inaccurate. To ensure that a MODIFY QUERY filter condition works properly, use a command to move the record pointer immediately after the MODIFY QUERY command. A simple GO TOP command, or a GO BOTTOM command followed by a GO TOP command, will suffice.

SEE ALSO

SET FILTER

The SEEK Command
Finding Data in an Index File

SEEK quickly locates data in an index file. This command allows memory variables and expressions.

SYNTAX

SEEK *expression*

where *expression* is literal data enclosed in quotation marks, the name of a memory variable containing the value to search for, or an expression defining the format of the value to search for.

VERSION

dBASE III PLUS, dBASE III

USAGE

SEEK works only with the master index file. By default, the first-listed index file in the USE or SET INDEX command is the master index file. However, the SET ORDER command can make any of several index files the master index file.

If the SEEK command is successful, the record pointer will be at the first record that matches the value being searched for. If SEEK is not successful, the FOUND( ) function is set to .F. and the EOF( ) function is set to .T. (until some other command moves the record pointer). If the SET TALK parameter is on, an unsuccessful search operation causes the message *No Find* to be displayed.

If SET EXACT is off, only the leftmost characters need to match for the search to be successful. If SET EXACT is on, only a character-for-character match will be successful.

SEEK will find a record marked for deletion only if the SET DELETED parameter is set to off. SEEK will not find a record hidden by a SET FILTER or MODIFY QUERY condition.

If the index file contains several keys, the field widths and formats of both the data being searched for and the key expression of the index file must match exactly. SEEK cannot locate characters embedded within the index expression.

You can use SEEK to create expressions that allow the search data to match the format of the key expression in the index file. For example, if an index file was created with the expression

INDEX ON UPPER(LName) + STR(Amount,9,2) TO AnyFile

the following commands will search for data in the index file using the proper format.

```
LName = "Smith"
Amount = 123.45
SEEK UPPER(LName) + STR(Amount,9,2)
```

SEEK locates an item in the master index file for the current database.

If you wish to seek data in an index file that is built from two or more character fields, the widths of the data in the characters being searched for must match the field widths in the database. In a command file, you can use the GET and READ commands to ensure appropriate widths.

To access the SEEK command from the Assistant menu, first open the appropriate database and index file, using the Database file option on the Set up pull-down menu. Then highlight Position on the top menu and select Seek from the pull-down menu. Enter a value to search for and press Return.

EXAMPLES

The following command attempts to locate the name Jones in the currently active index file.

SEEK "Jones"

The next commands also attempt to locate Jones in the currently active index file. However, in this example, the name to search for is stored in a memory variable named LookFor.

LookFor = "Jones"
SEEK LookFor

TIPS

Make sure that the format and length of the expression in the SEEK command matches those of the index key expression (see the discussion of the INDEX ON command in Chapter 7).

SEE ALSO

FIND
INDEX
SET INDEX
SET ORDER
SET EXACT

9

Commands for Performing Calculations

This chapter discusses commands that are used for performing calculations on database data. The SUM and AVERAGE commands calculate the sum and average of numeric fields in a database. The COUNT command counts the records in a database. TOTAL creates a summary (subtotaled) copy of a database. All commands support the scope, FOR, and WHILE options, so that you can select specific records to include in the calculation.

Note that these commands only calculate the data and do not necessarily display any results or reports. Chapter 5, "Commands for Printing Data," discusses techniques for displaying totals and subtotals in formatted reports.

The AVERAGE Command

Calculating the Average

AVERAGE calculates the average (arithmetic mean) of a numeric field.

SYNTAX

AVERAGE *expressions scope* [**WHILE** *condition*]
[**FOR** *condition*] [**TO** *memory variables*]

where *expressions* are field names or expressions of numeric fields, *scope* is a dBASE scope option, *condition* is a valid query criterion, and *memory variables* are names of memory variables in which to store the results.

VERSION

dBASE III PLUS, dBASE III

USAGE

The AVERAGE command calculates the average of a numeric field or fields. Up to five field names or expressions, separated by commas, can be included. If no field names or expressions are specified, all fields are averaged.

If TO is used, there must be a memory variable name for each field name or expression. If the SET TALK parameter is on, the results of the calculations are displayed on the screen. If SET TALK is off, the results are not displayed and therefore must be stored in memory variables to be accessible.

Records hidden by a SET FILTER, MODIFY QUERY, or SET DELETED ON command are not included in the calculation.

To access the AVERAGE command from the Assistant menu, open the database file of interest and highlight the Retrieve option on the top menu. Select Average from the pull-down menu.

EXAMPLES

The command

AVERAGE Ext_Price TO AvgPrice

calculates the average of the numeric field Ext_Price and stores the result in a numeric memory variable named AvgPrice.

TIPS

It is faster to use several fields or expressions in a single AVERAGE command than to use several separate AVERAGE commands. That is, the command

AVERAGE Sale,Salary TO AvgSale,AvgSalary

will run twice as fast as the commands

AVERAGE Sale TO AvgSale
AVERAGE Salary TO AvgSalary

SEE ALSO

SUM
COUNT

The COUNT Command
Counting Records

COUNT counts how many records meet a specified search criterion.

SYNTAX

COUNT *scope* [**WHILE** *condition*] [**FOR** *condition*]
[**TO** *memory variable*]

where *scope* is a dBASE scope option, *condition* is a valid query criterion, and *memory variable* is the name of a memory variable in which to store the result.

VERSION

dBASE III PLUS, dBASE III

USAGE

The COUNT command tallies the number of records in the database field that match a search criterion. If SET TALK is off, the results are not displayed and therefore must be stored in memory variables to be accessible. Records hidden by a SET FILTER, MODIFY QUERY, or SET DELETED ON command are not included in the tally.

To access the COUNT command from the Assistant menu, open the database file of interest, highlight the Retrieve option on the top menu, and select Count from the pull-down menu.

EXAMPLES

The command

COUNT FOR LName = "Smith" TO SmithNumb

counts the number of individuals in the database that have the last name Smith and stores this number in a variable named Smith-Numb. To view the results of the tally, use @ or ?, as follows:

? SmithNumb

SEE ALSO

RECCOUNT( )
AVERAGE

The SUM Command

Calculating the Sum

SUM calculates the sum of numeric fields.

SYNTAX

SUM *expressions scope* [**WHILE** *condition*]
[**FOR** *condition*] [**TO** *memory variables*]

where *expressions* are field names or expressions of numeric fields, *scope* is a dBASE scope option, *condition* is a valid query criterion, and *memory variables* are names of memory variables in which to store the results.

VERSION

dBASE III PLUS, dBASE III

USAGE

Up to five field names or expressions, separated by commas, can be included in the SUM command. If no field names or expressions are listed, all numeric fields are summed. If the TO portion of the command is used, there must be a memory variable name for each field name or expression, each separated by a comma. If the SET TALK parameter is on, the results of the calculation are displayed on the screen immediately. Otherwise, the results are not displayed and therefore must be stored in memory variables to be accessible.

Records hidden by a MODIFY QUERY, SET FILTER, or SET DELETED ON command are not included in the calculation.

To access the SUM command from the Assistant menu, open the database file of interest, highlight the Retrieve option on the top menu, and select Sum from the pull-down menu.

EXAMPLES

The command

SUM Age TO TotAge

calculates the sum of the numeric field Age and stores the result in a numeric memory variable named TotAge.

To display the results of the preceding calculations, use @ or ?, as follows:

? TotSale,TotTax

TIPS

It is faster to use several fields or expressions in a single SUM command than to use several separate SUM commands. That is, the command

SUM Sale,Salary TO TotSale,TotSalary

will run twice as fast as the commands

SUM Sale TO TotSale
SUM Salary TO TotSalary

SEE ALSO

TOTAL
REPORT FORM
UPDATE
AVERAGE

The TOTAL Command

Creating a Summary Database

TOTAL creates a new database with totals of numeric fields summarized by a key field or expression.

SYNTAX

TOTAL ON *key expression* **TO** *file name [scope]*
    *[*FIELDS *field names] [*WHILE *condition]*
    *[*FOR *condition]*

where *key expression* is the expression representing the field to be grouped, *file name* is the name of the file to copy totaled records to, *scope* is a scope option, *field names* are names of fields to include in the total, and *condition* is any valid search criterion.

VERSION

dBASE III PLUS, dBASE III

USAGE

Use the TOTAL command to create a database containing a single record for each unique value in a particular field in the original database. The numeric fields in the summary database contain the totals of numeric values in the original database file. The database is assumed to be in the current disk drive and directory unless otherwise specified in the file name.

The database must be sorted or indexed on the field or expression of interest (that is, on the key expression). Using TOTAL with an improperly indexed or sorted database will not generate an error message; instead, it will produce an incomplete summary database.

The structure of the generated summary database file is identical to that of the original database, except that memo fields are not copied.

Records hidden by a MODIFY QUERY, SET FILTER, or SET DELETED ON command are not included in the totals.

If the SET SAFETY parameter is on, dBASE asks for permission before overwriting a file with the name specified in the TO portion of the command. If SET SAFETY is off, dBASE automatically overwrites the named file.

The TOTAL command is not accessible from the Assistant menu.

EXAMPLES

The sample database shown here is named Sales and is indexed on the PartNo field.

Record#	PART_NO	QTY	UNIT_PRICE	DATE
1	A-111	5	10.00	01/31/87
2	A-111	5	10.00	01/31/87
3	B-222	1	100.00	01/01/87
4	B-222	1	100.00	01/02/87
5	C-333	10	50.00	01/01/87

To calculate how many of each item in the database were sold, you could enter these commands:

USE Sales INDEX PartNo
TOTAL ON PartNo TO SaleSumm FIELDS Qty

When the TOTAL command completes its job, the Sale-Summ.dbf file will contain a summary of the Sales database file, with a single record for each unique part number in the Sales database file. The contents of the SaleSumm database file generated by the TOTAL command in this example are shown here.

Record#	PART_NO	QTY	UNIT_PRICE	DATE
1	A-111	10	10.00	01/31/87
2	B-222	2	100.00	01/01/87
3	C-333	10	50.00	01/01/87

Note that the Qty field in the SaleSumm file contains the total of the Qty fields for each part number in the Sales file. The Unit_Price field is not totaled, however, because it was not included in the FIELDS portion of the TOTAL command.

SEE ALSO

MODIFY REPORT
SUM
AVERAGE
UPDATE

10

Commands for Managing Files

This chapter focuses on general-purpose commands used primarily for managing files. It also includes commands that are not easily categorized under a particular function.

The CLEAR Command
Clearing dBASE Parameters

CLEAR provides many basic functions depending on the optional second part of the command.

SYNTAX

CLEAR *[ALL] [FIELDS] [GETS] [MEMORY] [TYPEAHEAD]*

VERSION
---

dBASE III PLUS, dBASE III (FIELDS and TYPEAHEAD options only)

USAGE

When used by itself, CLEAR clears the screen. It can also be used to clear a portion of the screen. For example, the command

@ 12,0 CLEAR

clears only the bottom half of the screen (row 12, column 0, to the bottom of the screen). Chapter 4, "Commands for Custom Screens," provides additional examples.

CLEAR ALL closes all open files, including database, index, format, catalog, and memo files. It also erases all memory variables and sets the work area back to 1. Chapter 14, "Commands for Memory Variables," provides examples.

CLEAR FIELDS releases the settings specified in the SET FIELDS TO command and automatically issues a SET FIELDS OFF command. See Chapter 11, "Commands for Managing Multiple Database Files," for examples.

CLEAR GETS releases GET commands on the screen from access through the READ command. This command has no effect on the data stored in fields or memory variables. Chapter 4, "Commands for Managing Custom Screens," discusses this command.

CLEAR MEMORY releases all memory variables, both public and private (unlike RELEASE ALL, which releases only private variables). See Chapter 14, "Commands for Memory Variables," for additional details.

CLEAR TYPEAHEAD empties the typeahead buffer, ensuring that no old keystrokes affect new commands that accept data (such as READ, ACCEPT, WAIT, and so forth).

The CLEAR command is not accessible from the Assistant menu.

Consider this routine from a command file:

```
CLEAR
UserName = SPACE(30)
@ 10,10 SAY "Enter your name " ;
    GET UserName
READ

@ 20,2 SAY "Hello, " + UserName + "..."
?
CLEAR TYPEAHEAD
WAIT
```

The first CLEAR command clears the screen. The first @...SAY-
...GET combination waits for the user to type his or her name. The
second @...SAY combination displays a message with the user's
name. The CLEAR TYPEAHEAD command deletes any ex-
traneous keystrokes beyond the allowable length of the UserName
variable from the typeahead buffer, so that they will not affect the
WAIT command. The WAIT command displays the prompt *Press
any key to continue* and waits for the user to press any key.

CLOSE
@...SAY...GET
RELEASE
SET FIELDS
SET VIEW
SET TYPEAHEAD

The CLOSE Command

Closing a File

CLOSE closes the type of file specified, emptying any buffers and ensuring that the closed file is up to date. Each time a file is closed, the number of simultaneously open files is reduced by one.

SYNTAX

**CLOSE [ALL] [ALTERNATE] [DATABASES]
[FORMAT] [INDEX] [PROCEDURE]**

VERSION

dBASE III PLUS, dBASE III

USAGE

The CLOSE command allows you to close files that are no longer needed for immediate use. You can use CLOSE in conjunction with commands that will work only with closed files (such as ERASE, MODIFY, SELECT, and others) to close a particular file before issuing the command.

EXAMPLES

The following command closes all open files but has no effect on memory variables.

CLOSE ALL

To close only the open database, index, and format files, enter the command

CLOSE DATABASES

TIPS

Remember, CLOSE DATABASES closes *all* open files of the specified type. To close only files in a particular work area, select that work area and issue a USE command without a file name, as follows:

SELECT J
USE

The CLOSE command is not accessible from the Assistant menu.

SEE ALSO

CLEAR   SET PROCEDURE
INDEX   SET ALTERNATE
SET INDEX   SELECT
SET FORMAT   USE

The COPY Command
Copying a File

COPY makes a copy of an existing file on disk.

SYNTAX

COPY *[FILE] [STRUCTURE] [TO new file name scope]*
    [FIELDS field list]*
    [WHILE condition] [FOR* condition]*
    [TYPE file type] [STRUCTURE EXTENDED]*

where *new file name* is the name of the copy, *scope* is any valid scope option, *field list* is a list of field names delimited by commas, *condition* is any valid search criterion, and *file type* is a foreign file definition. The [FILE], [STRUCTURE], and [STRUCTURE EXTENDED] options are alternate versions of the COPY command.

VERSION

dBASE III PLUS, dBASE III

USAGE

The following paragraphs discuss each of the four versions of the COPY command.

COPY TO

The COPY TO command copies the currently selected database file to a new database file with the same structure, or at least a portion of the same structure. If the file the records are being copied to already exists, dBASE asks for permission before overwriting the existing file *only* if the SET SAFETY parameter is on. If SET SAFETY is off, the file is overwritten automatically.

Unless otherwise specified, all records are copied to the new file. If SET DELETED is on, records marked for deletion are not copied. If a SET FILTER condition is in effect, only records that meet the filter criteria are copied. If an index file is in use, the records on the copied database file will be in the sort order specified by the index file.

The FIELDS option limits the copy operation to particular fields. For example, the command

> **COPY TO Summary FIELDS CustNo, LName, FName, ;**
> **Address**

copies only the four listed fields to a database file named Summary.

The WHILE and FOR options limit the records copied to those that meet a search criterion. For example, the following commands copy only records in which the LName field begins with the letters A through M.

COPY TO A:Half FOR LName > = "A" .AND. ;
LName < = "M"

You can build a COPY TO command from the Assistant menu by highlighting Organize on the top menu and selecting Copy from the pull-down menu.

COPY TYPE

The COPY TYPE command allows you to export dBASE data to various other software systems and file formats. For example, to copy a database file to VisiCalc format, open the database with the USE command and enter the command

COPY TO *new file name* **TYPE DIF**

where *new file name* is the name of the new file. The dBASE program will add the extension .dif to the exported file. To export data from dBASE to Multiplan spreadsheets, use the SYLK option with the copy command. The file being exported must have been opened with the USE command before the COPY command is issued. The copied file will not have an extension unless you specify one in the *new file name* portion of the command.

To copy dBASE data to Lotus 1-2-3 format, use the WKS option with the COPY command.

The TYPE SDF and TYPE DELIMITED options allow you to export ASCII text file copies of dBASE data. See the discussion of APPEND FROM in Chapter 3 for a discussion of the TYPE options, which are the same for both APPEND FROM and COPY TO.

The FIELDS, FOR, and WHILE options can be used with TYPE, just as they can be with other versions of the COPY command. FOR and WHILE limit TYPE to certain records, and FIELDS limits TYPE to certain fields.

This version of the COPY command is not available from the Assistant menu.

COPY FILE

The COPY FILE command copies *any* file to a new file. You must include file-name extensions with both file names in the command. For example, the command

COPY FILE MyProg.prg TO A:MyProg.bak

copies the command file named MyProg.prg to a file named MyProg.bak on drive A.

If the SET SAFETY parameter is on, COPY FILE will ask for permission before overwriting an existing file. Otherwise, it automatically overwrites the existing file.

COPY FILE is somewhat faster than COPY TO if you wish to copy an entire database file. However, COPY FILE does not automatically copy memo field (.dbt) files, so you'll need to copy these separately. Furthermore, COPY FILE does not support the FOR, WHILE, or FIELDS option.

To access the COPY FILE command from the Assistant menu, highlight Tools on the top menu and select Copy File from the pull-down menu.

COPY STRUCTURE

The COPY STRUCTURE command copies only the structure of a database to a new file, not the records. Like the COPY TO command, COPY STRUCTURE allows you to limit the copy operation to particular fields using the FIELDS option.

COPY STRUCTURE is not available from the Assistant menu.

COPY STRUCTURE EXTENDED

The COPY TO *new file name* STRUCTURE EXTENDED command creates a new database with four fields named Field_Name, Field_Type, Field_Len, and Field_Dec. Each record in this new file defines a single field in the file it was copied from.

You can create a new database file from the structure-extended file using the CREATE FROM command.

EXAMPLES

The following commands copy the database file Mail.dbf to three smaller files named Part1, Part2, and Part3. The routine demonstrates a technique for storing a large database file from a hard disk on smaller files on floppy disks.

```
USE Mail
? "Place Part 1 disk in drive A"
WAIT
COPY TO A:Part1 FOR LName < = "J"
? "Place Part 2 disk in drive A"
WAIT
COPY TO A:Part2 FOR LName > = "K" .AND. LName < = "S"
? "Place Part 3 disk in drive A"
WAIT
COPY TO A:Part3 FOR LName > = "T"
```

The following command copies the memo field file Mail.dbt to a backup file named MailMemo.bak.

```
COPY FILE Mail.dbt TO MailMemo.bak
```

SEE ALSO

APPEND
FROM
CREATE
MODIFY STRUCTURE
RENAME

The DIR Command

Displaying File Names

DIR displays the names of files on the directory.

SYNTAX

DIR *drive path wildcard*

where *drive* and *path* are the disk drive and path designations and *wildcard* is an optional skeletal file name represented as a sequence of characters.

VERSION

dBASE III PLUS, dBASE III

USAGE

If no drive, path, or wild card is included in the command, DIR displays the names of database (.dbf) files only. For each database file, it displays the number of records, date of last update, and file size (in bytes). DIR also shows the number of files displayed, the total number of bytes that the files occupy, and the number of bytes remaining on the disk drive. If there are more files than will fit on the screen, DIR pauses before each screenful and displays the message *Press any key to continue.*

Use a wild card in the DIR command to display nondatabase files. In the wild card, ? matches any single character and * matches any group of characters. When displaying nondatabase files, the file sizes and latest update dates are not displayed.

To access the DIR command from the Assistant menu, highlight Tools and select Directory from the pull-down menu.

EXAMPLES

The command

DIR *.prg

displays the names of all program (.prg) files on the currently logged drive and directory.

The command

DIR B:\dbdata*.db?

displays the names of files on the dbdata directory of drive B that begin with the letters db in the file extension (for example, .dbf and .dbt files).

SEE ALSO

LIST
DISPLAY

The DISPLAY Command
Displaying Record Contents

The DISPLAY command displays the contents of a database record.

SYNTAX

DISPLAY *[scope] [fields/expressions]*
    *[**WHILE** condition]* *[**FOR** condition]*
    *[**OFF**]* *[**TO PRINT**]*

where *scope* is a scope option, *fields/expressions* is a list of field names or expressions separated by commas, and *condition* is a valid search criterion.

VERSION

dBASE III PLUS, dBASE III

USAGE

The DISPLAY command alone shows a single record from the database file. If a scope option such as ALL, NEXT, or REST is included, the command will display several records. The FOR and WHILE options limit the display to records that match a search criterion. The OFF option suppresses display of the database record numbers. The TO PRINT option directs output to the printer. To direct output to a text file, use the SET ALTERNATE command.

The contents of a memo field are not displayed unless the name of the field is specifically requested in the *fields/expressions* list.

If the output of the DISPLAY command is more than 20 lines long, the command will pause after each 20 lines and wait for a key to be pressed to continue.

Field names or expressions are listed above the data if the SET HEADING parameter is on. If SET HEADING is off, only the data are displayed.

If the record pointer is already at the end of the file when the DISPLAY command is entered, the screen shows nothing (or only field names if SET HEADING is on).

To build a DISPLAY command from the Assistant menu, highlight Retrieve on the top menu and select Display from the pulldown menu.

DISPLAY can also be used to show information other than the contents of databases, as illustrated in the "Examples" section.

EXAMPLES

The following command prints the CustNo, Qty, and Unit_Price fields, as well as the product of the Unit_Price field multiplied by the Qty field, adding 6 percent tax only if the Tax field is .T. Only records that have 1001 in the CustNo field are included in the display. Record numbers are not included.

DISPLAY ALL CustNo, Qty, Unit_Price,;
    IIF(Tax,(Qty＊Unit_Price)＊1.06,Qty＊Unit_Price) ;
    FOR CustNo = 1001 OFF TO PRINT

SEE ALSO

LIST
MODIFY REPORT
REPORT FORM

The ERASE Command

Deleting a File

ERASE deletes a file from the directory.

SYNTAX

ERASE *file name*

where *file name* is the complete name of the file, including the extension.

VERSION

dBASE III PLUS, dBASE III

Unless otherwise specified, ERASE searches only the currently logged drive and directory for the file to erase. Furthermore, ERASE does not search the path defined in a dBASE SET PATH or DOS PATH command.

An open file cannot be erased. Use the appropriate CLOSE command to close the file before erasing it.

If the name of the file to be erased is stored in a memory variable, use macro substitution in the ERASE command, as follows:

```
FileName = "Archive.bak"
ERASE &FileName
```

Unlike DOS, dBASE does not support wild-card characters in file names used with the ERASE command. To use wild-card characters in an ERASE command, use the RUN or ! command to access the DOS ERASE command.

Erasing a file that includes a memo field does not automatically erase the associated .dbt (memo field) files. These have to be erased separately.

To access the ERASE command from the Assistant menu, highlight Tools and select Erase from the pull-down menu.

The DELETE FILE command is identical to the ERASE command.

The following commands erase the Mail.dbf database and its memo field file from the disk in drive B.

```
ERASE B:Mail.dbf
ERASE B:Mail.dbt
```

CLOSE
DELETE

The EXPORT Command

Exporting a Database to PFS:FILE Format

The EXPORT command exports a dBASE database to PFS:FILE format.

SYNTAX

EXPORT TO *file name* **TYPE PFS**

where *file name* is the name of the PFS:FILE file to create.

VERSION

dBASE III PLUS only

USAGE

Before using the EXPORT command, open the database you want to export. If you wish to export a copy of the dBASE format (.fmt) file used for entering and editing records, that format file should also be open with the SET FORMAT TO command.

If SET SAFETY is on, EXPORT will ask for permission before overwriting an existing PFS:FILE file with the same name. If SET SAFETY is off, EXPORT overwrites the existing file automatically.

PFS:FILE files generally have no extension, so you should always follow the name of the file to be created with a single period, as shown in the "Examples" section.

To access EXPORT from the Assistant menu, highlight Tools and select Export from the pull-down menu.

The following commands export a copy of the Mail.dbf database and the MailScr.fmt format file to a PFS:FILE file named PFSMail.

USE Mail
SET FORMAT TO MailScr
EXPORT TO PFSMail. TYPE PFS

TIPS

If an exported file exceeds the maximum number of fields allowed by the external software package, the external package will likely truncate the fields in the exported database.

SEE ALSO

COPY TO
IMPORT

The GO/GOTO Commands
Moving the Pointer to a Specified Position

Both GO and GOTO position the pointer to a specified record number or position in the database file.

SYNTAX

GO TOP
GOTO TOP
GO BOTTOM

GOTO BOTTOM
GO *recno*
GOTO *recno*

where *recno* is the number (or an expression that evaluates to a number) of the record to move the record pointer to.

VERSION

dBASE III PLUS, dBASE III

USAGE

GO and GOTO can be used interchangeably. The TOP and BOTTOM options move the record pointer to the first or last record in the database file or to the first and last records as determined by the currently active index file. The GO or GOTO command used with a specified number always sends the record pointer to the record with that number; the command is unaffected by index file sequence.

The record number can be calculated in an expression, as in the following example, in which the pointer is moved seven records down from the current record position.

GOTO (RECNO( ) + 7)

If the record number is stored as a character string, use a macro, as in the following example.

MoveTo = "22"
GOTO &MoveTo

Attempting to go to a record that does not exist causes the *Record out of range* error message to be displayed. This error message will appear even when the record exists in the database file but not in the currently active index file.

The GO and GOTO commands can position the record pointer at a record that is marked for deletion, even if the SET DELETED parameter is on.

To access GOTO from the Assistant menu, highlight Position and select Goto.

EXAMPLES

The following command moves the record pointer to the top of the database file before the DO WHILE .NOT. EOF( ) loop begins processing.

GO TOP
DO WHILE .NOT. EOF( )
    commands...
SKIP
ENDDO (not eof)

SEE ALSO

SKIP
SET DELETED
RECNO( )

The LIST Command

Displaying the Contents of All Records

LIST displays the contents of all database records.

SYNTAX

LIST *[scope]* *[fields/expressions]*
    *[***WHILE*** condition]* *[***FOR*** condition]*
    [OFF] *[***TO PRINT***]*

where *scope* is a scope option, *fields/expressions* is a list of field names or expressions separated by commas, and *condition* is a valid search criterion.

VERSION

dBASE III PLUS, dBASE III

USAGE

When used without additional options, LIST displays every record in the database file. If a scope option is included, the display is limited to the number of records specified in the scope condition. The FOR and WHILE options limit the display to records that match a search criterion. The OFF option suppresses the display of the database record numbers. The TO PRINT option directs output to the printer. To direct output to a text file, use the SET ALTERNATE command.

Unlike the DISPLAY command, LIST does not pause for a keypress after every 20 lines.

The contents of memo fields are not displayed by the LIST command unless specifically requested in the *fields/expressions* list. The default width for memo fields is 50 characters, though this can be changed with the SET MEMOWIDTH command.

Field names or expressions are displayed above the data if the SET HEADING parameter is on. If SET HEADING is off, only the data are displayed.

Like DISPLAY, LIST can also be used to show information other than the contents of databases, as illustrated in the "Examples" section.

To access the LIST command from the Assistant menu, highlight the Retrieve option and select List from the pull-down menu.

EXAMPLES

The following command prints the CustNo, Qty, and Unit_Price fields and the product of the Unit_Price field multiplied by the Qty field, adding 6 percent tax only if the Tax field is .T. Only records that have 1001 in the CustNo field are included in the display. Record numbers are not included in the display.

```
LIST CustNo, Qty, Unit_Price, ;
    IIF(Tax,(Qty*Unit_Price)*1.06,Qty*Unit_Price) ;
    FOR CustNo = 1001 OFF TO PRINT
```

SEE ALSO

DISPLAY
MODIFY REPORT
REPORT FORM

The MODIFY STRUCTURE Command

Restructuring an Existing Database File

MODIFY STRUCTURE allows you to change the structure of an existing database file.

SYNTAX

MODIFY STRUCTURE

VERSION

dBASE III PLUS, dBASE III

USAGE

The MODIFY STRUCTURE command allows you to move the cursor freely and change the field names, data types, widths, and decimal places of any existing field. You can also add new fields or delete existing fields. The control keys used in MODIFY STRUCTURE are identical to those used with the CREATE command, as shown in Table 2.2.

Take care not to change both the name of a field and its width during a single session. Doing so will likely lead to data loss. Instead, use MODIFY STRUCTURE to change the name of the field and save the new database structure immediately. Then use MODIFY STRUCTURE again to change the width of the field, and again save the new structure immediately.

To access MODIFY STRUCTURE from the Assistant menu, highlight Modify on the top menu and select Database file from the pull-down menu.

EXAMPLES

The commands

USE Mail
MODIFY STRUCTURE

bring the structure of the Mail database to the screen ready for editing.

SEE ALSO

CREATE

The RENAME Command
Renaming a File

RENAME changes the name of a file on disk.

SYNTAX

RENAME *old file name* **TO** *new file name*

where *old file name* is the complete name of the file to rename, and *new file name* is the complete new name for the file.

VERSION

dBASE III PLUS, dBASE III

USAGE

RENAME requires the use of file-name extensions in both the original and new file names. The current disk drive and directory are assumed in both file names, unless otherwise specified. The RENAME command does *not* search paths specified in the DOS PATH or dBASE SET PATH commands.

If a database file that contains a memo field is being renamed, the associated .dbt file must be renamed separately.

The new file name must be unique to the currently logged drive and directory. If another file with the specified new file name already exists, an error message is displayed and both files remain as they were. An open file cannot be renamed. Use the appropriate version of the CLOSE command to close an open file before renaming it.

To access RENAME from the Assistant menu, highlight Tools and select Rename.

Unlike the DOS RENAME command, the dBASE RENAME command does not support the wild-card characters ? or *.

EXAMPLES

The following command changes the name of the MyProg.cmd file to MyProg.prg.

RENAME MyProg.cmd TO MyProg.prg

SEE ALSO

COPY

The SKIP Command

Moving the Pointer N Records

SKIP moves the record pointer a specified number of records from its current position.

SYNTAX

SKIP *n*

where *n* is the number of records to move the pointer (or an expression that calculates that number).

VERSION

dBASE III PLUS, dBASE III

USAGE

If the database file in use is indexed, SKIP moves the record pointer in the order defined by the index file expression. If the database is not indexed, SKIP moves the record pointer sequentially, based on record numbers.

The SKIP command alone moves the pointer forward one record. To move the record pointer backward, you must include a minus sign and a number.

To access SKIP from the Assistant menu, highlight Position and select Skip from the pull-down menu.

EXAMPLES

The following command moves the pointer forward 10 records.

SKIP 10

The next command moves the record pointer back one record.

   SKIP − 1

The next command calculates the number of records to skip, using a complex expression and memory variables named Cols and Rows.

   SKIP (((Cols − 1) * Rows) − 1) * − 1

SEE ALSO

   GO/GOTO
   DO WHILE
   BOF( )
   EOF( )
   RECNO( )

The TYPE Command
Displaying Text File Contents

The TYPE command displays the contents of a text file.

SYNTAX

   TYPE *file name* *[***TO PRINT***]*

where *file name* is the name of the text file whose contents you wish to view, and the TO PRINT option sends output to the printer.

VERSION

dBASE III PLUS, dBASE III

USAGE

TYPE displays the contents of any DOS text (or ASCII) file, including dBASE command files and text files created by the TO FILE option available with REPORT and LABEL. TYPE will also display output from an ALTERNATE file. ASCII files generated by dBASE generally include the extension .txt.

TYPE cannot display the contents of non-ASCII files, including dBASE .dbf and .ndx files and DOS file names with the .com, .exe, .bin, and .obj extensions. TYPE cannot display open files.

The current drive and directory are assumed unless otherwise specified. The file-name extension must be included.

The TYPE command is not accessible from the Assistant menu.

EXAMPLES

The command

TYPE MyProg.prg TO PRINT

prints the contents of the dBASE command file named MyProg.

TIPS

You can use the TYPE command to view the structure of external ASCII files before attempting to import them with the APPEND FROM...TYPE command.

SEE ALSO

APPEND FROM
COPY TO...TYPE
LABEL FORM
REPORT FORM
SET ALTERNATE

11

Commands for Managing Multiple Database Files

Multiple database files are generally set up to manage *one-to-many* relationships among data items. For example, in an accounts receivable system, you would probably store *many* transactions for each *one* customer. Figure 11.1 shows how two database files, named Customer.dbf and Charges.dbf, could be set up to store accounts receivable data.

Notice that both databases have a field named CustNo, for the customer's account number. This is the *common field*, or *key field*, that relates the two files. When you create databases that will be related in this manner, this common field must be identical in field name, data type, width, and number of decimal places (if applicable) in both database files.

Because there are *many* transactions for each *one* customer, we can say that the Charges database represents the *many side* of the relationship, and the Customer database represents the *one side*. Keeping these terms in mind when reading this chapter will help clarify the discussions of these commands. In almost all cases, you'll want to set up database relationships so that the file on the "many side" of the relationship *points into* the file on the "one side" of the relationship. Specifically, you want the common field on the "many side" of the relationship to point to the index file of the common field on the "one side" of the relationship.

```
        Customer.dbf (one record per customer)

   CustNo  LName    FName      Address              City        -->
  ►1001    Adams    Martha     P.O. Box 1107        Alameda     etc.
   1002    Smith    Albert     345 C St.            San Diego   etc.
   1003    Jones    Fred       345 Grape St.  '     Encinitas   etc.



        Charges.dbf   (one  record  per  charge)

      CustNo  Part_No   Qty   Unit_Price   Date
    ► 1001    A-111     3      10.00        07/05/87
      1003    B-222     10      4.95        07/07/87
    ► 1001    C-333     1      44.45        07/11/87
      1002    A-111     15     10.00        07/16/87
    ► 1001    B-222     2       4.95        07/18/87
```

Figure 11.1: Sample database design for storing accounts receivable data

The CREATE VIEW and MODIFY VIEW Commands

Setting Up a View File

The CREATE VIEW and MODIFY VIEW commands establish links among database files and store the parameters for setting up the relationship within a view (.vue) file. Once the view file is established, the two (or more) related database files can be handled as a single database file in many dBASE operations.

SYNTAX

CREATE VIEW/MODIFY VIEW *file name*
  [FROM ENVIRONMENT]

where *file name* is the name of the view file to create or modify.

VERSION

dBASE III PLUS only

USAGE

The CREATE VIEW and MODIFY VIEW commands (without the FROM ENVIRONMENT option) present a full-screen, menu-driven environment for defining the relationships among database files. CREATE VIEW creates a new view file, and MODIFY VIEW alters an existing view file. You can access CREATE VIEW and MODIFY VIEW from the Assistant menu by highlighting either Modify or Create on the top menu and selecting View from the sub-menu. Once the relationships are defined, the parameters necessary to establish the relationships are stored in the view file.

The default extension that dBASE provides for the view file name is .vue. The view file will contain all of the necessary elements to open the work areas, database files, and index files for the relationship, as well as the necessary relationship definitions. In addition, you can define a filter criterion, fields, and a format file for the view.

CREATE VIEW and MODIFY VIEW present the Set Up, Relate, Set Fields, Options, and Exit menus. Menu options can be selected by moving the highlight with the arrow keys. Each item, when highlighted, displays a pull-down menu. Options within a pull-down menu are selected by moving the highlight to the option and pressing Return. The ← and → keys will always exit a submenu and return you to the higher-level menu.

Views are automatically activated when you select Exit and Save from the top menu. You can also activate an existing view by issuing the SET VIEW command or by highlighting Set Up on the Assistant menu and selecting View on the pull-down menu.

Individual menu items on the CREATE/MODIFY VIEW screen are discussed in the following sections.

The Set Up Menu

The Set Up menu displays a list of all database files on the currently logged drive and directory. As soon as you select a database file, the screen displays a list of the names of all index files on the current drive and directory. You can select index files for the database using the usual method of highlighting and pressing Return. A triangle appears to the left of database and index file names selected for the view. Pressing ← leaves the submenu and returns to the higher-level menu.

When selecting database files for the view, the database file on the "many side" need not have an associated index file, unless you want to use an index file to specify a sort order for the display. However, any database on the "one side" of a relationship must be indexed on the common field, and that index must be selected from the Set Up menu.

If more than two database files are to be included in the view, they must be selected in a chain-like manner; never reselect a database file that has already been selected for the view.

The Relate Menu

Once the database and index files are selected for a view, the Relate menu displays the names of the selected database files and allows you to select fields from each database to define relationships. When you select a database file from the Relate menu, the screen displays remaining database files into which you can set a relationship. When you select a file, the screen asks you to define the expression relating the two files. You can press F10 for a list of field names to base the relationship on and select any field by highlighting it and pressing Return. You must select a field, or define an expression involving two or more fields, that the two files have in common. Furthermore, the field or expression you select *must* match the contents of the index file of the file being pointed into (that is, the index file for the file on the "one side" of the relationship). The contents of the index file are displayed at the bottom of the screen.

The Set Fields Menu

After the relationships are defined, the Set Fields menu lets you select fields from the database files to display. When you select this menu, it displays the names of all database files in the view file. Selecting a database file name displays a list of all fields in that database. All fields are initially marked with a triangle for display. To exclude a field from display, move the highlight to the field name and press Return. Fields without the triangle on the left are hidden while the view file is in effect. You can include as many fields in the display as you wish.

The Options Menu

The Options menu presents two options: Format and Filter. The Format option lets you select an existing format file that is automatically opened when the view file is opened. The Filter option allows you to define a Filter criterion for selecting records that should be displayed in the view. If no filter is specified, all records are accessible through the view. If a filter condition such as State = "CA" is defined, only records with CA in the State field are displayed when the view file is in effect.

The Exit Menu

The Exit menu presents the Save and Abandon options. The Save option saves the current view in the view file and automatically activates the view. The Abandon option abandons the currently defined view, does not save the current view in the view file, and does not activate the view.

Once the view is defined, the SET VIEW command opens the view and, consequently, all files defined for the view. On the Assistant menu, you can select the View option on the Set Up menu to activate a view. Once a view is activated, all future commands will treat the files in the view as a single database file.

CREATE VIEW FROM ENVIRONMENT

The alternative syntax CREATE VIEW *file name* FROM ENVIRONMENT creates a view file from the relationships that have already been determined in a series of SELECT, USE, and SET RELATION commands. This form of the command does not use a menu for defining the view. The "Examples" section demonstrates the use of this alternative syntax for the CREATE VIEW command.

Note that the FROM ENVIRONMENT parameter is used only with CREATE VIEW, not with MODIFY VIEW. However, once a view has been created with the CREATE VIEW *filename* FROM ENVIRONMENT command, that view can be altered using MODIFY VIEW *file name*.

EXAMPLES

The steps presented here would set up a relationship from the Charges.dbf database into the Customer.dbf database. Before building the view, enter the command **INDEX ON CustNo to Customer** to create an index file of the CustNo field for the Customer database.

To create the view file, first, at the dot prompt, enter the command **CREATE VIEW AR1**. The prompt reads *Select database files to be represented in this view*. From the Set Up menu select Charges.dbf and press ← to leave the index file submenu without selecting an index file. Also, select Customer.dbf as the second database and Customer.ndx as the index file.

Now select the Relate option. The prompt reads *Select the database that will initiate the relation*. This will be the database on the "many side" of the relationship, so highlight Charges.dbf and press Return.

Next, the instruction reads *Select the database file that will accept the relation*. This will be the file on the "one side" of the relationship, so highlight Customer.dbf and press Return.

You are now prompted to *Enter an expression* or *Press F10 for a field menu* and reminded that *The master index key expression is CustNo*. CustNo is, indeed, the common field, so press F10 and select CustNo from the list of field names. Then press Return. At this point, the action line reads *Relation chain: CHARGES.DBF->CUSTOMER.DBF*, indicating that the Charges.dbf database is "pointing into" the Customer database (that is, the "many side" is properly pointing into the "one side" of the relationship).

Next, select the Set Fields option. The instruction reads *Select a database from which to choose fields*. Select Charges.dbf and then select individual fields. Select Customer.dbf and select fields to display from this database as well. When you are done, press ←. You can now select Filter to define a permanent filter criterion for the view, Format to assign it an existing format file, or Exit and Save to complete it.

The alternative series of commands for setting up the identical view file for Customer.dbf and Charges.dbf is shown here.

```
SELECT A
USE Charges
SELECT B
USE Customer INDEX Customer
SELECT A
SET RELATION TO CustNo INTO Customer

*SET FIELDS TO field names
CREATE VIEW Ar1 FROM ENVIRONMENT
```

(The SET FIELDS option allows you to define field names for the view).

Regardless of which technique you use to create the view, you can use MODIFY VIEW to change it.

SEE ALSO

SELECT   SET FILTER
SET RELATION   SET FORMAT
SET VIEW   USE
SET FIELDS

The JOIN Command

Merging Two Databases

JOIN merges the contents of two database files into a new, third database file.

SYNTAX

JOIN WITH *alias* **TO** *file name*
    FOR *condition [***FIELDS** *field list]*

where *alias* is the name of the database file, alias, or work area of the file being combined with currently selected database files, *file name* is the name of the new file being created, *condition* is any valid search criterion that selects what will go into the merged file, and *field list* is an optional list of field names to include in the new file.

VERSION

dBASE III PLUS, dBASE III

USAGE ═══════════════════════

Both files to be joined must be open simultaneously. If the FIELDS option is not included, all fields from both database files are included in the newly created file.

The JOIN command is not accessible from the Assistant menu.

EXAMPLES ═══════════════════════

The following commands create a database file named BigFile consisting of the FName and LName fields from the Customer database and the Charge and Date fields from the Charges database.

```
SELECT A
USE Customer
SELECT B
USE Charges
SELECT A

JOIN WITH B TO BigFile FOR CustNo = B->CustNo ;
    FIELDS FName, LName, B->Charge, B->Date
```

SEE ALSO ═══════════════════════

SET RELATION
SELECT

The SELECT Command

Assigning Databases to Work Areas

The SELECT command is used both to assign databases to work areas and to move from one work area to another. By assigning databases to separate work areas with the SELECT command, you can open up to 10 database files simultaneously. You can define the 10 work areas as either 1 through 10 or A through J.

SYNTAX

SELECT *work area/alias*

where *work area* is a letter A through J or a number 1 through 10, and *alias* is the name of the database or an alias defined in the ALIAS portion of a USE command.

VERSION

dBASE III PLUS only; in dBASE III use SET

USAGE

Once you have defined work areas with the SELECT and USE commands, you can select a new work area without affecting the current record position of the pointer in the unselected work area.

Generally, any command that changes the contents of a field (APPEND, EDIT, BROWSE, READ, and so forth) works only for the currently active database (the one specified by the most recent SELECT command). However, you can *display* fields from any database by using a pointer. For example, the command

LIST Prod_No, B– >ProdName, C– >Vendor

displays the Prod_No field from the currently selected database, the ProdName field from the database in work area B, and the Vendor field from the database in work area C. You can use file name aliases in lieu of the B–> and C–> symbols. For example, if the Prod-Name field is stored in a database named Master.dbf, and the Vendor field is stored in a database named Vendors.dbf, you can use this LIST command:

LIST Prod_No, Master– >ProdName, Vendors– >Vendor

Aliases can be used with all dBASE commands that use field names, including MODIFY REPORT, MODIFY LABEL, DISPLAY, ?, SUM, AVERAGE, and COUNT.

In some cases, dBASE will not allow all 10 database files to be open. For example, if a catalog is in use, it occupies the tenth file position; hence, only 9 other files can be opened with the SELECT and USE commands. Furthermore, if the Config.sys file does not specify FILES = 20 and BUFFERS = 15, the error message *Too many files are open* will appear before 10 files are open. Command files, along with other open files, may also reduce the number of database files you can open.

EXAMPLES

In the following example, the Master database and Master index file are assigned to work area A. The Charges database and the Charges and ChrgDate index files are assigned to work area B.

SELECT A
USE Master INDEX Master
SELECT B
USE Charges INDEX Charges, ChrgDate

At this point, the Charges database and its index files are currently active. To make the Master database and Master index files active (so that commands such as LIST, APPEND, and EDIT access the Master database and its index file), you can enter the command

SELECT A

TIPS

Be sure to use the SELECT command rather than the USE command to switch among multiple open database files. Remember that USE opens a file in the current work area and closes whatever file was already open in that work area.

SEE ALSO

USE
SET RELATION
SET VIEW
CREATE/MODIFY VIEW
SET FIELDS

The SET RELATION Command

Defining a Relationship Between Two Open Databases

The SET RELATION command defines a relationship between two databases that are open simultaneously. The databases must have a field or group of fields common to both database files.

SYNTAX

SET RELATION TO *common field* **RECNO( )**
   INTO *file name*

where *common field* is the key field that both files share and is indexed on the linked file. In lieu of a common field, you can use RECNO( ), which sets a one-to-one relationship between multiple database files and is generally used to bypass the 128-field-per-record limitation. The *file name* parameter can be the name of the file being linked or the work area for that file or an alias specified in the USE command.

VERSION

dBASE III PLUS, dBASE III

SET RELATION links the currently active database (as defined by the SELECT command) to another open database. The active database should be the "many side" in a one-to-many relationship. The field name following the TO portion of the command indicates a common field that is identical in name, data type, and width for both databases; it may also indicate any combination of common fields in both databases. The index expression in the linked file must match the expression to the right of the TO portion of the SET RELATION command.

Once a relationship is set, any movement through the currently selected database file causes dBASE to move the record pointer to the corresponding record in the linked file. The positioning involves an index file; hence, the linked file must be indexed on the common field. If no value in the linked file matches the value in the active database, the record pointer in the linked file is set to EOF( ).

Only one relationship can be set from one work area into another. You can, however, set up relationships from *several* work areas into a *single* work area. The command SET RELATION TO without any following parameters ends the relationship in the currently selected work area.

The dBASE program allows up to seven relationships to be active at any given time. Hence, if at least eight database files are open simultaneously (SELECT A through SELECT H), seven SET RELATION commands can be issued, each one set from its own work area (A through H).

If you use RECNO( ) as the SET RELATION expression, the open files will be linked based on matching record numbers. This command allows you to bypass the 128-field-per-record limit.

When deleting and packing records, it is imperative that both database files be treated equally. If you delete and pack any records on one database but not the other, the two databases will have an unequal number of records, and the SET RELATION command will no longer accurately link records in the packed database to records in the unpacked database.

The SET RELATION command is not accessible from the Assistant menu.

The file named Products contains the part number (PartNo), part name (PartName), and selling price (Sel_Price) for each product sold in a store. Products was indexed on the PartNo field using the command INDEX ON Part_No TO Products. The Orders database contains a record for each order. Each record includes the part number (PartNo) and the quantity ordered (Qty), but not the part name and selling price. To see a list of all orders from Orders, with the part name and extended price (quantity × selling price), first set a relationship from Orders into the Products.dbf and Products.ndx files, as follows:

```
SELECT A
USE Orders
SELECT B
USE Products INDEX Products
SELECT A
SET RELATION TO PartNo INTO Products
```

To view the orders with part names and extended prices, enter the command

```
LIST PartNo,B->PartName,(Qty * B->Sel_Price)
```

The SET FIELDS command can be used with CREATE/MODIFY VIEW or SET RELATION.

Even when multiple database files are open and related, the APPEND and INSERT commands add data to the currently selected database file only.

SELECT   CREATE/MODIFY VIEW
USE   SET FIELDS
INDEX   SET VIEW

The UPDATE Command

Updating One Database File from Another

UPDATE changes the contents of one database file based on the contents of another database file.

SYNTAX

> **UPDATE ON** *key field* **FROM** *fromfile*
>   **REPLACE** *field* **WITH** *expression*
>   *[additional fields* **WITH** *expressions]*
>   *[RANDOM]*

where *key field* is the common field relating the two database files, *fromfile* is the name of the outside file containing the data used in the update operation, *field* is the name of a field to be changed, *expression* is the change to perform, and *additional fields* WITH *expressions* are additional fields and expressions in the update operation.

VERSION

dBASE III PLUS, dBASE III

USAGE

UPDATE is typically used to update values in a master file based on data stored in a transaction file. Both the master and transaction file must be open, and they must have a common field. Any field names from the transaction file must be preceded with an alias (B->).

Both files should be indexed on the key field that relates the two files. If only the master file (the one being updated) is sorted or indexed, the RANDOM option must be included at the end of the UPDATE command. When RANDOM is used with an unindexed file, the update operation will usually require more time.

The UPDATE command is not accessible from the Assistant menu.

EXAMPLES

In this example, the master database named MastFile, indexed on the PartNo field, contains the following records.

Record#	PartNo	PartName	In_Stock	Last_Sale	Ytd_Sold
1	1111	Apples	10	12/31/87	100
2	2222	Bananas	10	12/31/87	50

A transaction file called TranFile, which is also indexed on the PartNo field, contains the three sales transactions shown here.

Record#	PartNo	Qty_Sold	Date_Sold
1	1111	1	02/01/87
2	1111	5	02/02/87
3	2222	5	03/01/87

To subtract the quantities sold from the quantities in stock, replace the Last_Sale field with the date of the last sale, increment the Ytd_Sold field by the quantity sold for each part number, and enter these commands:

```
SELECT A
USE MastFile INDEX Mastfile
SELECT B
USE TranFile INDEX TranFile

SELECT A
UPDATE ON PartNo FROM Tranfile ;
    REPLACE In_Stock WITH In_Stock - B->Qty_Sold, ;
    Last_Sale WITH B->Date_Sold, ;
    Ytd_Sold WITH Ytd_Sold + B->Qty_Sold
```

When command execution is finished, the MastFile database will contain the data shown here.

Record#	PartNo	PartName	In_Stock	Last_Sale	Ytd_Sold
1	1111	Apples	4	02/02/87	106
2	2222	Bananas	5	03/01/87	55

Notice that the expression REPLACE In_Stock WITH In_Stock - B->Qty_Sold subtracted six units from the In_Stock quantity for part 1111 and five units from the In_Stock quantity for part number 2222. The second expression, REPLACE...Last_Sale WITH B->Date_Sold, replaced the Last_Sale dates with the dates in the Date_Sold field in the TranFile database. The last listed date for part number 1111 (02/02/87) is the one that remained in the MastFile database.

In the MastFile database, the Ytd_Sold field was incremented by 6 for part number 1111 and by 5 for part number 2222 because of the UPDATE expression REPLACE...Ytd_Sold WITH Ytd_Sold + B->Qty_Sold.

The key field, PartNo, matched the quantities and dates in the TranFile database to the appropriate records in the MastFile database to ensure that the update was accurate.

SEE ALSO

SET RELATION
SELECT

12

Programming Commands

The commands presented in this chapter are used only in conjunction with command files (or dBASE *programs*). None of these commands is accessible from the Assistant menu. The MODIFY COMMAND (or CREATE COMMAND) command allows you create a new command file or modify an existing one. The DO command is used to run the completed command file.

Within a program, commands such as ACCEPT, INPUT, and WAIT provide a means for presenting prompts to the user and storing the user's response to the prompts. Other commands, such as DO WHILE...ENDDO, IF...ELSE...ENDIF, and DO CASE...ENDCASE, provide a means for controlling the logical flow of a program.

The *, &&, and NOTE Commands

Adding Comment Lines

The NOTE, *, and && commands serve exactly the same purpose in a command file: They define a line as a programmer comment to be ignored by the dBASE interpreter.

SYNTAX

NOTE *any text*
* *any text*
dBASE command
&& *any text*

where *any text* is any information you wish to place in a program as a note to yourself or other programmers, and *dBASE command* is any dBASE command.

VERSION

* and NOTE: dBASE III PLUS, dBASE III; &&: dBASE III PLUS only

---

USAGE

NOTE and * define an entire line, beginning in the leftmost column of a command file, as a comment. The && command marks in-line comments to the right of an existing command.

EXAMPLES

In the following example, only the command ExtPrice = Qty *
U_Price is actually processed by dBASE.

> **NOTE: ExtPrice is the extended price of the transaction.**
> ***   Qty is the Quantity, U_Price is unit price.**
> **ExtPrice = Qty * U_Price   && Calculate extended price**

ACCEPT Command

Storing a Response to a Prompt

The ACCEPT command presents a prompt on the screen and waits
for the user to respond by typing some text and pressing the Return
key. Whatever the user types is stored in a memory variable.

SYNTAX

ACCEPT *[prompt]* **TO** *memory variable*

where *prompt* is optional and *memory variable* is the name of the
character memory variable that will store the user's entry.

VERSION

dBASE III PLUS, dBASE III

USAGE

Use ACCEPT to present a prompt to the user and wait for a response.
(Although technically the prompt is optional, it is generally included.)

The user's response is stored in a memory variable of the character data type. The data stored in the memory variable can be from 1 to 254 characters long.

The optional prompt can be surrounded by quotation marks, apostrophes, or brackets. The following examples are equivalent.

ACCEPT "Enter your name " TO Name
ACCEPT 'Enter your name ' TO Name
ACCEPT [Enter your name] TO Name

To embed an apostrophe or other character in the prompt, just use different characters for the outside delimiters:

ACCEPT "What's your name " TO Name

The prompt itself can be stored in a memory variable. Moreover, a macro can be placed anywhere in a prompt.

The character data that the user types in response to the prompt that ACCEPT presents can be treated as any other character-string memory variable.

EXAMPLES

The command line

ACCEPT "Enter your name " TO Name

displays the prompt *Enter your name* on the screen and waits for the user to type some text and press Return. Whatever the user types before pressing the Return key is stored in the variable Name as a character string.

TIPS

Any data entered via the ACCEPT command can be used for macro substitution.

ACCEPT will work with character strings of any length up to 254 characters. To restrict the size of the memory variable character string, use the @...READ command instead.

To convert the character data entered via the ACCEPT command to numeric or date data, use the VAL or CTOD function.

To detect whether the user pressed Return without entering any text in response to the ACCEPT command prompt, check for either a length greater than 0, an ASCII value greater than 0, or a null string ("").

SEE ALSO

@...READ
INPUT
WAIT

The CREATE COMMAND Command
Creating or Modifying Command Files

See the MODIFY COMMAND command later in this chapter.

The DO Command
Executing a Command File

The DO command tells dBASE to perform all of the commands stored in a command file or procedure. It can be entered directly at the dot prompt or used within a command file to call another command file.

SYNTAX

DO *program name* [**WITH** *parameters*]

where *program name* is the name of a command file with the assumed extension .prg, or a procedure within a procedure file, and the optional *parameters* are the data to be passed to the procedure or command file.

VERSION

dBASE III PLUS, dBASE III

USAGE

The DO command executes all commands in a command file or procedure. It cannot call a file that is already open (that is, you cannot call a command file or procedure file recursively in dBASE III PLUS).

If the DO command is entered at the dot prompt, the dot prompt reappears when the command file or procedure has finished running. If DO is used as a command in a command file, control returns to the first line beneath the calling DO command when the called program is finished running or a RETURN command passes control back to the calling program.

Every DO command opens a file, which counts as an open file within the limit of 15 total open files. Therefore, a series of DO commands may cause the *Too many files are open* error message to appear, even though only a few database and index files are actually open.

When a DO command is entered, dBASE searches only the current disk and directory for the appropriate file. To specify another disk drive, use the dBASE SET DEFAULT command or specify the disk drive in the file name. To specify another directory, include it in the file name or use a SET PATH command.

Pressing the Escape (Esc) key terminates a program and presents the options Cancel, Ignore, and Suspend.

The command DO MyProg first searches for a procedure named MyProg in the currently open procedure file. If no such procedure exists, or if there is no open procedure file, the command searches for a command file named MyProg.prg on disk. If neither a procedure nor a command file with the correct name can be found, dBASE returns the error message *File does not exist*.

DO...WITH   ON
RETURN   SET DOHISTORY
SET PROCEDURE   SET ECHO
PROCEDURE   SET DEBUG
PARAMETERS   SET STEP

The DO CASE... ENDCASE Command

Selecting One Option Among Alternatives

The DO CASE...CASE...OTHERWISE...ENDCASE construct selects a single course of action from a set of alternatives. It differs from the IF...ENDIF clause in that you can list many mutually exclusive options between the DO CASE and ENDCASE clauses.

```
DO CASE
    CASE condition
        commands...
```

```
     [CASE condition
          commands...]
     [OTHERWISE
          commands...]
  ENDCASE
```

where *condition* is a valid logical statement and *commands* are commands to be executed under the specified conditions. Any number of CASE commands can be listed between the DO CASE and END-CASE clauses. The OTHERWISE command is optional. A single ENDCASE command is required at the end of every DO CASE clause.

VERSION

dBASE III PLUS, dBASE III

USAGE

The DO CASE clause is used when only one option out of several alternatives is to be selected. As soon as a single CASE statement evaluates to true, dBASE performs all commands between that CASE statement and the next one in the clause. From that point on, all other CASE statements are ignored (whether they evaluate to true or not), and processing begins at the first command after the ENDCASE command.

If none of the CASE statements in a DO CASE clause evaluates to true, the commands listed after the optional OTHERWISE command are executed. If there is no OTHERWISE command and none of the CASE statements evaluates to true, all commands between DO CASE and ENDCASE are ignored.

Like the DO WHILE...ENDDO and IF...ENDIF constructs, DO CASE clauses can be nested inside one another as long as each clause begins with a DO CASE command and ends with an END-CASE command.

The DO CASE clause differs from a series of stacked IF clauses in that the alternatives in a DO CASE clause are always mutually exclusive.

EXAMPLES ═══════════════

The DO CASE clause is usually used to tell dBASE to take an action based on a user's menu selection. To test the DO CASE clause in a simple example, enter and run the following program.

```
*************************************** CaseTest.prg
*-------------- Test the DO CASE...ENDCASE Commands.
CLEAR
INPUT "Enter a number from 1 to 4 " TO X

DO CASE

   CASE X = 1
        ? "You entered one."

   CASE X = 2
        ? "You entered two."

   CASE X = 3
        ? "You entered three."

   CASE X = 4
        ? "You entered four."

   OTHERWISE
        ? "I said from one to four!"

ENDCASE
```

The INPUT command waits for a number between 1 and 4. If the user enters a number within this range, a CASE statement shows a message with the number in English (for example, *You entered one*). If the user does not enter a number between 1 and 4, the OTHER-WISE command displays the message *I said from one to four!*

SEE ALSO ═══════════════

IF...ELSE...ENDIF

The DO WHILE... ENDDO Command

Constructing Iterative Loops

The DO WHILE...ENDDO command is used to construct repetitive (*iterative*) loops in a program. As long as the condition that repeats the loop is true, all commands between the DO WHILE and ENDDO commands are executed repeatedly. When the looping condition becomes false, processing continues at the first command after ENDDO.

SYNTAX

DO WHILE *condition*
    commands...
    [LOOP]
    [EXIT]
    commands...
ENDDO

where *condition* is a logical statement that determines the condition under which the loop should continue repeating, and *commands...* are any commands to be repeated within the loop. The optional LOOP and EXIT commands are used to exit the loop before all the commands within the loop are executed. The ENDDO command marks the end of the commands to be repeated within the loop.

VERSION

dBASE III PLUS, dBASE III

USAGE

The DO WHILE loop is one of the most frequently used structures in dBASE programming. A loop tells dBASE to repeat a series of commands as long as a certain condition exists. The DO WHILE command marks the start of the loop, and the ENDDO command marks the end of the loop.

Every DO WHILE command must have one, and only one, END-DO command associated with it in the command file. The ENDDO command must be in the same command file as its associated DO WHILE command, and neither the DO WHILE nor ENDDO command should be enclosed within any conditional clause such as IF...ENDIF or DO CASE...ENDCASE.

If the DO WHILE condition is not true when the loop is entered, the loop will not be processed at all.

EXAMPLES

One of the most common programming constructs is the DO WHILE .NOT. EOF( ) loop, which repeats until the record pointer is beyond the last record in the currently open database. In the following example, the routine positions the record pointer at the first record in the currently open database (GO TOP). The loop condition repeats all commands between the DO WHILE and ENDDO commands until the record pointer is past the last record in the database.

```
GO TOP
DO WHILE .NOT. EOF( )
    ? PartNo, PartName
    ? Qty,U_Price,(Qty*U_Price)
    SKIP
ENDDO
```

Within the DO WHILE loop, the ? command displays the fields PartNo, PartName, Qty, and U_Price from a single record, as well as the extended price (Qty * U_Price). The SKIP command moves the pointer to the next record in the database.

If the SKIP command were excluded, the DO WHILE loop would simply redisplay the first record from the database forever.

The SKIP command moves the record pointer to the next record in the database, ensuring that dBASE eventually reaches the end of the database file (EOF( )), which in turn terminates the loop.

When placing loops inside of loops, be sure that each DO WHILE loop has an ENDDO associated with it. Also, keep in mind that a LOOP or EXIT command operates only on the loop at its own nesting level. Here is an example of a command file with nested loops.

```
******************************************* Nested.prg.
*--------------------------- Demonstrate nested loops.
SET TALK OFF
CLEAR
*--------- Set beginning value for outer loop.
OutLoop = 1
DO WHILE OutLoop <= 5
   ? "Outer loop = ",OutLoop
   ?
   ?
   *----- Set beginning value for inner loop.
   InLoop = 1
   DO WHILE InLoop <= 40
      ?? TRANSFORM(InLoop,"##")
      *------- Increment inner loop counter.
      InLoop = InLoop + 1
   ENDDO (InLoop)
   *--------- Increment outer loop counter.
   OutLoop = OutLoop + 1
ENDDO (OutLoop)
?
? "All done"
```

Indentations and comments next to the ENDDO commands help make the nesting more visible. In this example, the outer loop repeats 5 times, and the inner loop repeats 40 times within each outer loop.

If you place a RETURN command within a DO WHILE loop, the loop may still affect processing, even though control returned to the calling program. To avoid this, place the RETURN command beneath the ENDDO command. If necessary, you can use the EXIT or LOOP command from within the loop to exit the loop.

SEE ALSO

LOOP
EXIT

The EXIT Command

Terminating a Loop

The EXIT command passes control to the first line beneath the ENDDO command in a DO WHILE loop and terminates the loop regardless of the DO WHILE condition.

SYNTAX

EXIT

VERSION

dBASE III PLUS, dBASE III

USAGE

EXIT forces termination of a DO WHILE loop, regardless of the condition stated in the DO WHILE command. Whereas the LOOP command passes control back to the top of the loop, the EXIT command passes control on to the first command below the ENDDO command.

EXAMPLES

The following routine displays the message *Press Space Bar to stop printer* on the screen and then prints records from the currently open database using a DO WHILE .NOT. EOF( ) loop. If the user presses the space bar (ASCII 32) while the program is running, however, the enclosed EXIT command passes control to the SET PRINT OFF command beneath ENDDO.

```
************ Sample program to demonstrate EXIT command.
SET TALK OFF
CLEAR
@ 5,5 SAY "Press Space Bar to stop printer"
SET PRINT ON
SET CONSOLE OFF

DO WHILE .NOT. EOF()
   ? Name, Company, Address
   *--- If space bar pressed, exit the loop.
   IF INKEY() = 32
      EXIT
   ENDIF
   SKIP
ENDDO (not EOF())

*----- Set printer off and screen on.
SET PRINT OFF
EJECT
SET CONSOLE ON
```

The IF...ELSE... ENDIF Command

Executing Conditional Commands

The IF...ELSE...ENDIF command allows a program to make decisions while it is running.

SYNTAX

IF *condition*
    commands...
[ELSE]
    commands...
ENDIF

where *condition* is a valid dBASE logical expression, *commands...* are the commands to be executed under the specified conditions, ELSE is an optional branch to alternative commands, and ENDIF is the command required to close the IF clause. (If you forget to include the ENDIF command, dBASE will not present any error message, but your program will behave unpredictably.)

VERSION

dBASE III PLUS, dBASE III

USAGE

When dBASE encounters an IF command in a command file, it evaluates the condition as either true or false. What happens next depends on how the IF clause is structured. The examples in the next section demonstrate how to set up IF clauses.

Any text to the right of the ENDIF command is ignored, so you can place comments to the right of an ENDIF command without the leading && characters. (Do leave at least one space between ENDIF and the comment, however.)

EXAMPLES

In the following routine, the ACCEPT command asks whether the user wants to send output to the printer. If the user types **Y**, the IF clause sets the printer on line; otherwise, it does not. Either way, processing continues at the CLEAR command beneath the ENDIF command.

```
*----------------------------- Ask about printer.
ACCEPT "Send results to printer? (Y/N) " TO YesNo

*--- If user enters Y or y, set the printer on.
IF UPPER(YesNo) = "Y"
    SET PRINT ON
ENDIF (yesno)

CLEAR
```

Note that in this example, the text (yesno) to the right of the ENDIF command is a programmer comment.

IF clauses can be nested one inside the other as long as each IF command has an ENDIF command associated with it. Nesting IF clauses within one another has a very different effect than stacking IF clauses above one another.

For example, suppose you know the following to be true:

```
LName = "Smith"
State = "CA"
```

In the following routine, the command ? LName,State prints *Smith* and *CA*, because both IF clauses are true.

```
IF LName = "Smith"
    IF State = "CA"
        ? LName,State
    ENDIF (state)
ENDIF (lname)
```

In the next routine, the command ? LName,State is never encountered, because the outermost IF command evaluates to false. Because the outermost IF clause is evaluated as false, *all* commands between the outermost IF and the outermost ENDIF are completely ignored by dBASE.

```
IF LName = "Jones"
    IF State = "CA"
        ? LName, State
    ENDIF (state)
ENDIF (lname)
```

The effect of nesting one IF clause inside the other is the same as using .AND. in a single IF clause. That is, nesting the IF for the state inside the IF for the last name is the same as using the construction

```
IF LName = "Smith" .AND. State = "CA"
    ? LName, State
ENDIF (LName and State)
```

THE IF...ELSE...ENDIF COMMAND

If you *stack* IF clauses rather than nest them, you end up with an "or" relationship between conditions. Suppose dBASE is currently pointing to a database record with the name "Smith" in the LName field and "CA" in the State field. The following stacked IF clauses will print *Smith CA* on the screen, because it is true that LName is Smith and State is CA.

```
IF LName = "Smith"
    ? LName
ENDIF
IF State = "CA"
    ?? State
ENDIF
```

Now consider this modification of the upper IF clause:

```
IF LName = "Jones"
    ? LName
ENDIF
IF State = "CA"
    ?? State
ENDIF
```

The command ?? State prints *CA*, but the ? LName command is never executed, because LName in this example is Smith, not Jones.

SEE ALSO

DO CASE
IIF
& (macro substitution)

The INPUT Command

Storing Input

The INPUT command presents a message on the screen and waits for the user to enter some data and press the Return key. The data entered via the INPUT command is assumed to be numeric unless it is enclosed in quotation marks.

SYNTAX

INPUT *[prompt]* **TO** *memory variable*

where *prompt* is an optional character string enclosed in double or single quotation marks or brackets, and *memory variable* is any valid memory variable name.

VERSION

dBASE III PLUS, dBASE III

USAGE

INPUT is usually used to request numeric data from the user. The optional prompt can be enclosed in double quotation marks, apostrophes, or brackets. Hence, these three commands are identical:

```
INPUT "Enter your age " TO Age
INPUT 'Enter your age ' TO Age
INPUT [Enter your age ] TO Age
```

To embed an apostrophe or other character in the prompt, use different characters for the outside delimiters, as in the following example.

```
ACCEPT "What's your age " TO Age
```

The prompt can be stored in a memory variable, and a macro can be substituted directly into a prompt.

To enter nonnumeric data in response to the INPUT command, a user must enclose the entry in quotation marks.

If the user presses Return in response to the prompt that INPUT displays without first entering some data, dBASE will reject the entry and redisplay the prompt until the user types a value.

EXAMPLES

The following command displays the prompt *What's 5 + 5?* and waits for the user to enter an answer.

INPUT "What's 5 + 5? " TO Answer

The answer is stored in a numeric variable named Answer.

SEE ALSO

@...READ
ACCEPT
WAIT

The LOOP Command
Immediately Repeating a Loop

LOOP passes control within a DO WHILE loop back to the top of the loop. The looping condition is reevaluated before the loop is repeated.

SYNTAX

LOOP

VERSION

dBASE III PLUS, dBASE III

USAGE

LOOP is an optional command used to pass control back to the current DO WHILE command. It prevents a series of commands within a loop from being processed unnecessarily. It can be used only inside an IF...ENDIF or DO CASE...ENDCASE clause.

EXAMPLES

In the following routine, the READ command waits for the user to enter a person's last name and then stores that entry in a variable named Search. If the user enters a name, the SEEK command attempts to find the name, and the IF clause that follows responds accordingly. However, if the user presses Return without typing a last name to search for, the LOOP command passes control back to the top of the DO WHILE loop, ignoring the SEEK command and IF clause altogether (and terminating the DO WHILE Search # " " loop in this example as well).

```
*--- Sample program to demonstrate the LOOP command.
USE AnyFile INDEX LastName

Search = "X"
DO WHILE Search # " "
   Search = SPACE(20)
   a 5,5 SAY "Enter last name to search for ";
   GET Search
   READ

   *---- If no name entered, skip lower commands.
   IF Search = " "
      LOOP
   ENDIF (Search = " ")

   *--- Attempt to find entered name.
   SEEK UPPER(Search)

   *--- If found, edit it.
   IF FOUND()
      EDIT RECNO()
   *--- If not found, display message.
```

```
ELSE
    @ 23,1 SAY "No such person on file!"
ENDIF (found)

ENDDO (while Search # " ")

RETURN
```

SEE ALSO

EXIT
IF...ENDIF
DO CASE...ENDCASE
DO WHILE...ENDDO

The MODIFY COMMAND Command
Creating or Modifying Command Files

The MODIFY COMMAND command calls up the dBASE text editor for creating or modifying command files. The dBASE program automatically adds the extension .prg to command files created with the MODIFY COMMAND text editor. The MODIFY FILE command is similar to the MODIFY COMMAND, except that it does not assume the .prg extension when creating or searching for a file.

SYNTAX

MODIFY COMMAND *file name*

where *file name* is a valid DOS file name (up to eight characters long, with no spaces or punctuation).

VERSION

dBASE III PLUS, dBASE III

USAGE

Use MODIFY COMMAND to create and edit command files. When you enter the command, dBASE searches for the file specified. If the file is found, it is brought to the screen for editing. If the file is not found, dBASE creates it.

Unless specified, the current drive and directory are assumed. You can specify drive and directory designators at the beginning of the file name using the usual DOS sequence.

When saving edited command files, dBASE stores a copy of the previous (unedited) version of the command file using the same file name but with the extension .bak.

Pressing the F1 key toggles on and off the help screen of control key commands at the top of the screen. See Table 12.1 for a complete list of the control-key commands used within the dBASE text editor.

The MODIFY COMMAND editor cannot hold more than 5,000 characters. When the 5,000-character limit is exceeded, a warning message appears at the top of the screen. If you were typing new material when the 5,000-character warning appeared, you could save all text prior to the five thousandth character by typing Ctrl-W or Ctrl-End as usual. If you inadvertently load a command file using MODIFY COMMAND, not realizing the file contains over 5,000 characters, *do not* save the command file. Saving the command file at this point would cut off all characters beyond 5,000. Instead, abandon the command file with the Esc key or the Ctrl-Q combination.

The dBASE text editor automatically word-wraps command lines at the sixty-sixth character. When you press Return after typing a line, dBASE ends the line with a *hard carriage return.* This hard carriage return shows up as a < symbol at the extreme right edge of the screen. Lines that dBASE wraps automatically are broken by *soft carriage returns,* which do not show any symbol at the right edge of the screen.

Lines that are broken by soft carriage returns are treated as single command lines when the program is running. Any lines broken by hard carriage returns are considered two separate commands. If a

	KEY	ALTERNATE	FUNCTION
Cursor-Movement Commands	↑	Ctrl-E	Moves cursor up one line
	→	Ctrl-X	Moves cursor down one line
	↓	Ctrl-D	Moves cursor left one character
	↑	Ctrl-S	Moves cursor right one character
	Home	Ctrl-A	Moves cursor left one word
	End	Ctrl-F	Moves cursor right one word
	Ctrl-←	Ctrl-Z	Moves cursor to beginning of line
	Ctrl-→	Ctrl-B	Moves cursor to end of line
	PgUp	Ctrl-R	Scrolls screen up one page (18 lines)
	PgDn	Ctrl-C	Scrolls screen down one page (18 lines)
Insert Commands	Return	Ctrl-M	Ends line and begins new line; also inserts a new line if insert mode is on

Table 12.1: Keyboard Control Commands for the MODIFY COMMAND Editor

	KEY	ALTERNATE	FUNCTION
	Ins	Ctrl-V	Toggles insert mode on and off
		Ctrl-N	Inserts a blank line at cursor position
Delete Commands	Backspace	Rub	Deletes the character to the left of the cursor
	Del	Ctrl-G	Deletes the character under the cursor
		Ctrl-T	Deletes the word to the right of the cursor
		Ctrl-Y	Deletes the entire line under the cursor
File-Manipulation Commands	Ctrl-End	Ctrl-W	Saves command file with all changes
	Esc	Ctrl-Q	Returns to dot prompt without saving current changes to command file
		Ctrl-KB	Reformats text in a paragraph (used with memo fields rather than command files)
		Ctrl-KF	Locates the first occurrence of any words specified

	Ctrl-KL	Locates the next occurrence of words specified in Ctrl-KF
	Ctrl-KR	Reads an external command file stored on disk into the current command file starting at the cursor position
	Ctrl-KW	Saves a copy of the current command file with a new name
Help Screen Toggle	F1	
	Ctrl-\	Toggles help menu on and off

Table 12.1: Keyboard Control Commands for the MODIFY COMMAND Editor (continued)

single command line is broken with a hard carriage return, a semicolon character must end the top line. When you use the semicolon to break lines, be sure to place at least one space between words.

To print a hard copy of a file created with the MODIFY COMMAND editor, exit the editor so that the dot prompt reappears. Then use the TYPE command with the TO PRINT option to print the file.

TIPS

You can also use the "nondocument" mode of most word processors to create and edit command files.

SEE ALSO

Appendix A, "Configuring dBASE III PLUS."

The RETURN Command

Returning Control to the Calling Program

The RETURN command passes control back to the line beneath the DO command that called the program. If a command file was called directly from the dot prompt, the RETURN command simply passes control back to the dot prompt. When RETURN is used to terminate a command file, it closes the called command file and subtracts one file from the number of files currently open.

The command RETURN TO MASTER passes control from a called program all the way back to the highest-level program in an application (usually the main menu program). It also closes all open files along the way.

SYNTAX

RETURN [TO MASTER]

where the TO MASTER portion of the command is optional.

VERSION

dBASE III PLUS, dBASE III

USAGE

RETURN is generally used as the last command in a program (or procedure) to pass control back to the calling program, but it can be placed anywhere within a command file. However, you should avoid placing RETURN commands within DO WHILE loops. Forcing a program to return control to a calling program within a DO WHILE loop leaves the looping condition active. Hence, the old loop might still have some effect on the currently running program.

EXAMPLES

In the following example, the RETURN command passes control back to the calling program from within a DO WHILE loop, demonstrating a poorly structured loop:

```
DO WHILE .T.
    commands...
    IF Choice = "X"
        RETURN
    ENDIF
ENDDO
```

By structuring the loop properly, you not only tighten the routine, but you also ensure that the RETURN command is issued after the loop has run its course. All you have to do is move the IF condition to the DO WHILE condition and drop the RETURN command to beneath the loop, as follows:

DO WHILE Choice # "X"
    commands...
ENDDO
RETURN

When there is no elegant way to have control fall naturally out of a loop and to the RETURN command, you can still place the RETURN command outside the loop and use the EXIT command to force termination of the loop.

TIPS

Remember that every procedure in a procedure file must end with a RETURN.

SEE ALSO

DO
PROCEDURE
PARAMETERS
SET PROCEDURE

The WAIT Command
Suspending Processing

The WAIT command suspends processing of a program and waits for the user to press any key. It accepts only a single keystroke and does not require the Return key to be pressed.

SYNTAX

WAIT *[prompt]* **TO** *[memory variable]*

where both *prompt* and *memory variable* are optional.

VERSION

dBASE III PLUS, dBASE III

USAGE

When the WAIT command is used alone in a command file, it presents the message *Press any key to continue* on the screen and delays processing until the user presses any key. The user's keypress is not stored in any field or variable.

If the programmer specifies a prompt, either enclosed in double or single quotation marks or in brackets, the WAIT command displays that prompt in lieu of the default prompt.

If you want the WAIT command to pause without presenting any message at all, use a blank as the prompt, as follows:

WAIT " "

If you specify a variable name to store the keystroke in, the keystroke is stored in that memory variable as a character string (regardless of whether the user typed a letter or number). If the user presses a nonprinting character such as the Return key, the variable is stored as the single ASCII character 0 with a length of 0 (that is, "").

EXAMPLES

This routine asks the user whether he or she wishes to continue with some task. If the user presses the letter **N**, the IF clause returns control to the calling program.

```
WAIT "Do you wish to continue? (Y/N) " TO YesNo
IF UPPER(YesNo) = "N"
    RETURN
ENDIF
```

TIPS

To restrict the user's entry to a particular group of letters (for example, the letters A through F and X), initialize the variable used in the TO portion of the command to a blank and place the WAIT command in a DO WHILE loop that repeats as long as letters outside of the desired group are entered. In the following example, the WAIT prompt will reappear until the user enters one of the letters A, B, C, D, E, F, or X.

```
Choice = " "
DO WHILE .NOT. UPPER(Choice) $ "ABCDEFX"
    WAIT "Enter your choice (A–F or X) " TO Choice
ENDDO
```

SEE ALSO

ACCEPT
INPUT
@...READ
INKEY( )
ON KEY
READKEY( )

13

Commands for Procedures and Parameters

This chapter discusses commands relating to a special type of command file known as a *procedure file*. A procedure file is a single command file that contains small, very specialized routines that are stored in RAM. With the use of *parameter passing* (sending information to and from the procedures), you can develop many custom routines that are easily adapted to many different applications. Over time, you can build up a library of flexible routines that will accelerate your development of applications.

You create a procedure file in the same way that you create a command file: You simply use the MODIFY COMMAND editor or an external word processor. Give the file any valid DOS file name, along with the .prg extension. Within the procedure file, each procedure must begin with the PROCEDURE command followed by the name of the procedure. Each procedure must end with the RETURN command, which returns control to the dot prompt or calling program.

The CLOSE PROCEDURE Command

Closing a Procedure File

The CLOSE PROCEDURE command closes any currently open procedure file.

SYNTAX

CLOSE PROCEDURE

VERSION

dBASE III PLUS, dBASE III

USAGE

CLOSE PROCEDURE clears an open procedure file from RAM. (It does not affect the permanent disk copy of the procedure file.)

EXAMPLES

If you attempt to edit an open procedure file with the MODIFY COMMAND editor, the error message *File is already open* will appear. To close the procedure, enter the CLOSE PROCEDURE command and try again to use the MODIFY COMMAND editor.

SEE ALSO

CLOSE
CLEAR
SET PROCEDURE

The DO...WITH Command

Executing a Command File or Procedure

The DO...WITH command executes a command file or procedure and passes parameters to it. The PARAMETERS command in the called command file or procedure receives the passed values.

SYNTAX

DO *file name* **WITH** *parameter list*

where *file name* is the name of the command file or procedure to run, and *parameter list* is a list of up to seven parameters, separated by commas, to be passed.

VERSION

dBASE III PLUS, dBASE III

USAGE

The DO command executes a command file or a procedure. When the command is issued, dBASE checks whether a procedure file has been opened with the SET PROCEDURE command. If it has, dBASE checks whether a procedure with the given file name exists in the procedure file. If it does, dBASE executes that procedure. If no procedure file is open or no procedure with the given file name exists, dBASE checks the directory for a command file with the specified file name and .prg extension. If the command file exists, dBASE executes it. If neither the procedure nor the command file are available, dBASE returns the error message *File does not exist*.

The WITH portion of the command passes parameters to the PARAMETERS statement in the procedure or command file being executed. The number of items in the WITH portion of the

DO...WITH command must match the number of items in the
PARAMETERS command. The order of items in the DO...WITH
command must also match the order of items in the PARAME-
TERS command. Data in the WITH portion of the command can
be literal, variable, or calculated.

EXAMPLES

In the following PARAMETERS command, the variable Amount is
the numeric data type, Name is the character data type, and Date
is the date data type.

PARAMETERS Amount, Name, Date

In the following example, all three items of information are passed
literally. Note that the character data type is enclosed in quotation
marks, and the numeric and date data types are not.

DO Sample WITH 123.45, "Joe Smith", DATE()

SEE ALSO

PARAMETERS   PROCEDURE
DO   PUBLIC
SET PROCEDURE

The PARAMETERS Command
Assigning Local Variable Names

The PARAMETERS command assigns variable names to data
passed to a procedure. These variable names are local to the procedure (that is, they are known only to the procedure) and are not automatically passed back to the calling program. These local variable

names receive their values from those listed in the WITH portion of the DO...WITH command.

SYNTAX

PARAMETERS *parameter list*

where *parameter list* is a list of up to seven variable names, separated from each other by commas.

VERSION

dBASE III PLUS, dBASE III

USAGE

The PARAMETERS command must be the first executable command beneath the PROCEDURE command in a procedure (only programmer comments can be placed between the PROCEDURE and PARAMETERS commands). The PARAMETERS command assigns local variable names to the data passed to the procedure in a DO...WITH command. The number of parameters passed to a procedure must be the same in the DO...WITH and PARAMETERS commands.

If a variable name in the PARAMETERS statement is the same as a variable name already in the calling program, the original variable is used and its contents may be altered by the procedure. If the variable name used in the PARAMETERS command is unique, the variable is erased before control is returned to the calling program.

The information passed to a PARAMETERS command through a DO...WITH command can be literal data, data stored in variables, or calculated data.

Usually, field names and database names passed as parameters need to be treated as macros within the called procedure.

Though usually used with procedures, the PARAMETERS command can also be used in a command file, as long as it is the first executable line in the command file. The command file can be run and parameters passed using the usual DO...WITH command syntax.

The only difference is that the command file will take longer to load and execute than a procedure would, because the command file is stored on disk, and the procedure is stored in RAM.

EXAMPLES

The following procedure calculates the monthly payment on a loan using data passed as parameters named Principal, Interest, and Term, where Interest is the annual percentage rate and Term is the number of years. The Pmt parameter is used to store the results of the calculation.

```
*---- Payment procedure calculates
*---- monthly payment on a mortgage.
PROCEDURE Payment
PARAMETERS Principal,Interest,Term,Pmt
   *-- Convert APR to monthly rate.
   Interest = (Interest/12)/100
   *-- Convert years to months.
   Term = (Term*12)
   Pmt = Principal*Interest/(1-1/(1+Interest)^Term)
RETURN
```

SEE ALSO

DO...WITH
PROCEDURE
PUBLIC
SET PROCEDURE

The PROCEDURE Command

Naming a Procedure

The PROCEDURE command marks the beginning of a procedure and assigns a name to the procedure within a procedure file.

SYNTAX

PROCEDURE *procedure name*

where *procedure name* is no more than eight characters long.

VERSION

dBASE III PLUS, dBASE III

USAGE

Each individual procedure within a procedure file must begin with the PROCEDURE command followed by the name of the procedure. The procedure name must start with a letter and contain no more than eight characters. Numbers and underscores can be used in the procedure name.

Every procedure in a procedure file must end with a RETURN command, which passes control back to the calling command file or procedure. Within a procedure file, one procedure can call another. A single procedure file can contain no more than 32 procedures.

When dBASE encounters the PROCEDURE command within a command file that was not loaded with SET PROCEDURE, it ignores the command and instead immediately executes a RETURN command.

Once a procedure file is opened and a DO command is issued, dBASE scans the names of all procedures. If it finds no such procedure, dBASE checks the disk for a command file with the procedure name and the .prg extension. Therefore, if you attempt to call a procedure that is not in the currently open procedure file (or if there is no open procedure file), dBASE displays the error message *File does not exist.*

EXAMPLES

The following procedure file contains two procedures: one named Center and the other named ErrMsg.

```
************************************* GenProcs.prg
*------- Sample procedure file with two procedures.

*-------------- Center procedure centers any string.
PROCEDURE Center
PARAMETERS Title,RM
   Pad = SPACE((RM/2)-(LEN(Title)/2))
   ? Pad + TRIM(Title)
RETURN

*-- ErrMsg procedure beeps, displays error
*-- message, waits for a keypress.
PROCEDURE ErrMsg
PARAMETERS Msg
   @ 22,1 SAY Msg
   ? CHR(7)
   WAIT
   @ 22,1 CLEAR
RETURN
```

The name of the procedure file in this example is GenProcs.prg. To open the procedure file and display the error message *No such person on file!* using the ErrMsg procedure, you enter the following commands.

SET PROCEDURE TO GenProcs
DO ErrMsg WITH "No such person on file!"

SEE ALSO

SET PROCEDURE   DO...WITH
PARAMETERS   RETURN

The SET PROCEDURE Command

Loading a Procedure File

The SET PROCEDURE command loads a procedure file from a disk into RAM. Once loaded, all procedures within the file are accessible with the DO command.

SYNTAX

SET PROCEDURE TO *file name*

where *file name* is the name of the procedure file. The .prg file-name extension is assumed unless another is specified.

VERSION

dBASE III PLUS, dBASE III

USAGE

One of the biggest advantages of procedure files is speed. A DO command can locate and execute a procedure in RAM far more quickly than it can locate, load, and execute a command file stored on a disk.

The SET PROCEDURE command opens a procedure file and makes all procedures within that file accessible. If the SET PROCEDURE command is issued and another procedure file is already open, that procedure file is closed before the new one is opened. Only one procedure file can be open at a time.

A procedure file can have a maximum of 32 procedures within it. Each of these procedures must begin with the PROCEDURE command and the procedure name, and each must end with a RETURN command.

EXAMPLES

The command SET PROCEDURE TO GenProcs searches the disk for a file named GenProcs.prg. If dBASE finds the file, the command closes any currently open procedure file and then loads the GenProcs.prg procedure file into RAM.

TIPS

Although you can use the SET PROCEDURE command in any command file, you should never place it in a procedure file. In dBASE III PLUS version 1.0, using the command SET PROCE-DURE within a procedure file can cause the computer to stop. In version 1.1, a SET PROCEDURE command within a procedure file causes the error message *File is already open* to appear but does not stop the computer.

The DISPLAY STATUS command displays the name of any currently open procedure file.

SEE ALSO

PROCEDURE
RETURN
PARAMETERS
DO...WITH

14

Commands for Memory Variables

Data stored in a database file are stored on disk. With dBASE III PLUS, you can also store information in the computer's main memory, or RAM. Data stored in RAM are called *memory variables* (or memvars). Unlike database data, data stored in memory variables are usually erased as soon as you exit dBASE.

Memory variables are automatically assigned a data type (character, numeric, logical, or date) based on the context in which they are created. (There is no way to store dBASE memo fields in memory variables). For tips on combining data types with either fields or memory variables, see the STR( ), VAL( ), IIF( ), CTOD( ), DTOC( ), and IIF( ) functions in Chapter 16, "dBASE Functions."

The DISPLAY MEMORY Command
Displaying Memory Variables

The DISPLAY MEMORY command shows the names, data types, sizes, contents, and other information concerning currently active memory variables.

SYNTAX

DISPLAY MEMORY [TO PRINT]

where the optional TO PRINT command sends the output to the printer.

VERSION

dBASE III PLUS, dBASE III

USAGE

If the DISPLAY MEMORY command is used after a command file has terminated, only public memory variables are displayed. However, if it is used while a command file is suspended, all variables active at that moment are displayed.

The status of each variable is displayed as public (pub), private (priv), or hidden (hidden). The data type of each variable is also displayed as numeric (N), character (C), logical (L), or date (D).

Each number is displayed in two formats: as it is represented internally in memory and as it appears on the screen.

Very large numbers are displayed in scientific notation but stored internally as rounded numbers.

DISPLAY MEMORY pauses for a keypress after each screenful of information. If you don't want the display to pause, use LIST MEMORY instead.

Both the DISPLAY MEMORY and LIST MEMORY commands allow the TO PRINT option to send the display to the printer. To store a copy of the memory variable display on a disk file, use the SET ALTERNATE command with the DISPLAY or LIST MEMORY command.

EXAMPLES

Figure 14.1 shows the output from a DISPLAY MEMORY command executed after suspension of procedure processing. Variable names are listed in the left column. The status, data type, contents, and program in which the variable was created is also listed for each variable. The bottom of the screen describes both used and available memory variable space.

TIPS

To inspect the status of memory variables in a running program, press Esc while the program is running, select Suspend from your list of options, and then enter the DISPLAY MEMORY command.

```
. DISPLAY MEMORY
COMPANY     pub    C   "ABC Corporation"
AMOUNT      priv   N       123  (        123.00000000)          C:test.prg
MAYBE       priv   L   .T.                                      C:test.prg
TODAY       priv   D   03/23/87                                 C:test.prg
X           priv   (hidden)  C   "Original"                     C:test.prg
X           priv   C   "Now"                              C:GenProcs.prg
     6 variables defined,        52 bytes used
   250 variables available,    5948 bytes available

. ▪
```

Figure 14.1: Sample output from the DISPLAY MEMORY
command

SEE ALSO

STORE
PUBLIC
PRIVATE

The PRIVATE Command
Hiding a Public Memory Variable Value

The PRIVATE command temporarily hides the current value of a public memory variable so that a lower-level command file or procedure can use the variable name.

SYNTAX

PRIVATE *variable list* [**ALL**[**LIKE/EXCEPT** *skeleton]]*

where *variable list* is a list of variable names, each separated by a comma. The optional ALL command declares all variables as private. The optional LIKE and EXCEPT commands can be used to define a group of variable names using the ★ and ? wild-card characters in a *skeleton* name.

VERSION

dBASE III PLUS, dBASE III

USAGE

PRIVATE is used in general-purpose procedures and programs to keep local variable names from interfering with existing public or higher-level variables with the same names. Once a variable is declared private, the value in the public or higher-level variable retains its value, but is temporarily hidden. Any new operations take place only on the private variable. As a result, when the program or procedure that created the private variable ends, the public or higher-level memory value resumes its original value, unaffected by changes in the private variable with the same name.

When creating skeletons for use with the optional LIKE and EXCEPT components, ∗ stands for any combination of characters, and ? stands for any single character.

EXAMPLES

The command PRIVATE ALL declares all public variables currently in use as private (hidden) from variable names being created at the current program level and lower. The command PRIVATE ALL LIKE C∗ hides all memory variables that begin with the letter C.

The following procedure includes a memory variable named Counter declared as PRIVATE. When this procedure completes its task, any variable named Counter that existed before the procedure was called will resume its original value when the procedure returns control to the calling program.

```
*---------- Pause for a few seconds.
PROCEDURE Pause
   *-- Don't disrupt outside Counter variable.
   PRIVATE Counter
   Counter = 1
   *-- Count to 500 to take up time.
   DO WHILE Counter < 500
      Counter = Counter + 1
   ENDDO (counter)
   *-- Counter in calling program will now
   *-- retain its original value, because the Counter
   *-- variable in this procedure is private
   *-- (local) to this procedure.
RETURN
```

SEE ALSO

PUBLIC
STORE
RELEASE

The PUBLIC Command

Making a Variable Accessible to Any Command File in a System

The PUBLIC command defines a variable as accessible to and modifiable by all lower levels of command files within a system. Public memory variables are not automatically erased when the command file or procedure that created them ends.

SYNTAX

PUBLIC *variable names*

where *variable names* is a list of variable names separated by commas.

VERSION

dBASE III PLUS, dBASE III

USAGE

By default, all dBASE variables are private. This means that they are accessible only to the command files that created them and to programs at a lower level. A RETURN command erases all variables created in the current program. Memory variables created in the highest-level program are erased as soon as control is returned to the dot prompt.

Public memory variables are available to programs and procedures at all levels, as well as at the dot prompt. Variables created at the dot prompt are public by default. To create public variables within a command file, you must use the PUBLIC command. The placement of the PUBLIC command in the command file is also important. It must come *before* the variable is assigned a value. Typically, all variables that are to be public in a given application are declared at the beginning of the highest-level program in the application (usually the main menu program).

Once a memory variable is declared public, only the RELEASE, CLEAR MEMORY, CLEAR ALL, or QUIT command can erase the memory variable.

Hidden memory variables are those that have the same names as variables in lower-level programs but are temporarily set aside or hidden while the lower-level programs are running.

You must issue the PUBLIC command before the STORE command or the = assignment operator that creates the variable. When first declared public, memory variables are defined as the logical data type with the type accordingly.

EXAMPLES

To declare several variables as public simultaneously, list the variable names separated by commas, as follows:

PUBLIC Qty, Unit_Price, Tax, Ext_Price

TIPS

To avoid any potential problems when trying to declare existing variables as public, declare all public variables early in an application, perhaps at the top of the main menu program that the user sees first.

SEE ALSO

PRIVATE
STORE
DISPLAY MEMORY
SUSPEND
DO...WITH

The RELEASE Command

Removing Memory Variables and Assembly Language Subroutines

The RELEASE command erases memory variables and reclaims the space they had occupied. RELEASE is also used to remove assembly language subroutines from memory (as discussed in Chapter 20, "Commands for Running External Programs").

SYNTAX

RELEASE *variable list [* **ALL[LIKE/EXCEPT** *skeleton]] ;*
[**MODULE** *subroutine name]*

where *variable list* is the name of the variable to release or a list of variable names separated by commas. The ALL, LIKE, and EXCEPT components are optional. The *skeleton* parameter allows you to define variables using the ★ and ? wild-card characters. The *subroutine name* is the name of an assembly language subroutine to be released from memory using the RELEASE MODULE combination.

VERSION

dBASE III PLUS, dBASE III

USAGE

The RELEASE command removes memory variables from memory to make room for new ones. When entered at the dot prompt, RELEASE ALL releases all memory variables. When used in a command file, however, it erases only those variables created by the current program or procedure.

EXAMPLES

The command

RELEASE Choice, X, MyVar

erases the memory variables Choice, X, and MyVar and frees the memory used by them. The command

RELEASE ALL LIKE Month∗

releases all memory variables beginning with the letters Month.

SEE ALSO

CLEAR
STORE
PRIVATE

The RESTORE Command
Loading Memory Variables into Memory

RESTORE loads memory variables from disk into memory.

SYNTAX

RESTORE FROM *file name* [ADDITIVE]

where *file name* is the name of the memory (.mem) file from which the variables are retrieved. The ADDITIVE component is optional.

VERSION

dBASE III PLUS, dBASE III

USAGE

Any memory variables that were stored on disk with a SAVE command can be loaded into memory using the RESTORE command. Unless you specify the ADDITIVE option, all memory variables currently in memory are erased before the new variables are retrieved. If ADDITIVE is used, retrieved variables are combined with existing variables. If both a retrieved and an existing variable have the same name, the retrieved variable overwrites the existing variable.

Restored variables are always private to the level at which they were restored. To treat restored variables as public to an entire system, you can either restore them at the highest-level program in an application or declare them public before they are restored.

RESTORE searches the currently logged disk drive and directory for the specified file unless a drive or directory are specified in the file name. RESTORE will also search the path specified in a dBASE SET PATH command.

EXAMPLES

The command

RESTORE FROM SetUp

deletes all variables currently in memory and reads in memory variables stored on the file named SetUp.mem. The command

RESTORE FROM SetUp ADDITIVE

reads in memory variables from the file named SetUp.mem without first deleting existing memory variables.

TIPS

If you receive the error message *Out of memory variable slots* while using a RESTORE FROM...ADDITIVE command, you've exceeded the 256-variable limit. Use SAVE and RELEASE to make room for the incoming variables.

The error message *Out of memory variable memory* means you've exceeded the 6,000-byte limit while trying to restore saved variables. Again, you can use the SAVE and RELEASE commands to make more room, or you can extend the amount of memory available for variables through the Config.db file.

SEE ALSO

SAVE   RELEASE
STORE

The SAVE Command
Saving Active Memory Variables

The SAVE command places a copy of active memory variables in a disk file.

SYNTAX

SAVE TO *file name [***ALL LIKE/EXCEPT** *skeleton]*

where *file name* is the name of the file to store the variables in, and *skeleton* is a variable name specified with wild-card characters; *skeleton* is used with the ALL LIKE or ALL EXCEPT options to specify a group of memory variables to be stored.

VERSION

dBASE III PLUS, dBASE III

USAGE

The SAVE command can store all or some of the currently active memory variables in a disk file. The disk file will have the name you supply followed by the extension .mem. Saving memory variables has no effect on data stored in database files.

File names must be valid DOS file names. Unless otherwise specified, the file will be created on the currently logged disk drive and directory.

If you do not use the ALL LIKE or ALL EXCEPT options, all currently active memory variables are stored in the file. The ALL LIKE and ALL EXCEPT options allow you to specify skeletal file names with the ? and * wild-card characters, where the ? symbol represents a single character, and * represents any group of characters.

EXAMPLES

The command

SAVE TO MemVars

stores a copy of all active memory variables in a disk file named MemVars.mem. The command

SAVE ALL LIKE New* TO SetUp

stores all memory variables starting with the letters New in a disk file named SetUp.mem.

SEE ALSO

RESTORE
RELEASE
CLEAR MEMORY

The STORE Command

Placing a Value in a Memory Variable

The STORE command, like the assignment operator (=), places a value into a memory variable.

SYNTAX

STORE *expression* **TO** *variable name*

where *expression* is a value (either numeric or string), a variable name, an expression, or a field name, and *variable* is the name of the variable, or several variables, that will store the value.

VERSION

dBASE III PLUS, dBASE III

USAGE

STORE can be used to create a new variable and place a value in it or to place a new value into an existing memory variable. An alternative to the STORE command is the assignment operator (=), with the following syntax:

variable name = *expression*

A maximum of 256 memory variables can be active at any one time. Unless otherwise modified in the Config.db file, the amount of space allotted for memory variables is 6,000 bytes.

The STORE command and the assignment operator always place their values into a memory variable, even if the open database includes a field with the same name. On the other hand, commands that display or use memory variables give a field precedence over a memory variable when the field and memory variable have the same name. When a field and memory variable have the same name, you can use the M->alias to specify the memory variable (for example, the expression M->LName refers to the memory variable, rather than the field, named LName).

The data type of the memory variable being stored is assumed by the data itself. Memo field data cannot be stored in a memory variable.

When assigning values to variables, numbers can be added to themselves, and character strings can be concatenated with themselves, as some of the examples in the following section demonstrate.

EXAMPLES

The command

STORE 123.45 TO Amount

stores the value 123.45 in a memory variable named Amount, with the numeric data type. The command

Amount = 123.45

performs exactly the same task as STORE 123.45 TO Amount.

With the STORE command, you can place a value in many variables:

STORE 0 TO Top, Bottom, Left, Right

This command creates four memory variables named Top, Bottom, Left, and Right and assigns each the numeric value of 0. The assignment-operator (=) technique does not allow you to assign a value to multiple memory variables.

SEE ALSO

PUBLIC
PRIVATE
DISPLAY MEMORY
RELEASE
SAVE
RESTORE
REPLACE

15

Debugging Commands

When dBASE encounters an error in a program, it stops processing the program and displays the offending line with a question mark above the approximate location of the error and an error message that briefly describes the problem. The screen also displays the series of command files that led to the error, with the name of the program containing the error listed first.

Beneath the error information, the screen presents the options Cancel, Ignore, and Suspend (C, I, and S). You select an option by typing its letter. The options are summarized here.

Cancel   Terminates program execution, erases all private memory variables (those created within this program), and returns to the dot prompt. The program can be edited immediately with MODIFY COMMAND or another editor.

Ignore   Ignores the line with the error in it and continues processing the program at the next line.

Suspend   Leaves the command file open and all
           memory variables intact and returns to the
           dot prompt. DISPLAY, LIST, and all other
           commands display the status of the program
           environment when the error occurred. The
           command file cannot be edited immediately,
           however, because it is still open. To resume
           processing, enter the RESUME command.
           To cancel processing and edit the command
           file immediately, enter the CANCEL
           command.

Either Suspend or Cancel will return you to the dot prompt,
where you can enter one of the debugging commands to help isolate
and correct the error. Note that if you suspend the program, the
DISPLAY MEMORY command will show the status of all memory
variables, whereas Cancel erases all variables local to the program.

dBase offers several debugging commands and techniques to help
you isolate and fix errors. Note that all debugging commands can be
inserted directly into command files to isolate particular problem
areas. The rest of this chapter discusses the individual commands
used in debugging.

The CANCEL Command
Terminating a Command File

CANCEL terminates execution and closes all command files.

SYNTAX

CANCEL

VERSION

dBASE III PLUS, dBASE III

USAGE

The most common use of the CANCEL command is to close a suspended command file so that it can be edited. (CANCEL does not, however, close open procedure files; the CLOSE PROCEDURE command does that.) It can be used directly in a command file to terminate all program execution, close all program files, and return control to the dot prompt. Doing so also erases all private memory variables.

SEE ALSO

SUSPEND
RESUME
CLOSE PROCEDURE

The DISPLAY STATUS Command

Displaying the Status of Parameters

The DISPLAY command displays the current status of dBASE parameters, pausing with each full screen.

SYNTAX

DISPLAY STATUS [TO PRINT]

where the TO PRINT option echoes the display to the printer.

VERSION

dBASE III PLUS, dBASE III

USAGE

The DISPLAY STATUS command shows the following information about each currently open database file:

- Database name
- Active index files
- Index file keys
- SELECT area
- Alias name
- Relations set
- Open memo file names

If no databases are open, no information is displayed.

DISPLAY STATUS also shows the status of the following parameters.

- ALTERNATE file in use (if any)
- SET PATH command
- Default disk drive
- Print destination
- SET MARGIN setting
- Currently selected work area (from SELECT)
- ON ERROR destination
- Current settings for most SET commands
- Function-key assignments

The LIST STATUS command is equivalent to DISPLAY STATUS, except that it does not pause for a filled screen, which is why it is preferred when the TO PRINT option is used.

EXAMPLES

Following is a sample display from the DISPLAY or LIST STATUS command.

```
Currently Selected Database:
Select area:  1, Database in Use: C:ABCTemp.dbf    Alias: ManySide
     Related into: ABCProd
     Relation: Product

Select area:  2, Database in Use: C:ABCProd.dbf    Alias: OneSide
     Master index file:  C:ABCProd.ndx  Key: product

Alternate file: C:TaxRept.txt
File search path: C:\DBFILES
Default disk drive: C:
Print destination:  LPT1:
Margin =    0
Current work area =    1
On Error:     DO ErrProc

ALTERNATE  - ON    DELETED     - OFF   FIXED      - OFF   SAFETY      - OFF
BELL       - ON    DELIMITERS  - OFF   HEADING    - ON    SCOREBOARD  - ON
CARRY      - OFF   DEVICE      - SCRN  HELP       - OFF   STATUS      - OFF
CATALOG    - OFF   DOHISTORY   - OFF   HISTORY    - ON    STEP        - OFF
CENTURY    - OFF   ECHO        - OFF   INTENSITY  - ON    TALK        - OFF
CONFIRM    - OFF   ESCAPE      - ON    MENU       - ON    TITLE       - ON
CONSOLE    - ON    EXACT       - OFF   PRINT      - OFF   UNIQUE      - OFF
DEBUG      - OFF   FIELDS      - OFF

Programmable function keys:
F2  - assist;
F3  - list;
F4  - dir;
F5  - display structure;
F6  - display status;
F7  - display memory;
F8  - display;
F9  - append;
F10 - edit;
```

TIPS

To store a copy of the DISPLAY STATUS command output in a disk file, use the SET ALTERNATE command.

SEE ALSO

DISPLAY MEMORY
DISPLAY STRUCTURE
SUSPEND

The DISPLAY STRUCTURE Command

Displaying the Structure of a Database File

DISPLAY STRUCTURE displays the structure of the currently open database file.

SYNTAX

DISPLAY STRUCTURE TO [PRINT]

where the TO PRINT option echoes the display to the printer.

VERSION
---

dBASE III PLUS, dBASE III

USAGE

The DISPLAY STRUCTURE command displays the name, disk drive, location, number of records, date of last change, and total number of bytes per record for the database, as well as the name, data type, width, and number of decimal places for each field. The total number of bytes per record includes the extra byte used to store the deletion marker.

If SET FIELD is on, a triangle appears to the left of the currently accessible fields. The LIST STRUCTURE command presents the same display but does not pause between full screens.

EXAMPLES

The following display shows the results of the DISPLAY STRUCTURE command used with a database file name Customer.

```
Structure for database: C:Customer.dbf
Number of data records:      999
Date of last update   : 03/09/87
Field  Field Name  Type       Width    Dec
    1  CUSTNO      Numeric       4
    2  LNAME       Character    15
    3  FNAME       Character    10
    4  ADDRESS     Character    25
    5  CITY        Character    20
    6  STATE       Character     2
    7  ZIP         Character    10
    8  PHONE       Character    13
    9  LAST_UPDAT  Date          8
   10  START_BAL   Numeric       8      2
```

TIPS

To store a copy of the structure in a text file, use the SET ALTERNATE command. This command is useful for incorporating copies of database structures into technical documentation.

SEE ALSO

DISPLAY STATUS
COPY

The RESUME Command

Resuming Execution of a
Suspended Command File

The RESUME command continues processing a suspended command file.

SYNTAX

RESUME

VERSION

dBASE III PLUS, dBASE III

USAGE

Use the RESUME command to restart execution of a suspended command file at the first line beneath the one that caused the error or the first line beneath the SUSPEND command.

EXAMPLES

If you want to continue running a program after suspending it and experimenting with some commands at the dot prompt, type **RESUME** at the dot prompt.

SEE ALSO

SUSPEND

The SET DEBUG Command

Sending Echoed Output to the Printer

SET DEBUG sends the output from a SET ECHO command to the printer rather than the screen.

SYNTAX

SET DEBUG ON/OFF

where ON sends echoed output to the printer and OFF sends it to the screen.

VERSION

dBASE III PLUS, dBASE III

USAGE

Use the SET DEBUG ON command to view the normal screen activity of a program while generating a printed copy of SET ECHO command output. (If SET ECHO is not on, SET DEBUG does nothing.) Like the SET ECHO and SET STEP commands, SET DEBUG command can be placed anywhere within a command file, allowing you to print only part of the file.

You can use the printed output from SET ECHO and SET DEBUG to follow each line in the program as dBASE processed it. This provides an exact picture of how dBASE executed the command file and should help you isolate logical errors that might otherwise be difficult to find.

EXAMPLES

The following routine is surrounded by SET ECHO and SET DEBUG commands.

```
SET ECHO ON
SET DEBUG ON
COUNT FOR DELETED() TO DelRecs
DO WHILE DelRecs > 0 .AND. .NOT. EOF()
   IF DELETED()
      ? "Deleted - ",RECNO(),CustNo,LName,FName
   ENDIF
   SKIP
ENDDO
SET DEBUG OFF
SET ECHO OFF
EJECT
```

After the program is run, the printout displays

COUNT FOR DELETED( ) TO DelRecs
DO WHILE DelRecs > 0 .AND. .NOT. EOF( )
SET DEBUG OFF

indicating that none of the commands within the DO WHILE loop was processed and therefore the WHILE condition was false before the loop was performed.

SEE ALSO

SET ECHO
SET DOHISTORY
SET ALTERNATE
SET TALK
DISPLAY STATUS

The SET DOHISTORY Command

Recording Commands in a History File

SET DOHISTORY records commands from the command file being processed in a history file, in the same manner that interactive commands are stored in a history file.

SYNTAX

SET DOHISTORY ON/OFF

where ON records command file commands in the history file, and OFF terminates the recording.

VERSION

dBASE III PLUS only

USAGE

The dBASE III PLUS program records all interactive commands in a history file that can be reviewed with the LIST HISTORY command or with the ↑ and ↓ keys. If SET DOHISTORY is on, commands from command files are recorded in the history file as well.

The default number of commands recorded in the history file is 20. However, the SET HISTORY command allows you to set this value to any number within the range 0 to 16,000.

EXAMPLES

To record 500 command lines from a command file in the history file, enter the following commands

SET HISTORY TO 500
SET DOHISTORY ON

at the dot prompt before running the command file.

When the command file is finished running, enter the following commands to terminate the recording of program commands and to review the commands as they were processed.

SET DOHISTORY OFF
DISPLAY HISTORY

SEE ALSO

SET HISTORY
DISPLAY HISTORY
SUSPEND
RESUME
SET DEBUG

The SET ECHO Command

Displaying Command File Lines During Processing

The SET ECHO command displays each line in a command file as it is being processed.

SYNTAX

SET ECHO ON/OFF

where ON turns echoing on and OFF turns it off.

VERSION

dBASE III PLUS, dBASE III

USAGE

To see an entire program echoed, type SET ECHO ON at the dot prompt before running the program. If you have already isolated the error, you can place the SET ECHO command directly in the command file so that echoing begins and ends in the vicinity of the error.

EXAMPLES

In the following program, a DO WHILE loop is causing problems in a command file. To view the processing, you can surround the routine with SET ECHO commands.

```
SET ECHO ON
DO WHILE .NOT. EOF( )
    ? LName, FName
ENDDO (eof)
SET ECHO OFF
```

TIPS

SET ECHO displays its output quickly. Unless the program or segment you want to view with SET ECHO is very short, you may want to use the SET STEP and SET DEBUG commands to slow it down.

SEE ALSO

SET TALK
SET STEP
SET DEBUG
SET DOHISTORY

The SET STEP Command
Pausing Program Execution by Line

SET STEP pauses program execution after each line is processed, allowing you to view processing one line at a time.

SYNTAX

SET STEP ON/OFF

where ON starts the stepping process and OFF disables it and returns to normal processing.

VERSION

dBASE III PLUS, dBASE III

USAGE

When STEP is on, each line in a program is individually processed, its results (if any) are displayed, and the screen displays this message before processing the next line: *Press SPACE to step, S to suspend, or Esc to cancel....* Pressing the space bar simply moves processing to the next line in the command file. Pressing the Esc key terminates processing, closes the command file, erases all private memory variables, and returns to the dot prompt.

Typing **S** to suspend processing returns control to the dot prompt without closing the command file or erasing any memory variables. You can use the DISPLAY MEMORY, DISPLAY STRUCTURE, DISPLAY STATUS, and other commands at that point to analyze the environment. To resume processing, enter **RESUME**. To stop processing and edit the command file, enter **CANCEL**.

When ECHO is on, the SET STEP command displays each command line before processing it, displaying the results and presenting the stepping options.

EXAMPLES

To view each line in a command file as it is processing and step through each line as well, enter the commands

    SET ECHO ON
    SET STEP ON

directly at the dot prompt.

TIPS

SET STEP offers not only a technique for pausing execution but also a technique for suspending program execution at a specific location. If you select Suspend from the SET STEP options, remember to type **C** for Cancel before editing the command file. (If you suspend a procedure file, you'll need to close it with CLOSE PROCEDURE.) If you don't want to close the file, however, you can use the RESUME command to continue processing.

SEE ALSO

SET ECHO
SET DEBUG
SUSPEND
RESUME

The SUSPEND Command
Suspending Command File Execution

The SUSPEND command suspends execution of a command file without closing the file or erasing any memory variables.

SYNTAX

SUSPEND

VERSION

dBASE III PLUS only

USAGE

The SUSPEND command forces suspension of a program at a specific place (presumably at a location where you've isolated an error). When dBASE encounters a SUSPEND command, it displays the message *Do suspended,* and the dot prompt reappears. All commands, including DISPLAY MEMORY, DISPLAY STRUCTURE, DISPLAY STATUS, DISPLAY HISTORY, and ?, then display information about the program environment at that exact point in the program.

To edit a suspended command file, first close the file with the CANCEL command. If you suspend a procedure file, you must close it with the CLOSE PROCEDURE command prior to editing. To resume processing without editing, enter **RESUME**.

If you create any memory variables at the dot prompt while a command file is suspended, those memory variables will be private to the suspended command file.

EXAMPLES

After isolating a program bug near a particular routine, you can check parameters by placing a SUSPEND command near that routine, as follows:

```
SEEK Search
SUSPEND
LIST WHILE .NOT. EOF( )
```

When the program runs, it is suspended immediately after the SEEK command is executed. You can then enter any useful DISPLAY commands or commands such as ? FOUND( ) or ? EOF( ) to determine whether the item was found or the end of the file was encountered.

SEE ALSO

RESUME
CANCEL
DISPLAY HISTORY
DISPLAY MEMORY
DISPLAY STATUS
DISPLAY STRUCTURE

16

dBASE Functions

The dBASE functions are used in conjunction with dBASE commands to perform operations on individual data items. When discussing functions, the term *argument* refers to the data that the function operates on, which is always stored within parentheses.

All functions *return* some value. The data type of the value returned depends on the individual function.

Functions that do not accept arguments still require the use of parentheses.

The & (Macro Substitution) Function

Substituting Text into a Command

The ampersand (&) allows a character string stored in a memory variable to be substituted into a command line.

SYNTAX

&*variable*

where *variable* is the name of a memory variable containing a character string.

VERSION

dBASE III PLUS, dBASE III

USAGE

This function substitutes the contents of the memory variable following the & symbol into a command line, so that the substituted text actually becomes part of the command.

EXAMPLES

The following commands tell dBASE to open a database file named MyData.dbf.

```
FileName = "MyData"
USE &FileName
```

If the & macro symbol had not been used, dBASE would have attempted to open a database file named FileName.dbf.

The ABS( ) Function

Returning the Absolute Value

The ABS( ) function returns the absolute value of a number or numeric expression.

SYNTAX

ABS(*number*)

where *number* is any number, numeric expression, or variable.

VERSION

dBASE III PLUS only

USAGE

The absolute value function converts negative numbers to positive. It has no effect on positive numbers.

EXAMPLES

To find the positive difference between two numbers, regardless of the order in which the subtraction occurs (larger number minus smaller number or vice versa), perform the subtraction inside the ABS argument, as the following steps demonstrate.

```
STORE 12 TO first
STORE 18 TO second
? ABS(first − second)
    6

? ABS(second − first)
    6
```

SEE ALSO

SQRT( )

The ACCESS( ) Function
Determining the User's Access Level

ACCESS( ) returns the access level (1–8) of the user, based on the user profile established in the PROTECT program. See Chapter 19, "Commands for Networking," for further information.

The ASC( ) Function
Returning the ASCII Code for a Character

ASC returns the ASCII code value of the leftmost character of any character string.

SYNTAX

ASC(*character***)**

where *character* is any character data or character expression or a variable containing character data.

VERSION

dBASE III PLUS, dBASE III

ASC( ) accepts any character string and returns the decimal ASCII code number for that character string. If the argument is longer than one character, ASC returns the ASCII code for the first character only.

Both of the following commands store the number 42 in a variable named AsciiVal, because 42 is the ASCII number for the asterisk character.

```
AsciiVal = ASC("*")
? AsciiVal
    42
AsciiVal = ASC("*------- comment")
? AsciiVal
    42
```

CHR( )

The AT( ) Function

Returning the Position of One String Within Another

AT( ) returns the starting position of one character string within another character string.

SYNTAX

AT(*character1,character2*)

where *character1* is the value to search for and *character2* is the string
to be searched. Either argument can be an expression that results in
a character string or the name of a memory variable containing a
character string.

VERSION

dBASE III PLUS, dBASE III

USAGE

The AT( ) function searches the second character string for the starting position of the first character string (or the substring expression).
If no starting point is found, a zero (0) is returned.

EXAMPLES

The following commands return the number 14, because the B in
Bob starts at the fourteenth character in the memory variable
FNames.

```
FNames = "JoeLarrySteveBobFrank"
? AT("Bob",FNames)
   14
```

SEE ALSO

SUBSTR( )
LEFT( )
RIGHT( )

The BOF( ) Function

Determining Whether the Beginning-of-File Has Been Reached

BOF( ) determines whether the beginning-of-file marker has been reached (that is, whether the record pointer is above record 1 or the top record in indexed order).

SYNTAX

BOF( )

VERSION

dBASE III PLUS, dBASE III

USAGE

If the record pointer has been moved to the beginning-of-file marker (which precedes the first record in a database), the function will yield a logical true (.T.) value; otherwise, it will return a logical false (.F.) value.

EXAMPLES

The following commands demonstrate that the beginning-of-file marker is located one record before the first record in a database file.

```
USE AnyFile INDEX AnyIndex
? BOF( )
    .F.
```

```
SKIP  – 1
? BOF( )
    .T.
```

SEE ALSO

EOF( )

The CDOW( ) Function

Returning the Day of the Week as a Character String

CDOW( ) returns the name of the day of the week from the date passed to the function.

SYNTAX

CDOW(date)

where *date* is of the date data type.

VERSION

dBASE III PLUS, dBASE III

USAGE

The argument must be of the date data type. The day of the week returned is of the character data type.

To convert a date in mm/dd/yy format to a format such as Monday, October 19, 1987, use the expression in the following example.

```
Date = CTOD("10/19/87")
FullDate = CDOW(Date) + ", " + CMONTH(Date) + " ";
    + LTRIM(STR(DAY(Date),2)) + ;
    ", " + LTRIM(STR(YEAR(Date)))
```

SEE ALSO

DOW( )   CMONTH( )
DAY( )   YEAR( )
CTOD( )

The CHR( ) Function

Returning the Character for an ASCII Number

CHR( ) returns the ASCII character for a number.

SYNTAX

CHR(*number***)**

where *number* is any number, numeric expression, or numeric variable.

VERSION

dBASE III PLUS, dBASE III

USAGE

CHR( ) returns the ASCII character assigned to the number (0–255) in the argument; it can be used to display graphics and other special-effects characters found on most printers and monitors. ASCII characters in the range 0 to 128 are standard on most printers and monitors. The extended ASCII character set, in the range 129 to 255, varies on different screens and printers.

EXAMPLES

The command ? CHR(7) causes the computer to beep.

SEE ALSO

ASC( )

The CMONTH( ) Function
Returning the Month as a Character String

CMONTH( ) returns the name of the month from a date passed to the function.

SYNTAX

CMONTH(*date***)**

where *date* is any data of the date data type.

VERSION

dBASE III PLUS, dBASE III

The date passed to the function must be a memory variable, a field, or the system date function. The value returned is always the month name as a character string.

The following expression displays the current system date in the format October 31, 1987.

```
? CMONTH(DATE( )) + ;
"  " + LTRIM(STR(DAY(DATE( )),2)) + ;
", " + LTRIM(STR(YEAR(DATE( ))))
```

MONTH( )	CDOW( )
DAY( )	DATE( )
DATE( )	DAY( )

The COL( ) Function

Returning the Column Position of the Cursor

The COL( ) function returns the current cursor column position.

```
COL( )
```

VERSION

dBASE III PLUS, dBASE III

USAGE

The COL( ) function accepts no argument; it returns only a numeric value.

EXAMPLES

The COL( ) function is commonly used for relative addressing on the screen. The following routine creates five highlighted bars in the fifth row of the screen. Each bar will be 10 spaces wide and separated from the previous bar by 5 spaces.

```
Blanks = SPACE(10)
Row = 5
DO WHILE COL( ) < 70
    @ Row,COL( ) + 5 GET Blanks
ENDDO
```

SEE ALSO

ROW( )
PROW( )
PCOL( )

The CTOD( ) Function

Converting a Character String to a Date

CTOD( ) converts a character variable in date format to the date data type.

SYNTAX

CTOD(*character***)**

where *character* is any character data in a format resembling a valid date.

VERSION

dBASE III PLUS, dBASE III

USAGE

The character expression that is passed to the function must be in the date format currently determined by the SET DATE and SET CENTURY commands.

EXAMPLES

When dBASE is set to its default date format, which is SET DATE AMERICAN, the following command will convert the character string 12/31/87 to the date data type.

Date = CTOD("12/31/87")

SEE ALSO

SET DATE
DTOC( )

The DATE( ) Function
Returning the DOS System Date

DATE( ) returns the DOS system date.

SYNTAX

DATE( )

VERSION

dBASE III PLUS, dBASE III

USAGE

The DATE( ) function always returns the system date using the
dBASE date data type.

EXAMPLES

The following commands display the current system date as a
default entry and allow the user to change that date.

```
DatePaid = DATE( )
@ 12,5 SAY "Enter date paid " GET DatePaid
READ
```

SEE ALSO

SET CENTURY
SET DATE
RUN

The DAY( ) Function

Returning the Day of the Month as a Number

DAY( ) returns the numeric value of the day of the month from a date passed to the function.

SYNTAX

DAY(*date*)

where *date* must be of the date data type.

VERSION

dBASE III PLUS, dBASE III

USAGE

The date passed to the DAY( ) function must be a memory variable, a field, or the system date using the date data type.

The following commands store the number 15 in the variable X, because the date falls on the fifteenth day of the month.

Date = CTOD("12/15/88")
X = DAY(Date)

CDOW( )
DOW( )

The DBF( ) Function

Returning the Name of the Current Database File

DBF( ) returns the name of the currently selected database file.

DBF( )

dBASE III PLUS only

The character string returned by DBF( ) contains the current drive designator with the file name, but not the current directory. A null string is returned if no database file is in use in the current work area.

The following commands illustrate values returned by the DBF( ) function.

```
USE AnyFile
? DBF( )
    C:AnyFile.dbf
CLOSE DATABASES
? DBF( )
    &&(null string is returned)
```

AT( )
SUBSTR( )

The DELETED( ) Function

Finding Records Marked for Deletion

DELETED( ) returns a logical true (.T.) value if the current record has been marked for deletion; otherwise, it returns a logical false (.F.) value.

DELETED( )

VERSION

dBASE III PLUS, dBASE III

USAGE

From within programs, you can use the DELETED( ) function as a condition for including or excluding records marked for deletion during any process, such as LIST, SUM, COUNT, and REPORT, that accesses multiple records. During debugging, records can be checked to determine their deletion status.

EXAMPLE

The following command lists records that have been marked for deletion.

LIST FOR DELETED( )

SEE ALSO

SET DELETED

The DISKSPACE( ) Function
Determining Available Disk Space

DISKSPACE( ) returns the number of bytes available on the default disk drive.

SYNTAX

DISKSPACE( )

VERSION

dBASE III PLUS only

USAGE

In routines that involve backing up data to floppy disks, this function can ensure that the target disks have sufficient room for the file transfer.

Checking the available disk space is also recommended before attempting a SORT command on a floppy disk. SORT requires twice the disk space of the file being sorted. Unless enough space is available, a disk-full error will occur.

EXAMPLES

Assuming that you need a minimum of 25K to sort a database file, you can use the following routine before sorting.

```
FileSize = 25000
IF DISKSPACE( ) > FileSize * 2
    SORT ON Name,Date TO NewFile
ELSE
    ? "Not enough room on disk!"
ENDIF
```

SEE ALSO

GETENV( )
RECCOUNT( )

The DOW( ) Function
Returning the Day of the Week as a Number

DOW( ) returns a number that indicates the day of the week.

SYNTAX

DOW(*date*)

where *date* is of the date data type.

VERSION

dBASE III PLUS only

USAGE

The date passed to the DOW( ) function must be of the date data type. The value returned is a number between 1 and 7, with Sunday being 1.

EXAMPLES

The following command lists all records with dates that fall on a weekend (assuming that the Date field is of the date data type).

LIST FOR DOW(Date) = 1 .OR. DOW(Date) = 7

SEE ALSO

CDOW( )
DAY( )

The DTOC( ) Function

Converting a Date to a Character String

DTOC( ) converts any date to a character string.

SYNTAX

DTOC(*date***)**

where *date* is any data of the date data type.

VERSION
---

dBASE III PLUS, dBASE III

USAGE

The DTOC( ) function converts date data to character data, usually so that dates can be compared to character strings in date format.

EXAMPLES

The following commands ask the user to enter starting and ending dates; they then display records with dates that fall within that range.

```
STORE SPACE(8) TO Start,End
@ 2,1 SAY "Enter starting date " ;
    GET Start PICTURE "99/99/99"
@ 4,1 SAY "Enter ending date " ;
    GET End PICTURE "99/99/99"
READ

*--- Search the field named Date.
LIST FOR DTOC(Date) > = Start .AND. ;
    DTOC(Date) < = End
```

SEE ALSO

CTOD( )
SET CENTURY

The EOF( ) Function

Determining Whether the End-of-File Has Been Reached

EOF( ) determines whether the end-of-file marker has been reached.

SYNTAX

EOF( )

VERSION

dBASE III PLUS, dBASE III

USAGE

If the record pointer has been moved to the end-of-file marker, the function will yield a logical true (.T.) value; otherwise, it will return a logical false (.F.) value. The end-of-file marker is at the first record position beneath the last record (RECCOUNT( ) + 1).

EXAMPLES

The following example shows that the end-of-file marker is located one record after the last record in a database file.

```
USE AnyFile INDEX AnyIndex
GO BOTTOM
? EOF( )
   .F.

SKIP
? EOF( )
   .T.
```

SEE ALSO

DO WHILE
BOF( )
FOUND( )

The ERROR( ) Function

Returning Error Numbers

ERROR( ) returns the number corresponding to an error that triggered an ON ERROR condition.

SYNTAX

ERROR( )

VERSION

dBASE III PLUS only

USAGE

When an ON ERROR condition is triggered, the ERROR( ) function contains a number that corresponds to the error.

EXAMPLES

The following command tells dBASE to pass control to a program or procedure named ErrProcs when an error occurs.

ON ERROR DO ErrProcs

The ErrProcs procedure file (or command file) can then include a DO CASE clause to respond to various types of errors, as follows.

```
*********************************** ErrTrap.prg
*----- Sample procedure to trap common errors.
PROCEDURE ErrProcs
   a 19,0 CLEAR
   a 19,0 TO 19,79 DOUBLE
   ? CHR(7)
   DO CASE

      CASE ERROR() = 4   && EOF() encountered.
         ? "End of file encountered unexpectedly."
         ? "Will try to repair. Please wait."
         *-- If index file open, may be corrupted.
         IF NDX() # " "
            REINDEX
         ENDIF
         RETRY

      CASE ERROR() = 114  && Damaged index file.
         ? "Damaged index file!"
         ? Please wait while rebuilding..."
         REINDEX
         RETRY

      CASE ERROR() = 6   && Too many files open.
         ? "Check the Config.db file on your root"
         ? "directory, as discussed in the manual."
         CANCEL
         CLOSE ALL
         ON ERROR

      CASE ERROR() = 29   && File inaccessible.
         ? "Disk directory is full, or an illegal"
         ? "character appears in file name!"
         ? "Check file name and directory, then try again."
```

```
OTHERWISE    && Unknown error: display dBASE message.
   ? "Unexpected error in program..."
   ? MESSAGE()
   WAIT "Press Esc to abort, any key to continue..."

ENDCASE
RETURN
```

SEE ALSO

ON ERROR
MESSAGE( )

The EXP( ) Function

Returning an Exponent

EXP( ) returns the value of the constant *e* raised to the power specified in the argument. It represents the inverse of the LOG( ) function.

SYNTAX

EXP(*number*)

where *number* is any number, numeric expression, or numeric variable.

VERSION

dBASE III PLUS, dBASE III

USAGE

The EXP( ) function uses the constant e, which is approximately equal to 2.7182818285. The number passed to the function is the value of the exponent (x in the expression e^x).

EXAMPLES

Note the varying accuracy of the values returned by the following EXP( ) functions.

```
SET DECIMALS TO 2        && the default
? EXP(1)
    2.72

? EXP(1.000)
    2.718

? EXP(1.0000000)
    2.7182818
```

SEE ALSO

LOG( )
SET DECIMALS
SET FIXED

The FIELD( ) Function

Returning a Field Name

FIELD( ) returns the name of a field corresponding to a numeric position in the file structure of the active database file.

FIELD(*number*)

where *number* is any number, numeric expression, or numeric
variable.

dBASE III PLUS only

The first field in a database file is number 1, or FIELD(1). The largest possible field number is 128. If you pass a number to the function
that is greater than the number of fields in the database file, the function will return a null string.

The following routine counts the fields in the currently active database and stores the result in a memory variable named No_Fields.

```
USE &AnyFile
No_Fields = 0
DO WHILE LEN(TRIM(FIELD(No_Fields + 1))) > 0
    No_Fields = No_Fields + 1
ENDDO
```

DBF( )
NDX( )
RECCOUNT( )

The FILE( ) Function
Determining Whether a File Exists

FILE( ) returns a logical true (.T.) value if dBASE finds the file name passed to the function; otherwise, it returns a logical false (.F.) value.

SYNTAX

FILE(*file name***)**

where *file name* is the file name used as a string or the name of a variable containing the name of the file to search for.

VERSION

dBASE III PLUS, dBASE III

USAGE

If the file name passed to the function is not contained in a memory variable, it must be enclosed in single or double quotation marks or brackets. The file name must include the file extension. Also, you must explicitly state the drive or directory if the default drive or directory is not used.

EXAMPLES

The following example ensures that a specific transaction file exists before dBASE attempts to use it. TranStru.dbf is an empty database that is used to create identical databases as needed. If Tran0714.dbf does not exist, the program creates it by copying the structure of TranStru.dbf.

```
IF .NOT. FILE("Tran0714.dbf")
    USE TranStru
    COPY STRUCTURE TO Tran0714
ENDIF
USE Tran0714
```

SEE ALSO

DIR
SET PATH

The FKLABEL( ) Function
Returning the Function-Key Label

FKLABEL( ) returns the name assigned to the function key specified by the numeric argument.

SYNTAX

FKLABEL(*number***)**

where *number* is any number, numeric expression, or numeric variable.

VERSION

dBASE III PLUS only

USAGE

Although most keyboards use the standard names F1, F2, F3, and so
forth for function keys, some use different names. The FKLABEL( )

function returns the label that appears on the user's keyboard. FKLABEL( ) can access only programmable function keys. On terminals that use the F1 key as the Help key, the lowest-number programmable function key is number 2, and because F2 is the first programmable function key in this case, the function FKLABEL(1) actually refers to the F2 key.

EXAMPLES

The following commands display the prompt *Press F2 to Exit*, assuming the user's keyboard uses F2 as the label for function key number 1. If the label for function key number 1 is *User 1*, then the prompt displays the message *Press User 1 to Exit*.

```
SET FUNCTION 2 TO "QUIT;"
Prompt = "Press " + FKLABEL(1) + " to exit"
@ 2,1 SAY Prompt
```

SEE ALSO

FKMAX( )
SET FUNCTION

The FKMAX( ) Function

Returning the Maximum Number of Programmable Function Keys

FKMAX( ) returns the maximum number of programmable function keys on the terminal in use.

SYNTAX

FKMAX( )

VERSION

dBASE III PLUS only

USAGE

The largest number that can be assigned to the special function keys in dBASE III PLUS for most ordinary IBM PC/XT/AT computers is 9.

EXAMPLES

The following DO WHILE loop repeats once for each programmable function key available on the current keyboard and waits for a command string to be assigned to each key.

```
SET TALK OFF
KeyNo = 1
DO WHILE KeyNo < = FKMAX( )
    Prompt = "Command for " + FKLABEL(KeyNo) + " Key "
    ACCEPT Prompt TO String
    SET FUNCTION FKLABEL(KeyNo) TO String
    KeyNo = KeyNo + 1
ENDDO
```

SEE ALSO

FKLABEL( )
SET FUNCTION

The FLOCK( ) Function

Determining Whether a File Is Locked

FLOCK( ) determines whether a file is locked. If the file is not already locked, FLOCK( ) locks the file if possible. See Chapter 19, "Commands for Networking," for further information.

The FOUND( ) Function

Determining the Results of a Search

FOUND( ) determines whether commands that searched for a particular record found that record.

SYNTAX

FOUND( )

VERSION

dBASE III PLUS only

USAGE

FOUND( ) tests whether the previous SEEK, LOCATE, CONTINUE, or FIND command was successful. It returns a logical true (.T.) value if the search was successful; otherwise, it returns a logical false (.F.) value.

EXAMPLES

The following routine illustrates how the FOUND( ) function can be used in a simple validation process.

```
USE AnyFile INDEX LNames
Search = SPACE(20)
@ 5,5 SAY "Enter name to look for " GET Search
READ
SEEK UPPER(Search)
IF FOUND( )
    DISPLAY
ELSE
    ? "Can't find that name!"
ENDIF
```

SEE ALSO

LOCATE
CONTINUE
SEEK
FIND

The GETENV( ) Function
Returning DOS Environmental Variables

GETENV( ) returns the contents of a DOS environmental variable.

SYNTAX

GETENV(*character*)

where *character* is a DOS environmental variable.

VERSION

dBASE III PLUS only

USAGE

GETENV( ) returns a character string containing the setting or definition of the environmental variable specified by the character argument. The argument can be a literal string, a string variable, or a string expression. If the argument does not match a DOS environmental variable, the function returns a null string.

EXAMPLES

The following command displays the DOS PATH setting.

```
? GETENV("PATH")
C:\ROOT
```

SEE ALSO

OS( )
VERSION( )

The IIF( ) Function

Executing an Immediate IF Command

IIF( ) makes an IF...ELSE decision within a command line or LABEL/REPORT definition.

IIF(*expression,value1,value2***)**

where *expression* is any expression that yields a .T. or .F. result, *value1* is the value returned if *expression* evaluates to .T., and *value2* is the value returned if *expression* evaluates to .F. The *value1* and *value2* parameters must be of the same data type.

dBASE III PLUS only

If either *value1* or *value2* is an executable expression (such as a formula), the expression is executed as well.

Note that IIF( ) cannot be used to execute dBASE commands. To execute commands based on a conditional expression, use the IF...ELSE...ENDIF command.

The following command, whether used in a program or a MODIFY REPORT or MODIFY LABEL column, calculates the extended price with 6 percent tax added if a logical variable named Tax is true. Otherwise, it displays the extended price without tax added.

IIF(Tax,(Qty∗UPrice)∗1.06,Qty∗UPrice)

IF...ELSE...ENDIF

The INKEY( ) Function

Checking for a Keypress

INKEY( ) returns an integer that corresponds to the most recent key pressed by the user.

SYNTAX

INKEY( )

VERSION

dBASE III PLUS only

USAGE

The INKEY( ) function accepts input from the keyboard at any time during an operation and is often used in programming for branching. The integer value returned by INKEY( ) is the ASCII value (in decimal format) of the key pressed. The nonprinting keys return the integer values shown in Table 16.1. If no key is pressed, INKEY( ) has a value of zero. The range of INKEY( ) values extends from 0 to 255.

EXAMPLES

The following command prints a report until the user presses any key to interrupt the report.

REPORT FORM AnyRep WHILE INKEY( ) = 0

SEE ALSO

ON KEY
READKEY( )

KEY PRESSED	EQUIVALENT KEY	INKEY( ) VALUE
→	Ctrl-D	4
←	Ctrl-S	19
↑	Ctrl-E	5
↓	Ctrl-X	24
Ctrl-→	Ctrl-B	2
Ctrl-←	Ctrl-Z	26
PgUp	Ctrl-R	18
PgDn	Ctrl-C	3
Ctrl-PgUp	Ctrl--	31
Ctrl-PgDn	Ctrl- ^	30
Ins	Ctrl-V	22
Del	Ctrl-G	7
Home	Ctrl-A	1
End	Ctrl-F	6
Home	Ctrl-]	29
End	Ctrl-W	23

Table 16.1: Keypresses and Their INKEY( ) Values

The INT( ) Function

Truncating Integer Values

INT( ) converts any numeric expression to an integer by truncating all digits after the decimal place.

SYNTAX

INT(*number***)**

where *number* is any number, numeric expression, or numeric variable.

VERSION

dBASE III PLUS, dBASE III

USAGE

To filter out or display every odd or even record in a database, use INT( ) to determine whether a number is odd or even.

EXAMPLES

The following commands test whether a number is even or odd.

```
IF INT (x/2) = x/2
    ? "Number is even."
ELSE
    ? "Number is odd."
ENDIF
```

SEE ALSO

ROUND( )
MOD( )

The ISALPHA( ) Function

Determining Whether a String Begins with an Alphabetic Character

ISALPHA( ) determines whether the first character in a string is a letter.

SYNTAX

ISALPHA(*character*)

where *character* is any character data or character expression or a variable containing character data.

VERSION

dBASE III PLUS, dBASE III

USAGE

If an argument begins with a letter, ISALPHA( ) returns .T. Otherwise, ISALPHA( ) returns .F.

EXAMPLES

The following commands return .F., because the Address variable begins with a number.

```
Address = "123 Oak Tree Lane"
? ISALPHA(Address)
    .F.
```

SEE ALSO

ISLOWER( )	UPPER( )
ISUPPER( )	VAL( )
LOWER( )	

The ISCOLOR( ) Function

Determining Whether a Color Monitor Is Available

ISCOLOR( ) returns a logical true (.T.) value if the computer is currently using a color video card, and a logical false (.F.) value if the computer is using a monochrome video card.

SYNTAX

ISCOLOR( )

VERSION

dBASE III PLUS only

EXAMPLES

The following routine illustrates the typical method of setting video attributes.

```
IF ISCOLOR( )
    SET COLOR TO GR/B,W/R,GR
ELSE
```

```
     SET COLOR TO W +
ENDIF
```

SEE ALSO

SET COLOR

The ISLOWER( ) Function

Determining Whether an Expression Begins with a Lowercase Letter

ISLOWER( ) returns a logical true (.T.) value if the character expression passed to the function begins with a lowercase letter; otherwise, it returns a logical false (.F.) value.

SYNTAX

ISLOWER( )

VERSION

dBASE III PLUS only

EXAMPLES

The following commands demonstrate the values returned by ISLOWER( ) under different conditions.

```
MemVar = "12345"
? ISLOWER(MemVar)
     .F.

MemVar = "ABCDE"
? ISLOWER(MemVar)
     .F.

MemVar = "aBCDE"
? ISLOWER(MEMVAR)
     .T.
```

SEE ALSO

ISALPHA( )   LOWER( )
ISUPPER( )   UPPER( )

The ISUPPER( ) Function

Determining Whether an Expression Begins with an Uppercase Letter

ISUPPER( ) returns a logical true (.T.) value if the argument begins with an uppercase letter; otherwise, it returns a logical false (.F.) value.

SYNTAX

ISUPPER( )

VERSION

dBASE III PLUS only

The following commands demonstrate the different values returned
by ISUPPER( ) under different conditions.

```
MemVar = "12345"
? ISUPPER(MemVar)
    .F.

MemVar = "ABCDE"
? ISUPPER(MemVar)
    .T.

MemVar = "abcde"
? ISUPPER(MemVar)
    .F.
```

ISALPHA( )   LOWER( )
ISLOWER( )   UPPER( )

The LEFT( ) Function

Returning the Specified Leftmost Characters

LEFT( ) returns a specified number of characters, starting from the
leftmost character.

LEFT(*character,number***)**

where *character* is any data of the character data type, and *number* is
an expression yielding a number.

VERSION

dBASE III PLUS only

USAGE

The numeric expression in the argument defines how many characters are to be extracted from the left side of the character expression. LEFT( ) simulates the SUBSTR( ) function with a starting position of 1. If the numeric expression is larger than the length of the character expression, the whole character string is returned. If the numeric expression is zero or a negative number, a null string is returned.

EXAMPLES

To extract the seven leftmost characters from a character expression, enter

```
? LEFT("abcdefghijklm",7)
abcdefg
```

SEE ALSO

AT( )   STUFF( )
LTRIM( )   SUBSTR( )
RIGHT( )   TRIM( )
RTRIM( )

The LEN( ) Function
Returning the Length of a Character String

LEN( ) returns the length of a character string.

LEN(_character_**)**

where _character_ is any character data or character expression or a variable containing character data.

dBASE III PLUS, dBASE III

The character string being measured can be stored in any character memory variable or field. The length of a null string is zero.

The LEN( ) function can be used as a conditional test for branching. The following sample routine closes the database and returns control to the calling program if the user presses Return rather than typing a name.

```
CustName = SPACE(20)
@ 5,15 SAY "Enter name" GET CustName
READ
*———— If no name entered, return to calling program.
IF LEN(TRIM(CustName)) = 0
    CLOSE DATABASE
    RETURN
ENDIF
```

STUFF ( )
STR( )
SUBSTR( )

The LOCK( ) Function

Determining Whether a Record Is Locked

LOCK( ) determines whether a record is locked. If the record is not already locked, LOCK( ) locks the record if possible. See Chapter 19, "Commands for Networking," for further information.

The LOG( ) Function

Returning the Natural Logarithm

LOG( ) returns the natural logarithm of the number passed to it.

SYNTAX

LOG(*number***)**

where *number* is any number, numeric expression, or numeric variable.

VERSION

dBASE III PLUS, dBASE III

USAGE

The natural logarithm has a base of *e* (a mathematical constant approximately equal to 2.7182818285). In the following equation, *y* is the numeric expression passed to the function, and x is the number returned by the function.

$$e^x = y$$

The following command displays the natural logarithm of 2.71828.

```
? LOG(2.71828)
    1.00000
```

EXP( )
SET DECIMALS
SET FIXED

The LOWER( ) Function

Converting to Lowercase Letters

LOWER( ) converts any character expression to lowercase.

SYNTAX

```
LOWER( )
```

VERSION

dBASE III PLUS, dBASE III

EXAMPLES

If you enter all values into a field such as FName in uppercase and you want to convert them all to mixed case (with only a single leading uppercase letter), use a routine like the following:

```
USE AnyFile
REPLACE ALL FName WITH UPPER(LEFT(FName,1)) + ;
    LOWER(RIGHT(FName,LEN(FName) – 1))
```

SEE ALSO

ISALPHA( )   LTRIM( )
ISLOWER( )   UPPER( )
ISUPPER( )

The LTRIM( ) Function
Trimming Leading Blanks

LTRIM( ) removes leading blanks from a character string.

SYNTAX

LTRIM( ) (*char*)

where *char* is any character data or character expression or a variable containing character data.

VERSION

dBASE III PLUS only

EXAMPLES

The following commands demonstrate how the LTRIM( ) function can be used to combine character data with data originally stored as a number.

```
Amount = 1234.56
? "You won $" + LTRIM (STR(Amount,9,2)) + " dollars!"
You won $1234.56 dollars!
```

SEE ALSO

STR( )
TRIM( )
RTRIM( )

The LUPDATE( ) Function

Returning the Date of Last Change

LUPDATE( ) returns the date, using the date data type, of the last update of the currently selected database file.

SYNTAX

```
LUPDATE( )
```

VERSION

dBASE III PLUS only

USAGE

The LUPDATE( ) function is useful for controlling processes that should occur either not more or not less than once a day. In either case, simply compare the current date to the date returned by the function to satisfy the condition for executing the process.

EXAMPLES

The LUPDATE( ) function can be used effectively in a database file backup routine. Use the IF LUPDATE( ) # DATE( ) expression as a condition for backing up the file, as follows:

```
USE AnyFile
IF LUPDATE( ) # DATE( )
    DO <backup procedure>
ENDIF
```

SEE ALSO

DISPLAY STRUCTURE
LIST STRUCTURE

The MAX( ) Function
Returning the Larger of Two Numbers

MAX( ) returns the larger of two numeric expressions.

MAX(*number1,number2***)**

where both *number1* and *number2* are numbers or expressions that result in numeric values.

dBASE III PLUS only

The MAX( ) function determines the higher of two numeric expressions. A practical use of the MAX( ) function is in establishing a lower limit (or floor) to a numeric expression, as illustrated in the "Examples" section.

The following routine calculates and displays an overhead cost using either 10 percent or the value stored in the field named Overhead, whichever is higher.

```
LIST "Total with overhead = ",Cost * MAX(.10,Overhead)
```

MIN( )

The MESSAGE( ) Function
Returning Error Messages

MESSAGE( ) returns the error message describing the error that triggered an ON ERROR condition.

SYNTAX

MESSAGE( )

VERSION

dBASE III PLUS only

USAGE

The MESSAGE( ) function returns a character expression identifying the error that has occurred. You can store the error message in a variable, display it immediately as is, or even display another message that may help clarify the error to the user (if the error occurs within a program).

EXAMPLES

In the example for ERROR( ), presented earlier in this chapter, the OTHERWISE condition displays the error message that triggered an ON ERROR condition if none of the preceding CASE clauses traps the error.

SEE ALSO

ERROR( )
ON ERROR

The MIN( ) Function
Returning the Smaller of Two Numbers

MIN( ) returns the lower value of two numeric expressions.

MIN(_number1,number2_**)**

where _number1_ and _number2_ are either numbers or expressions that result in numeric values.

dBASE III PLUS only

MIN( ) returns the smaller of two numeric arguments passed to it. It can be used to place a ceiling (maximum value) on a value, as illustrated in the "Examples" section.

The following command calculates interest on a field named Cost, using either 6 percent or the value stored in the field named Tax-Amt, whichever is smaller.

LIST "Total with tax = ",Cost * MIN(.06,TaxAmt)

MAX( )

The MOD( ) Function

Returning the Modulus

MOD( ) returns the remainder, or *modulus*, of the division of the numbers specified in the argument.

SYNTAX

MOD(*number1,number2*)

where *number1* is the dividend and *number2* is the divisor. The parameters *number 1* and *number 2* are either numeric values or expressions that result in numeric values. The sign of the result is the same as the sign of the divisor.

VERSION

dBASE III PLUS only

EXAMPLES

The MOD( ) function can be used to determine whether a number is evenly divisible by some other number. For example, the following IF command acts only on numbers that are evenly divisible by 10.

IF MOD(X,10) = 0

SEE ALSO

INT( )
TIME( )

The MONTH( ) Function

Returning the Month as a Number

MONTH( ) returns the number of the month in the date expression passed to the function.

SYNTAX

MONTH(*date*)

where *date* is the date data type.

VERSION

dBASE III PLUS, dBASE III

USAGE

The date expression must be a memory variable, a field, or the system date function. The value returned is a number between 1 and 12, inclusive, where 1 is January, 2 is February, and so forth.

EXAMPLES

The following command displays the month number of the system date.

? MONTH(DATE( ))

SEE ALSO

CMONTH( )   YEAR( )
DAY( )

The NDX( ) Function

Returning an Index File Name

NDX( ) returns the name of the index file corresponding to the number passed to the function.

NDX(*number*)

where *number* is an integer value between 1 and 7.

dBASE III PLUS only

The number is the position of the index file in the index file list in the currently selected work area. If no index files are open, the function returns a null string. The number returned is always between 1 and 7, because only seven index files can be open at a time.

The following example displays the names of all index files connected to the open database.

```
I = 1
DO WHILE (I < = 7) .AND. " " # NDX (I)
    ? NDX (I)
    I = I + I
ENDDO
```

SEE ALSO

DBF( )
SET INDEX
SET ORDER

The OS( ) Function

Returning the Name of the Current Operating System

OS( ) returns the name and version number of the operating system currently in use.

SYNTAX

OS( )

VERSION

dBASE III PLUS only

USAGE

The OS( ) function is generally used within an IF clause to perform different commands under different operating systems, thereby allowing you to make your applications portable to a variety of computers.

EXAMPLES

The general structure of the following IF clause can be used to perform different commands under the DOS and UNIX operating systems.

```
SET EXACT OFF
IF OS( ) = "DOS"
   <do these commands>
ENDIF
IF OS( ) = "UNIX"
   <do these commands>
ENDIF
```

SEE ALSO

GETENV( )
VERSION( )

The PCOL( ) Function

Returning the Printer Column Position

PCOL( ) returns the current column position of the printer print head.

SYNTAX

PCOL( )

VERSION

dBASE III PLUS, dBASE III

In relative addressing for printed output, the location of the next printed row depends on the location of the current row. You can store the value of PCOL( ) in a memory variable.

When you print reports with @...SAY and SET DEVICE TO PRINT commands, PCOL( ) allows you to define spaces between columns without specifying exact column locations, as follows:

```
@ PROW( ),1 SAY Name
@ PROW( ),PCOL( ) + 5 SAY Address
@ PROW( ),PCOL( ) + 5 SAY TRIM(City) + ", " + State,Zip
```

PROW( )
COL( )
ROW( )

The PROW( ) Function

Returning the Printer Row Position

PROW( ) returns the current row position of the printer print head.

PROW( )

VERSION

dBASE III PLUS, dBASE III

USAGE

The PROW( ) function is usually used for relative addressing in printed output. This means that the location of the next row to be printed depends on the current row. You can store the value of PROW( ) in a memory variable. You cannot use negative numbers in relative addressing with the PROW( ) function. The printer's platen can scroll forward only.

EXAMPLES

The following commands use relative printer addressing to print a double-spaced report on the printer using the @...SAY and SET DEVICE TO PRINT commands.

```
USE AnyFile
SET TALK OFF
SET DEVICE TO PRINT
DO WHILE .NOT. EOF( )
    @ PROW( ) + 2,1 SAY Name
    @ PROW( ),PCOL( ) + 5 SAY Address
    SKIP
ENDDO
```

SEE ALSO

PCOL( )
COL( )
ROW( )

The READKEY( ) Function

Returning the Key Used to Exit Full-Screen Operation

READKEY( ) returns an integer corresponding to the key that was pressed to exit from a full-screen command (APPEND, BROWSE, CHANGE, CREATE, EDIT, INSERT, MODIFY, or READ). The READKEY( ) function also indicates whether changes were made in the data during execution of the full-screen command.

SYNTAX

READKEY( )

VERSION

dBASE III PLUS only

USAGE

READKEY( ) returns one of two possible values for a single key-press, depending on whether any data on the screen were altered. If no changes were made to the data, READKEY( ) has a value between 0 and 36. If any field on the screen was changed, the READKEY( ) value is increased by 256. Table 16.2 lists the values returned by READKEY( ), for both unchanged and changed, records.

EXAMPLES

In the following routine, the value 15 (which indicates that the user typed past the end of the last field on the screen) is assigned to the

KEY PRESSED	READKEY( ) (RECORD UNCHANGED)	READKEY( ) (RECORD CHANGED)	ACTION
Ctrl-H	0		Moves backward one character
Ctrl-S	0		Moves backward one character
Backspace	0		Moves backward one character
Ctrl-D	1	257	Moves forward one character
Ctrl-L	1	257	Moves forward one character
→	1	257	Moves forward one character
Ctrl-A	2	258	Moves backward one word
Home	2	258	Moves backward one word
Ctrl-F	3	259	Moves forward one word
End	3	259	Moves forward one word
Ctrl-E	4	260	Moves backward one field
↑	4	260	Moves backward one field

Table 16.2: READKEY( ) Values for Unchanged (Column 2) and Changed (Column 3) Records

KEY PRESSED	READKEY( ) (RECORD UNCHANGED)	READKEY( ) (RECORD CHANGED)	ACTION
Ctrl-K	4	260	Moves backward one field
Ctrl-J	5	261	Moves forward one field
Ctrl-X	5	261	Moves forward one field
↓	5	261	Moves forward one field
Ctrl-R	6	262	Moves backward one screen
PgUp	6	262	Moves backward one screen
Ctrl-C	7	263	Moves forward one screen
PgDn	7	263	Moves forward one screen
Ctrl-Z	8	264	Pans left
Ctrl-←	8	264	Pans left
Ctrl-B	9	265	Pans right
Ctrl-→	9	265	Pans right

Table 16.2: READKEY( ) Values for Unchanged (Column 2) and Changed (Column 3) Records (continued)

KEY PRESSED	READKEY( ) (RECORD UNCHANGED)	READKEY( ) (RECORD CHANGED)	ACTION
Ctrl-U	10	266	Deletes something
Ctrl-V	11	267	Inserts something
Ctrl-Q Esc	12	268	Terminates without save
Rturn (←—)	13	Not used	Presses Return key
Ctrl-W Ctrl-End	14	270	Terminates with save
Ctrl-M (past end)	15	271	Recognizes that user typed past end of screen
Return (←—) (at start)	16	272	Empties APPEND, MODIFY STRUCTURE, MODIFY REPORT screen

Table 16.2: READKEY( ) Values for Unchanged (Column 2) and Changed (Column 3) Records (continued)

KEY PRESSED	READKEY( ) (RECORD UNCHANGED)	READKEY( ) (RECORD CHANGED)	ACTION
Ctrl-Home	33	289	Toggles menu display
Ctrl-]	33	289	Toggles menu display
Ctrl-PgUp	34	290	Zooms out
Ctrl- -	34	290	Zooms out
Ctrl-PgDn	35	291	Zooms in
Ctrl- ^	36	292	Accesses HELP function keys
F1	36	292	Accesses HELP function keys

Table 16.2: READKEY( ) Values for Unchanged (Column 2) and Changed (Column 3) Records (continued)

variable RK_Filled. If the user types past the end of the screen without making any changes, the routine simply skips to the next record. If the user made changes in the record first, the routine presents a prompt that allows the user to make further changes by pressing ↑.

```
RK_Filled = 15
SET FORMAT TO AnyScrn
READ
IF READKEY( ) = RK_Filled
    SKIP
ENDIF
IF READKEY = RK_Filled + 256
    Decide = " "
```

```
   @ 22,1 SAY "Press up arrow to make more changes ";
      GET Decide
   READ
ENDIF
```

SEE ALSO

INKEY( )   READ
ON KEY

The RECCOUNT( ) Function

Returning the Number of Records
in a Database

RECCOUNT( ) returns the total number of records in the currently
selected database file.

SYNTAX

RECCOUNT( )

VERSION

dBASE III PLUS only

USAGE

The total returned by RECCOUNT( ) includes all records, regard-
less of the number of deleted records hidden with SET DELIM-
ITED ON or by a MODIFY QUERY or SET FILTER condition.
If the database is empty, RECCOUNT( ) is zero.

In many applications, it is useful to move sequentially forward or backward through a database file. To display a status notice that tells you which record you are viewing out of the total number of records in the file, you can use the following routine.

```
GO TOP
DO WHILE .NOT. EOF( )
@ 5,55 SAY "Record " + STR(RECNO( ),5) + ;
    " of " + STR(RECCOUNT( ),5)
* <any other dBASE commands>
SKIP
ENDDO
```

SEE ALSO

RECNO( )
RECSIZE( )

The RECNO( ) Function

Returning the Current Record Number

RECNO( ) returns the number of the record currently in use.

SYNTAX

RECNO( )

VERSION

dBASE III PLUS, dBASE III

USAGE

If the database file contains no records, RECNO( ) returns 1, and
EOF( ) returns .T. If the record pointer is moved past the last record
in a nonempty database file, RECNO( ) returns the last RECNO( )
value plus 1. If the record pointer is moved backward beyond the
first record in a nonempty database file, RECNO( ) returns 1.

EXAMPLES

The following commands locate the first record with the name Jones
in the LName field and display the number of that record.

```
Use Mail INDEX Names
FIND Jones
IF FOUND( )
    ? "Jones is at record ",RECNO( )
ELSE
    ? "Can't find Jones"
ENDIF
```

SEE ALSO

RECCOUNT( )

The RECSIZE( ) Function

Returning the Record Size

RECSIZE( ) returns the number of bytes used by a single record in
the currently selected database file.

RECSIZE( )

dBASE III PLUS only

Use the RECSIZE( ) function with the RECCOUNT( ) and DISK-SIZE( ) functions to calculate the total disk space required to back up a given database file to floppy disks.

Assuming that you know the number of fields in the database you want to back up, you can calculate the header size for a dBASE III PLUS database file as follows:

```
FieldCount = X        &&(where X is the number of fields)
HeadSize = 32 * FieldCount + 35
```

DISKSPACE( )
RECCOUNT( )

The REPLICATE( ) Function

Repeating a Character String

REPLICATE( ) repeats a character string a specified number of times.

SYNTAX

REPLICATE(*character,number***)**

where *character* is the character or character string to repeat, and *number* is a number or numeric expression defining the number of times to repeat that character pattern.

VERSION

dBASE III PLUS only

USAGE

The REPLICATE( ) function returns a character expression consisting of *number* repetitions of *character*. The maximum length of the string is 254 characters.

EXAMPLES

To place a row of double lines across the top of a report, use the command

@ 4,0 SAY REPLICATE(" = ",80)

SEE ALSO

SUBSTR( )

The RIGHT( ) Function

Returning the Specified Rightmost Characters

RIGHT( ) returns a specified number of characters, starting from the rightmost point in a character expression.

SYNTAX

RIGHT(*character,number***)**

where *character* is any character string or expression, and *number* is a number or numeric expression that specifies the number of characters to return.

VERSION

dBASE III PLUS only

USAGE

The numeric expression in the argument defines the number of characters to extract from the right side of the character expression. If the numeric expression is less than 1, a null string is returned. If the numeric expression is greater than the length of the character expression, the entire character expression is returned.

The following routine pads any number stored in the variable
named X with sufficient leading zeros to give the number an exact
width of 15 characters.

```
Leader = "000000000000000"
INPUT "Enter a number " TO X

? RIGHT(Leader + LTRIM(STR(X,16,2)),15)
```

LEFT( )	SUBSTR( )
LTRIM( )	RTRIM( )
STUFF( )	TRIM( )

The RLOCK( ) Function
Determining Whether a Record Is Locked

RLOCK( ) determines whether a record is locked. If the record is
not already locked, RLOCK( ) locks the record if possible. See
Chapter 19, "Commands for Networking," for further information.

The ROUND( ) Function
Rounding a Number

ROUND( ) rounds a number to the nearest decimal place specified.

SYNTAX

ROUND(*number1,number2***)**

where *number1* is the number to round, and *number2* is the number of decimal places to round to.

VERSION

dBASE III PLUS, dBASE III

USAGE

The ROUND( ) function rounds the first number to the number of decimal places specified by the second number. If the second number is negative, the function begins rounding the integer portion of the number, as shown in the "Examples" section.

EXAMPLES

The following commands demonstrate the various effects of the ROUND( ) function on the number 12.3456.

```
? ROUND(12.3456,3)
    12.3460

? ROUND(12.3456,0)
    12.0000

? ROUND(12.3456, – 2)
    0.0000
```

SEE ALSO

SET DECIMALS
SET FIXED
INT( )

The ROW( ) Function

Returning the Row Position of the Cursor

The ROW( ) function returns the current row position of the cursor on the screen.

SYNTAX

ROW( )

VERSION

dBASE III PLUS, dBASE III

USAGE

The ROW( ) function is commonly used for relative addressing on the screen. For example, the expression @ ROW + 2,5 refers to two rows below the current row (and the fifth column).

You can also store the value of ROW( ) in a memory variable.

EXAMPLES

The following routine creates 10 variables named Var1 through Var10, each 10 spaces wide. The DO WHILE loop displays these variables on the screen, in two columns and five double-spaced rows, for data entry. After filling in the prompts, the LIST MEMORY command displays the values entered.

```
*----------- Create and display ten blank variables
*--5-------- on the screen for entering data.
SET TALK OFF
CLEAR
Counter = 1
a 3,5 SAY ""
```

```
DO WHILE Counter <= 10
   Sub = LTRIM(STR(Counter,2))
   Var&Sub = SPACE(10)
   @ ROW()+2,5 GET Var&Sub
   Counter = Counter + 1
   S5b = LTRIM(STR(Counter,2))
   Var&Sub = SPACE(10)
   @ ROW(),20 GET Var&Sub
   Counter = Counter + 1
ENDDO
READ
LIST MEMORY
```

[Ed: This is Desktop Companion Figure 17.7].

SEE ALSO

PROW( )
COL( )
PCOL( )

The RTRIM( ) Function

Removing Trailing Blanks

RTRIM( ) removes trailing blanks from a character expression.

SYNTAX

RTRIM(*character***)**

where *character* is any character data or character expression or a variable containing character data.

VERSION

dBASE III PLUS only; in dBASE III use TRIM( ).

USAGE

The RTRIM( ) function is equivalent to the TRIM( ) function.

SEE ALSO

LEFT( )   RIGHT( )
LTRIM( )   TRIM( )

The SPACE( ) Function
Creating Blank Spaces

SPACE( ) creates a character string composed of a specified number of blanks.

SYNTAX

SPACE(*number*)

where *number* is any number, numeric expression, or variable smaller than 254.

VERSION

dBASE III PLUS, dBASE III

USAGE

SPACE( ) creates a character string containing a specified number of blank spaces. SPACE( ) is usually used to initialize character memory variables.

Assuming that the LName field in a database has a width of 20, the
following routine allows a user to enter a last name to search for and
to store that entry in a memory variable named Search. The user's
entry cannot exceed 20 characters.

```
USE Mail INDEX LNames
Search = SPACE(20)
@ 10,5 SAY "Enter name to search for ";
    GET SEARCH READ
SEEK UPPER(TRIM(Search))
```

REPLICATE( )

The SQRT( ) Function

Returning the Square Root

SQRT( ) returns the square root of the number passed to the function.

SQRT(number**)**

where *number* is a positive number, an expression resulting in a positive number, or the name of a variable containing a positive number.

dBASE III PLUS, dBASE III

USAGE

The SQRT( ) function returns a number with either the default number of decimal places or the number of decimal places in the expression, whichever is larger.

Use the ABS( ) function to change a negative number to positive before taking its square root.

EXAMPLES

The following commands calculate and display the square root of 3213.56.

```
Numb = 3213.56
? SQRT(Numb)
    56.69
```

SEE ALSO

ABS( )   SET FIXED
SET DECIMAL

The STR( ) Function

Converting a Number to a String

STR( ) converts any numeric expression into a character string.

SYNTAX

STR(*number,[length],[decimal]*)

where *number* is the number to convert, *length* is the length of the converted number, and *decimal* is the number of decimal places in the number, if any.

VERSION

dBASE III PLUS, dBASE III

USAGE

The *length* parameter sets the total length of the character expression (including any decimal digits, the decimal point itself, and the minus sign), and the *decimal* parameter sets the number of decimal places to be included. If either parameter is omitted, dBASE uses the default setting (10 characters and 0 decimal places).

If you specify a length smaller than the number of digits to the left of the decimal point in the numeric expression, dBASE returns asterisks in place of the number. If you specify fewer decimal digits than are in the numeric expression, dBASE rounds the result to the specified number of decimal places.

EXAMPLES

The following commands demonstrate the effect of the STR function, using various arguments, on the number 1234.56.

```
Number = 1234.56

? STR(Number)
              1235 (10 characters wide, 0 decimal places)
? STR(Number,15,1)
                 1234.6 (15 characters, 1 decimal place)
 ? STR(Number,4,2)
     1235  (4 characters only; decimal digits don't fit)
```

TIPS

The STR( ) function is usually used to combine numeric data with character data. To prevent leading blanks in the converted number from appearing in the character string, use the LTRIM function with the STR function, as follows:

Prize = 100.00
Prompt = "You have won " + LTRIM(STR(Prize)) + "dollars!"

The command ? Prompt then displays *You have won 100 dollars!*.

STR( ) can also be used to define an exact column width for displaying numbers in printed reports.

SEE ALSO

LTRIM( )
TRANSFORM( )
VAL( )

The STUFF( ) Function

Inserting or Replacing a String

STUFF( ) combines two character expressions to produce a third character expression.

SYNTAX

STUFF(*character1,number1,number2,character2***)**

where *character1* is the target string, *character2* is the string being inserted, *number1* identifies the character position at which *character2* will be "stuffed" into *character1*, and *number2* identifies how many (if any) characters in *character1* will be deleted or overwritten.

VERSION

dBASE III PLUS only

USAGE

Essentially, the STUFF( ) function lets you "stuff" the second expression into the first expression. The first number describes where to insert the second expression into the first, and the second number determines how many characters are overwritten in the first expression. If the second number is zero or a negative number, no characters in the target string are overwritten. If the string being inserted is a null string, STUFF removes characters from the target string, because the overwritten characters are replaced by nothing.

EXAMPLES

The following commands illustrate examples of the outcome of various STUFF( ) operations with two strings named Target and Bullet.

```
Target = "This is a long sentence"
Bullet = "<inserted>"

? STUFF(Target,5,0,Bullet)
    This<inserted> is a long sentence

? STUFF(Target,5,0," " + Bullet)
    This <inserted> is a long sentence

? STUFF(Target,6,4,Bullet)
    This <inserted> long sentence
```

SEE ALSO

LEFT( )
RIGHT( )
SUBSTR( )

The SUBSTR( ) Function

Extracting a Substring

SUBSTR( ) extracts a smaller string from a larger string.

SYNTAX

SUBSTR(*character,number1,[number2]***)**

where *character* is the character string, *number1* is the starting location for the substring, and *number2* is the length of the substring.

VERSION

dBASE III PLUS, dBASE III

USAGE

The first numeric expression is the starting point of the string to be extracted. The optional second numeric expression signifies how many characters will be extracted. If *number2* is omitted, SUBSTR( ) will extract the maximum number of characters remaining in the character string.

EXAMPLES

In the following example, SUBSTR( ) displays DOG, a three-character substring beginning at the sixth character.

```
String = "YOUR DOG HAS FLEAS"
? SUBSTR(String,6,3)
   DOG
```

SEE ALSO

AT( )   RIGHT( )
LEFT( )   STUFF( )

The TIME( ) Function

Returning the System Time

TIME( ) returns the system time as a character string.

SYNTAX

TIME( )

VERSION

dBASE III PLUS, dBASE III

USAGE

TIME( ) returns a character string in the format hh:mm:ss (for example, 12:55:01). Because TIME( ) is returned as a character string, you cannot perform time arithmetic directly. Instead, you must first convert individual portions of the time string to numbers.

EXAMPLES

To time stamp a printed display, enter the command **? TIME( )** in your report heading. To include the time on a report printed by the REPORT FORM command, enter the option **HEADING TIME( )** in the REPORT FORM command.

SEE ALSO

MOD( )
DATE( )

The TRANSFORM( ) Function
Formatting Data

TRANSFORM( ) offers picture formatting features of numeric or character expressions without using the @...SAY command.

SYNTAX

TRANSFORM(*data,format***)**

where *data* is the item to be formatted, and *format* is the format to use.

VERSION

dBASE III PLUS only

USAGE

TRANSFORM extends picture formatting to commands such as ?, ??, DISPLAY, LABEL, LIST, and REPORT. The first argument can be a numeric or character variable. The second argument is a template, or the name of a variable containing the template, that defines the format.

Table 16.3 lists the picture functions that can be used with the TRANSFORM function. As with the PICTURE command, these function characters must be preceded by an @ sign. Table 16.4 lists

SYMBOL	DATA TYPE	EFFECT IN TRANSFORM
@(	N	Displays negative number in parentheses
@B	N	Left-justifies a number
@C	N	Displays CR (credit) after positive number
@X	N	Displays DB (debit) after negative number
@Z	N	Displays a zero as a blank space
@!	C	Displays all letters in uppercase
@R	C	Inserts template characters into displayed data
@S*n*	C	Displays the left *n* characters of data

Table 16.3: Picture Functions Used in TRANSFORM( )

SYMBOL	DATA TYPES	EFFECT IN TRANSFORM
X	C	Displays any character
!	C	Displays all letters in uppercase
9	N	Displays digit locations
#	N	Same as 9
$	N	Displays leading dollar signs if space permits
★	N	Displays leading asterisks if space permits
,	N	Displays comma if digits are present on both sides

Table 16.4: Picture Template Characters Used in TRANSFORM( )

the individual picture template characters that can be used in TRANSFORM functions.

EXAMPLES

Table 16.5 displays examples of the output of various TRANS-FORM functions.

SEE ALSO

@...SAY
STR

TRANSFORM OUTPUT	DISPLAYED
TRANSFORM(−123.45,"@(")	(123.45)
TRANSFORM(−123.45,"@B(")	(123.45)
TRANSFORM(−123.45,"@X")	123.45 DB
TRANSFORM(123.45,"@C")	123.45 CR
TRANSFORM(0,"@Z")	
TRANSFORM("cat","@!")	CAT
TRANSFORM("cat","@R X X X")	c a t
TRANSFORM("abcdefg","@S3")	abc
TRANSFORM(1234567.89,"999,999.99")	123,567.89
TRANSFORM(1234.56,"$999,999.99")	$$$1,234.56
TRANSFORM(1234.567,"* ###,###.##")	* * *1,234.57
TRANSFORM(−123,"@X 999,999.99")	123.00 DB
TRANSFORM(123,"@CX 999,999.99")	123.00 CR

Table 16.5: Example of Various TRANSFORM( ) Function
Formats

The TRIM( ) Function
Trimming Off Trailing Blanks

TRIM( ) removes trailing blanks from a character expression.

SYNTAX

TRIM(*character***)**

where *character* is any character data or character expression or a variable containing character data.

VERSION

dBASE III PLUS, dBASE III

USAGE

This function removes trailing blanks from a character expression. The trailing blanks are typically those used to pad the string to a width defined in a database field or to a predefined width created by a SPACE function before a READ command.

EXAMPLES

A common use of the TRIM( ) function is to create the last line of a mailing label. Separate fields usually exist for the city, state, and zip code, but the TRIM( ) function allows you to create a single line in the format Los Angeles, CA   92122, as in the following line.

    ? TRIM(City) + ", " + TRIM(State) + "   " + Zip

TIPS

Never use TRIM( ) in an index key expression, as this produces unequal key lengths within the index file, with unpredictable results.

SEE ALSO

LTRIM( )
RTRIM( )

The TYPE( ) Function

Returning the Data Type

TYPE( ) returns a single character code indicating the data type of the expression passed to the function.

SYNTAX

TYPE(*expression***)**

where *expression* is an expression of any type or the name of a database field or memory variable enclosed in quotation marks or brackets.

VERSION

dBASE III PLUS, dBASE III

USAGE

The TYPE( ) function tests for the existence of an expression, field, or variable; if the item does not exist, a U (for undefined) is returned.

If the item does exist, the appropriate data type is returned.

The possible data types returned by the function are C (Character), N (Numeric), D (Date), L (Logical), M (Memo), U (Undefined).

EXAMPLES

The following commands typed at the dot prompt demonstrate the TYPE( ) function.

```
STORE 0 TO memvar
? TYPE("memvar")
   N
STORE .F. TO Expired
? TYPE("expired")
   L
? TYPE("Today")
   U
? TYPE("DATE( )") = "D"
   .T.
```

SEE ALSO

FIELD( )

The UPPER( ) Function

Converting to Uppercase

UPPER( ) converts any lowercase letters in a character expression to uppercase.

SYNTAX

UPPER( )

VERSION

dBASE III PLUS, dBASE III

USAGE

UPPER converts all lowercase letters in a character string to upper-case. It has no effect on numbers or uppercase letters. It is often used in index file expressions to prevent case distinctions from affecting sort orders and searches.

EXAMPLES

The following commands demonstrate how UPPER works.

```
Name = "SuSiTa, 123 Apple St."
Name = UPPER(Name)
? Name
    SUSITA, 123 APPLE ST."
```

SEE ALSO

ISALPHA( )
ISLOWER( )
ISUPPER( )
LOWER( )

The VAL( ) Function

Converting a Character String to a Number

VAL( ) converts numbers stored as character strings to the numeric data type.

SYNTAX

VAL(*character***)**

VERSION

dBASE III PLUS, dBASE III

USAGE

If an argument contains leading numeric characters followed by nonnumeric characters, VAL( ) returns the leading numeric characters as a number. If the argument consists of leading nonnumeric characters (other than blanks), the function returns 0. The number of decimal digits returned by the function is determined by the SET DECIMALS command.

EXAMPLES

The following commands store the street address number as a numeric variable in a variable called StreetNo and then display that number.

```
Address = "34567 Adams St."
StreetNo = VAL(Address)
? StreetNo
   34567
```

SET DECIMALS
STR( )
TIME( )

The VERSION( ) Function

Returning the Version Number of the Current Program

VERSION( ) returns a character expression containing the version number of the dBASE III PLUS program in use.

VERSION( )

dBASE III PLUS only

VERSION( ) can be used to make sure that certain commands are used only with the versions of dBASE III PLUS that support the commands.

The following command displays the version number of dBASE III PLUS currently in use.

? VERSION( )
   dBASE III PLUS version 1.1

OS( )
GETENV( )

The YEAR( ) Function

Returning the Year as a Number

YEAR( ) returns the numeric value of the year from a date expression.

YEAR(*date*)

where *date* is any data of the date data type.

dBASE III PLUS, dBASE III

The YEAR( ) function returns a four-digit representation of the year.

EXAMPLES

The following example displays the year for the current system date.

```
? YEAR(DATE( ))
   1987
```

SEE ALSO

MONTH( )
DAY( )
SET CENTURY
INDEX

17

SET Commands

The dBASE SET commands allow you to define general parameters that affect the current session with dBASE III PLUS. When you issue a SET command, it stays in effect until you either quit dBASE or change the status of the parameter with another SET command.

You can also predefine many SET parameters so that they are automatically activated when you first run dBASE. To do so, you need to modify the Config.db file, as discussed in Appendix A, "Configuring dBASE III PLUS."

The SET Command
Setting Any dBASE Parameter

The SET command, when used alone, displays all current parameter settings and allows them to be changed through a menu.

SYNTAX

SET

VERSION

dBASE III PLUS, dBASE III

USAGE

SET provides a full-screen, menu-driven technique for viewing and changing current parameter settings. Figure 17.1 shows the screen displayed by the SET command.

The → and ← keys move the highlight across the top-menu options. Each top-menu option has a pull-down menu associated with it. The ↑ and ↓ keys move the highlight through pull-down menu options. Pressing Return selects the currently highlighted item. To toggle the parameter between settings, press Return. Additional instructions appear at the bottom of the screen as you work. For more help with a particular item, see the related SET command in this chapter. (For example, for additional information about the CENTURY option, see SET CENTURY.)

EXAMPLES

At the dot prompt, enter the command **SET** to view or alter SET parameters.

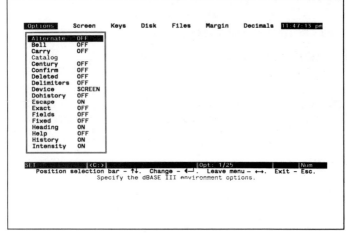

Figure 17.1: Screen displayed by the SET command

SEE ALSO

LIST STATUS
DISPLAY STATUS

The SET ALTERNATE Command

Capturing Displays in a File

SET ALTERNATE determines whether ensuing screen text is stored in the currently active alternate file.

SYNTAX

SET ALTERNATE [OFF][ON]

where the default setting is OFF.

VERSION

dBASE III PLUS, dBASE III

USAGE

The SET ALTERNATE ON command tells dBASE to record all screen entries and displays, except the output of @...SAY...GET commands, in the currently open alternate file. The SET ALTERNATE OFF command temporarily deactivates the alternate file so that ensuing screen displays are not recorded. The SET ALTERNATE ON command reactivates the file. Once an alternate file is closed, new data cannot be added to it. (The next SET ALTERNATE TO command to open the file would cause that file to be overwritten.)

Remember that SET ALTERNATE TO *file name* must precede the SET ALTERNATE ON command. SET ALTERNATE ON is required to start recording text.

EXAMPLES

The following commands create an alternate file named Text.txt, open that file, and copy the ? commands and their output into that file. The CLOSE ALTERNATE command then closes the alternate file.

```
SET ALTERNATE TO Text
SET ALTERNATE ON
? SQRT(144)
? "This is only a test."
SET ALTERNATE OFF
CLOSE ALTERNATE
```

SEE ALSO

SET ALTERNATE TO

The SET ALTERNATE TO Command

Naming an Alternate File

SET ALTERNATE TO creates an ASCII text file to which dBASE can direct output.

SYNTAX

SET ALTERNATE TO *[file name]*

where *file name* is the name of the text file to create.

VERSION

dBASE III PLUS, dBASE III

USAGE

The SET ALTERNATE TO command must be used before the SET ALTERNATE ON command for the text to be created. The text file name will have a .txt extension unless otherwise specified.

Not using the *file name* clause closes the alternate file. (The CLOSE ALTERNATE command also closes the file.)

If a file of the requested name already exists when the SET ALTERNATE TO command is issued, that file will be overwritten when SET ALTERNATE ON activates it.

Make sure that you close the alternate file when you are done recording text to ensure that the information is properly saved.

EXAMPLES

The command

SET ALTERNATE TO AltFile

creates a text file named AltFile.txt, which will capture screen text when SET ALTERNATE is on.

SEE ALSO

SET ALTERNATE

The SET BELL Command
Controlling the Bell

SET BELL determines whether the warning bell sounds when you type beyond the width of a field or enter invalid data.

SYNTAX

SET BELL *[OFF]/[ON]*

where the default setting is ON.

VERSION

dBASE III PLUS, dBASE III

USAGE

Use SET BELL OFF to prevent the bell from ringing repeatedly in screen displays that include many fields.

EXAMPLES

In the following example, the bell will ring if the user fills any of the memory variables completely, but not when the user answers the yes/no question.

```
STORE SPACE(20) TO Name, Address, City
YesNo = " "
SET BELL ON
@ 5,5 SAY "Enter name:" GET Name
@ 6,5 SAY "Enter address:" GET Address
@ 7,5 SAY "Enter city:" GET City
READ
SET BELL OFF
@ 10,5 SAY "Continue ? " GET YesNo
READ
```

SEE ALSO

SET CONFIRM

The SET CARRY Command

Carrying Data from One New Record to the Next

SET CARRY copies data from the previous record to the next record when the APPEND or INSERT command is used.

SYNTAX

SET CARRY *[OFF]/[ON]*

where the default setting is OFF.

VERSION

dBASE III PLUS, dBASE III

USAGE

The new record appended or inserted will not be saved unless some changes are made or a Ctrl-W or Ctrl-End command is entered.

EXAMPLES

The following commands set the carry option to ON before data are entered using the custom form MailScr.

USE MAIL
SET FORMAT TO MailScr
SET CARRY ON
APPEND

TIPS

When the INSERT BEFORE command is issued with SET CARRY ON, the contents of the preceding record are copied to the newly inserted record. For example, the commands

GOTO 20
SET CARRY ON
INSERT BEFORE

create a new record 20 with the same contents as record 19.

SEE ALSO

APPEND   READ
INSERT   SET FORMAT

The SET CATALOG Command

Storing File Names in a Catalog

The SET CATALOG command determines whether files are added to an open catalog.

SYNTAX

SET CATALOG [OFF]/[ON]

where the default setting is OFF. However, using the SET CATALOG TO *file name* command automatically sets CATALOG to ON.

VERSION

dBASE III PLUS only

USAGE

If CATALOG is set to ON and is used in conjunction with the SET CATALOG TO command, the open catalog is updated automatically by commands such as CREATE, INDEX, and CREATE/ MODIFY REPORT. If you issue the SET CATALOG OFF command, the files used by these commands will not be entered into the catalog.

In the following commands, the Mail database and Names and Zips index files are stored in the MailList catalog, but the Temp index file is not stored in the catalog.

```
SET CATALOG TO MailList
USE Mail
INDEX ON UPPER(LName + FName) TO Names
INDEX ON Zip TO Zips
SET CATALOG OFF
INDEX ON City TO Temp
```

SEE ALSO

SET CATALOG TO
SET TITLE

The SET CATALOG TO Command
Naming the Catalog File to Use

SET CATALOG TO creates and activates a new catalog, activates an existing catalog, or closes an open catalog.

SYNTAX

SET CATALOG TO *[file name]*

where *file name* is the name of the catalog file, with the .cat extension.

VERSION

dBASE III PLUS only

USAGE

Catalog files are used to group the names of files belonging to a particular application into a single file. The command SET CATALOG TO *file name* opens the catalog file if it exists, or creates it if it doesn't exist, and activates the catalog in the same way as SET CATALOG ON. The first time you create a catalog file in a directory, dBASE automatically creates a file called Catalog.cat. The names of all future catalog files created in that directory are stored in the Catalog.cat file.

SET CATALOG TO lets you query a catalog and see a menu of all files related to the database file in use. When the SET CATALOG ON command is used, all files opened or created are added to the catalog. This includes index (.ndx) and report (.frm) files. As new files are added, you are prompted for a descriptive name up to 49 characters long to store in the open catalog.

Once a SET CATALOG TO *file name* command is issued, you can use the ?, known as the query clause, in many commands to ask the catalog for a display of all related files.

To access the SET CATALOG TO command from the Assistant menu, highlight the Set Up option and select Catalog.

EXAMPLES

The following commands open an existing catalog named My_File.cat and check the catalog for existing database, report, and index file names.

```
SET CATALOG TO My_File
USE ?                       && Select a file from the menu
SET CATALOG OFF             && Catalog can still be queried
REPORT FORM ? TO PRINT      && Select a report from the menu
SET INDEX TO ?              && Select an index from the
                              menu
SET CATALOG ON
```

SEE ALSO

SET CATALOG
SET TITLE

The SET CENTURY Command

Displaying Dates in mm/dd/yy or mm/dd/yyyy Format

SET CENTURY allows the entry and display of century prefixes in the year portion of dates.

SYNTAX

SET CENTURY *[OFF]/[ON]*

where the default setting is OFF.

VERSION

dBASE III PLUS only

USAGE

Using SET CENTURY ON displays a four-digit year. Using SET CENTURY OFF displays a two-digit year and assumes the twentieth century.

The following commands accept two dates from the screen: one in mm/dd/yy format and the other in mm/dd/yyyy format.

```
STORE DATE( ) TO MDate1,MDate2
SET CENTURY ON
@ 12,5 SAY "Enter date:" GET MDate1
READ
SET CENTURY OFF
@ 13,5 SAY "Enter date:" GET MDate2
READ
@ 16,5 SAY "First date was " + MDate1
@ 17,5 SAY "Second date was " + MDate2
```

SEE ALSO

CTOD( )
DATE( )
DTOC( )

The SET COLOR Command
Activating or Deactivating Color Displays

SET COLOR selects either color or monochrome display on computers that have both options.

SYNTAX

SET COLOR *[OFF]/[ON]*

where the default setting depends on the monitor in use when dBASE is started.

VERSION
═══════════

dBASE III PLUS only

USAGE
═══════════

SET COLOR can be used to suppress color displays on computers that
have color capabilities but have a monochrome monitor attached.

EXAMPLES
═══════════

The command SET COLOR OFF prevents screen colors, which
would normally disrupt a monochrome screen, from affecting the
display.

SEE ALSO
═══════════

SET COLOR TO
ISCOLOR( )

The SET COLOR TO Command

Determining Screen Colors

SET COLOR TO allows you to change the colors displayed on the
screen.

SYNTAX
═══════════

SET COLOR TO *[standard][,enhanced][,border][,background]*

where *standard* is the basic dBASE screen display, *enhanced* is reversed video display, *border* is the screen border, and *background* is the background color setting (used on only some monitors).

VERSION

dBASE III PLUS, dBASE III (with differences)

USAGE

To display a particular color combination, use the letter codes in the following table. In the command, the color of the text comes first, followed by a slash and the background color. For example, entering **R/W** displays red letters on a white background. The U (underline) and I (inverse) options work only on monochrome monitors.

COLOR	CODE
Black	N
Blue	B
Green	G
Cyan	BG
Red	R
Magenta	RB
Brown	GR
White	W
Underline	U (Monochrome)
Inverse	I (Monochrome)
Blank	X
Blinking	*
High intensity	+

The *standard* portion of the command affects the usual text display, including displays by the ?, LIST, REPORT, and SAY commands. The *enhanced* portion of the command affects those characters displayed in reverse video, such as highlighted menu options and data displayed by the GET command. The *border* portion affects the border color (assuming the particular monitor in use has a border). The *background* portion applies to color monitors that can't set the individual background colors for standard and enhanced display. The * symbol for blinking and + character for high-intensity apply only to the foreground display (the actual typed letters).

EXAMPLES

To set the standard video display with yellow letters on a red background, the enhanced video display with white text against a red background, and a yellow border, type the following from the dot prompt:

SET COLOR TO GR + /R,W/R,GR +

TIPS

The X color combination can be used for password entry to make any typed characters invisible.

SEE ALSO

SET INTENSITY
SET

The SET CONFIRM Command
Determining Confirmation Requirements

SET CONFIRM determines whether a user can type beyond the end of a field prompt without pressing the Return key.

SET CONFIRM *[OFF]/[ON]*

where the default setting is OFF.

dBASE III PLUS, dBASE III

When you use the SET CONFIRM ON command, you must press Return to finish entering data into any field. When you use SET CONFIRM OFF, filling the field prompt will automatically move the cursor out of the field, even if you do not press Return.

The following commands let the user enter a Y or N character but require that the user also press Return after entering the character.

```
YesNo = .F.
SET CONFIRM ON
@ 23,1 SAY "Return to menu now? ";
   GET YesNo PICTURE "Y"
READ
```

@...SAY...GET

The SET CONSOLE Command
Enabling or Disabling Screen Display

SET CONSOLE turns the screen display off or on for other than @...SAY commands.

SYNTAX

SET CONSOLE [OFF]/[ON]

where the default setting is ON.

VERSION

dBASE III PLUS, dBASE III

USAGE

This command is normally used to turn off the screen so that only @...SAY...GET commands are displayed. The SET CONSOLE command does not affect output to a printer.

EXAMPLES

The following commands display the message *Press End to terminate report* on the screen and print a formatted report. The report is displayed only on the printer.

```
SET CONSOLE OFF
@ 2,2 SAY "Press End to terminate report"
REPORT FORM AnyRep WHILE INKEY( ) # 6 TO PRINT
SET CONSOLE ON
```

TIPS

The SET CONSOLE OFF command can be used when sending special control characters to the printer so that graphic characters are not unintentionally displayed on the screen.

SEE ALSO

SET PRINT
SET DEVICE

The SET DATE Command
Determining Date Format

SET DATE determines the format of date expressions.

SYNTAX

SET DATE *format*

where *format* is any valid dBASE date format.

VERSION

dBASE III PLUS, dBASE III

Regardless of the format used to enter a date, the SET DATE command will display all dates in the specified format. The following date formats are available.

SETTING	FORMAT
AMERICAN	mm/dd/yy
ANSI	yy.mm.dd
BRITISH	dd/mm/yy
ITALIAN	dd-mm-yy
FRENCH (dBASE III PLUS)	dd/mm/yy
FRENCH (dBASE III)	dd.mm.yy
GERMAN	dd.mm.yy

EXAMPLES

The following commands demonstrate the effect of SET DATE ANSI on a date variable.

```
Date = CTOD("01/28/89")
? Date
     01/28/89
SET DATE ANSI
? Date
     89.01.28
```

SEE ALSO

DATE( )
INDEX

The SET DEBUG Command

Echoing Command File Execution on the Printer

SET DEBUG determines whether output from SET ECHO ON is sent to the screen or the printer. See Chapter 15, "Debugging Commands," for further information.

The SET DECIMALS Command

Determining the Number of Decimal Places to Display

SET DECIMALS determines the minimum number of decimal places displayed in the results of numeric functions and calculations.

SYNTAX

SET DECIMALS TO *width*

where *width* is a number representing the number of decimal places to display.

VERSION

dBASE III PLUS, dBASE III

USAGE

SET DECIMALS is generally used with the SET FIXED command to set a fixed number of decimal places for the display of calculation results. If SET FIXED is not on, SET DECIMALS will not affect multiplication results.

EXAMPLES

The following commands demonstrate the result of a calculation first in the default mode and then after a decimal width is defined with the SET DECIMALS and SET FIXED commands.

```
? 123.456 * 22.8
    2814.7968
SET DECIMALS TO 2
SET FIXED ON
? 123.456 * 22.8
    2814.80
```

SEE ALSO

SET FIXED
ROUND( )

The SET DEFAULT Command
Specifying the Default Disk Drive

SET DEFAULT selects a disk drive for storing and accessing files.

SYNTAX

SET DEFAULT TO *drive*

where *disk drive* is a letter representing the disk drive. The default setting is the currently logged drive. The colon that usually follows a disk drive name (for example, A:) can be omitted in the SET DEFAULT command.

VERSION

dBASE III PLUS, dBASE III

USAGE

Use the SET DEFAULT command to change the drive used for reading and writing database, index, memory, procedure, format, and alternate files.

To access the SET DEFAULT command from the Assistant menu, highlight Tools on the top menu and select Set Drive from the pull-down menu.

EXAMPLES

The following command searches the disk in drive B for a database file named MyFile.

SET DEFAULT TO B
USE MyFile

SEE ALSO

SET PATH

The SET DELETED Command
Hiding or Displaying Deleted Records

SET DELETED determines whether records marked for deletion are hidden.

SYNTAX

SET DELETED [OFF][ON]

where the default setting is OFF.

VERSION

dBASE III PLUS, dBASE III

USAGE

Use the SET DELETED command as a filter on the database to mask records marked for deletion. Once the SET DELETED ON command is issued, such records are invisible to all dBASE commands until a SET DELETED OFF command is issued.

EXAMPLES

The following commands exclude records marked for deletion from the SUM and AVERAGE calculations.

SET DELETED ON
SUM Qty * Unit_Price TO TotSale
AVERAGE Qty * Unit_Price TO AvgSale

SEE ALSO

SET FILTER

The SET DELIMITERS Command
Hiding or Displaying Prompt Delimiters

SET DELIMITERS determines whether delimiters are displayed around data-entry and editing fields.

SYNTAX

SET DELIMITERS *[OFF]/[ON]*

where the default setting is OFF.

VERSION

dBASE III PLUS, dBASE III

USAGE

The SET DELIMITERS ON command places delimiters around the highlighted entry field displayed by a GET command, as well as around the highlighted fields on the default screens for APPEND, EDIT, and INSERT.

The following commands enclose all data-entry fields in curly braces when an APPEND, EDIT, READ, or INSERT command is issued.

SET DELIMITERS TO "{ }"
SET DELIMITERS ON

SET DELIMITERS TO

The SET DELIMITERS TO Command
Selecting Prompt Delimiters

SET DELIMITERS TO defines the characters that delimit the data-entry and editing fields.

SET DELIMITERS TO *[characters]* **[DEFAULT]**

where *characters* are the delimiters to display enclosed in quotation marks, and DEFAULT represents the default colon (:) characters.

dBASE III PLUS, dBASE III

USAGE

Either one or two characters can be specified in the SET DELIM-ITERS command. If only one character is specified, that character is used on both sides of the field display. If two characters are entered, the first represents the delimiter on the left side, and the second represents the delimiter on the right side.

EXAMPLES

The following commands display square brackets around data-entry fields when an APPEND, EDIT, READ, or INSERT command is issued.

    SET DELIMITERS TO "[ ]"
    SET DELIMITERS ON

SEE ALSO

    SET DELIMITERS
    SET INTENSITY
    @...SAY...GET

The SET DEVICE Command

Channeling @...SAY Displays to the Screen or Printer

SET DEVICE determines whether the @...SAY command will be displayed on the screen or the printer.

SYNTAX

SET DEVICE TO *[PRINT]/[SCREEN]*

where the default setting is SCREEN.

VERSION

dBASE III PLUS, dBASE III

USAGE

The SET DEVICE TO SCREEN command channels all output from @...SAY commands to the screen. SET DEVICE TO PRINT channels all @...SAY command displays to the printer.

EXAMPLES

The following commands display the message *Hi there...* on the screen and *I'm over here now...* on the printer.

```
@ 10,10 SAY "Hi there..."
SET DEVICE TO PRINT
@ 10,10 SAY "I'm over here, now..."
EJECT
SET DEVICE TO SCREEN
```

SEE ALSO

SET PRINT ON
@...SAY

The SET DOHISTORY Command

Recording Command File Execution in a History File

SET DOHISTORY determines whether commands from command files are recorded as they are executed. See Chapter 15, "Debugging Commands," for further information.

The SET ECHO Command

Displaying Command File Execution on the Screen

SET ECHO displays command lines from dBASE III PLUS programs on the screen or printer while the programs are being run. See Chapter 15, "Debugging Commands," for further information.

The SET ESCAPE Command

Activating or Deactivating the Escape Key

SET ESCAPE determines whether the Esc key interrupts processing.

SYNTAX

SET ESCAPE *[OFF]*/*[ON]*

where the default setting is ON.

VERSION

dBASE III PLUS, dBASE III

USAGE

If the Esc key is pressed while a program is running and SET ESCAPE ON is in effect, the program stops, and the following message is displayed.

Called from - <file name.prg>
Cancel, Ignore, Suspend? (C,I, or S)

If you choose Cancel, the program terminates and returns you to the dot prompt. If you select Ignore, the program resumes immediately. If you select Suspend, you can view memory variables or change the pointers in the database file from the dot prompt and then resume processing by typing **RESUME**.

If you press Esc while executing a command from the dot prompt and SET ESCAPE ON is in effect, the message ★★★ *INTER-RUPTED* ★★★ is displayed, and the dot prompt appears.

If the SET ESCAPE OFF command is in effect, pressing Esc does nothing.

EXAMPLES

The command

SET ESCAPE OFF

near the top of an application program prevents the user from interrupting processing by pressing the Esc key.

SEE ALSO

ON ESCAPE

The SET EXACT Command

Specifying the Character String Matching Technique

SET EXACT determines how a comparison between two character expressions is evaluated.

SYNTAX

SET EXACT *[OFF]/[ON]*

where the default setting is OFF.

VERSION

dBASE III PLUS, dBASE III

USAGE

The SET EXACT OFF command matches two character strings if the shorter string matches the characters on the left side of the longer string during all queries, including FOR, WHILE, FIND, SEEK, LOCATE, and SET FILTER queries.

The following commands list all individuals whose last names begin with the letters Black (for example, Black, Blackwell, Blacksmith).

SET EXACT OFF
LIST FOR LName = "Black"

The following commands display only the individuals with the last name Black.

SET EXACT ON
LIST FOR LName = "Black"

TRIM( )
LTRIM( )
RTRIM( )

The SET FIELDS Command

Activating or Deactivating the SET FIELDS TO Command

SET FIELDS allows you to use or ignore the list of fields defined with the SET FIELDS TO command.

SET FIELDS *[OFF]/[ON]*

where the default setting is OFF.

VERSION ═══════════════

dBASE III PLUS, dBASE III

USAGE ═══════════════

If SET FIELDS is off, all fields of the active database are available for display, entry, and editing.

If SET FIELDS is on, the fields available for display or entry are limited to those listed with the SET FIELDS TO command. If multiple related database files are in use, fields from related files are available for display and editing, but not for entering new data.

EXAMPLES ═══════════════

The following commands hide all fields from the currently open database except the CustNo, Qty, Unit_Price, and Date fields.

    SET FIELDS TO CustNo, Qty, Unit_Price, Date
    SET FIELDS ON

SEE ALSO ═══════════════

    SET FIELDS TO
    SET VIEW

The SET FIELDS TO Command
Specifying Fields to Hide or Display

SET FIELDS TO defines a list of fields to be displayed.

SET FIELDS TO *[field list/***ALL***]*

where *field list* is a list of names, separated by commas, of fields to include in displays. The optional ALL parameter permits access to all fields.

dBASE III PLUS, dBASE III

SET FIELDS TO defines only fields to be displayed. The field definition is not activated until a SET FIELDS ON command is issued. Additional SET FIELDS TO commands add new field names to the existing field name list. The SET FIELDS TO ALL command makes all fields accessible.

To include fields from a separate, related database file, select that work area with the SELECT command or use the file's alias with the field names. When the SET FIELDS TO command includes fields from multiple files, all fields are available as though they were from a single file. However, records can be appended to and inserted into only the currently selected database file.

When you use LIST or DISPLAY STRUCTURE with a SET FIELDS ON command in effect, those fields on the field list will display a greater-than ($>$) symbol to the left of the field name.

In the following commands, the SET FIELDS command specifies the PartNo and Qty fields from the Sales database and the PartName, Unit_Price, and Taxable fields from the Master database. The commands beneath the SET FIELDS ON command display data and perform calculations using the five defined fields.

```
*--- Open two database files.
SELECT A
```

```
USE Sales
SELECT B
USE Master INDEX Master
* – - Define relationship between files.
SELECT A
SET RELATION TO PartNo INTO Master
* – - Define available fields, and activate.
SET FIELDS TO PartNo,B->PartName,Qty, ;
                B->Unit_Price, B->Taxable
SET FIELDS ON

* – - Display the five fields.
LIST
* – - Calculate total sale.
SUM (Qty * Unit_Price) * IIF(Taxable,1.06,1) TO Total
```

SEE ALSO

@...SAY...GET   SELECT
MODIFY VIEW   SET RELATION
SET VIEW

The SET FILTER Command

Specifying Records to Hide

SET FILTER hides records in a database file that do not match a specified condition.

SYNTAX

SET FILTER TO *[condition]*[**FILE** *file name]*

where *condition* is any valid dBASE search criterion, and *file name* is the name of a query (.qry) file created by **MODIFY QUERY.**

| VERSION |

dBASE III PLUS, dBASE III

| USAGE |

If a condition is given, the SET FILTER command will mask the database so that only those records that meet the condition will be shown. SET FILTER applies only to the database file open in the work area where the command is issued. If several database files are open simultaneously, a separate filter can be set for each work area. Optionally, the SET FILTER command can include fields from related databases.

SET FILTER TO FILE *file name* reads the filter condition from a query (.qry) file established by the CREATE/MODIFY QUERY command. The *file name* must be the name of a query (.qry) file that contains expressions that are valid for the currently open database file (or files).

The SET FILTER TO FILE command can be built from the Assistant menu by highlighting Set Up and selecting Query.

Specifying SET FILTER TO without a condition turns off the filter on the active database and allows all records to be accessed.

| EXAMPLES |

The following example masks the LIST display to show only those records that fit the prescribed condition. In this case, monthly sales commissions must exceed $10,000 to be displayed.

```
USE Salesmen INDEX Sales_name
SET FILTER TO "Mth_Comm > = 10000"
GO TOP
LIST
```

| TIPS |

Because filters are not activated until the record pointer is moved, the command GO TOP should be used immediately after a SET

FILTER command to reposition the record pointer at the top of the newly filtered database.

SEE ALSO

CREATE/MODIFY QUERY

The SET FIXED Command

*Activating or Deactivating the
SET DECIMALS Command*

SET FIXED determines whether numbers are displayed with the fixed number of decimal places set by the SET DECIMALS command.

SYNTAX

SET FIXED *[OFF]/[ON]*

where OFF is the default value.

VERSION

dBASE III PLUS, dBASE II

USAGE

IF SET FIXED is on, all numeric values are displayed with the number of decimal places specified in the most recent SET DECIMALS command.

The following commands demonstrate the results of calculations before and after the FIXED parameter is specified as ON.

```
? 123.456 * 456.321
   56335.565376

SET DECIMALS TO 2
SET FIXED ON

? 123.456 * 456.321
   56335.57
```

SET DECIMALS
ROUND( )

The SET FORMAT Command

Opening a Format File

SET FORMAT selects a custom format previously stored in a format (.fmt) file. See Chapter 4, "Commands for Custom Screens," for further information.

The SET FUNCTION Command

Programming the Function Keys

SET FUNCTION allows each function key to be reprogrammed to represent a character expression up to 30 characters long.

SET FUNCTION *key* **TO** *string[;]*

where *key* is the name of the function key to program, *string* is the string of up to 30 characters that the key is to type, and the optional semicolon represents a Return keypress.

dBASE III PLUS, dBASE III

The first expression, which identifies the function key, can be a numeric or character expression, depending on whether your terminal has numbered function keys. If you have numbered function keys, use the key number to enter the name of the programmable function key; otherwise, use a character expression.

The semicolon generates a carriage return when you press the function key. It must follow the command and be inside the quotation marks surrounding the string.

The inside front cover shows the default function key assignments used by dBASE. Any key except F1 can be changed with the SET FUNCTION command.

EXAMPLES

The following example allows you to run WordStar from the dot prompt so that you need not leave dBASE III PLUS to edit a command file with WordStar.

SET FUNCTION 10 TO "RUN WS;"

TIPS

Multiple commands can be chained together in the character expression as long as their total length does not exceed 30 characters. Be sure to separate the commands with semicolons.

SEE ALSO

FKLABEL( )
FKMAX( )

The SET HEADING Command
Displaying Field Names

SET HEADING determines whether column titles appear above each field for the DISPLAY, LIST, SUM, and AVERAGE commands.

SYNTAX

SET HEADING *[OFF]/[ON]*

where the default setting is ON.

VERSION ═══════════

dBASE III PLUS, dBASE III

USAGE ═══════════

Normally, the commands DISPLAY, LIST, SUM, and AVERAGE display a column title for each displayed field, memory variable, or expression. When SET HEADING is OFF, the column titles are not displayed.

EXAMPLES ═══════════

In the following example, the LIST command displays field names and expressions above each column, as shown.

SET HEADING ON
LIST PartNo,Qty,B– >Unit_Price,(Qty*B– >Unit_Price)

PartNo Qty B– >Unit_Price (Qty*B– >Unit_Price)
A-111   1   100.00   100.00
B-222   2   150.00   300.00

Specifying HEADING OFF displays only the actual data, as follows:

SET HEADING OFF
LIST PartNo,Qty,B– >Unit_Price,(Qty*B– >Unit_Price)
A-111   1 100.00   100.00
B-222   2 150.00   300.00

SEE ALSO ═══════════

LIST
DISPLAY

The SET HELP Command

Activating or Deactivating the
Immediate Help Prompt

SET HELP determines whether the query *Do you want some help?*
(Y/N) appears when a command is incorrectly entered at the dot
prompt.

SYNTAX

SET HELP /OFF]/[ON]

where the default setting is ON.

VERSION

dBASE III PLUS, dBASE III

USAGE

When you choose help in response to the error prompt, the HELP
screen for the command in the line being executed is displayed,
regardless of the actual cause of the error.

SEE ALSO

HELP

The SET HISTORY Command

Activating or Deactivating the History File

SET HISTORY turns the HISTORY feature on and off.

SYNTAX

SET HISTORY [OFF]/[ON]

where the default setting is ON.

VERSION

dBASE III PLUS only

USAGE

The HISTORY feature allows commands that have been entered at the dot prompt to be recalled, edited, and reexecuted. To recall a command, press the ↑ key repeatedly at the dot prompt until the command you want is displayed. You can use the arrow, Ins, and Del keys to edit the command; press Return to reexecute the command.

EXAMPLES

The HISTORY feature is useful when you want to create a new index file that resembles the one just created. For example, you might have just created an index file as follows:

USE My_file
INDEX ON Zip + UPPER(LName + FName) TO Index1

To enter a similar command without retyping, press ↑ until the INDEX command line reappears. Then, using the arrow keys and the Del and Ins keys, change the command as in the following line to create the second index file.

INDEX ON STR(Age,2) UPPER(LName + FName) TO Index2

SEE ALSO

DISPLAY HISTORY   SET DOHISTORY
LIST HISTORY   SET HISTORY TO

The SET HISTORY TO Command

Specifying the Size of the History File

SET HISTORY specifies the number of command lines to be stored in the history file.

SYNTAX

SET HISTORY TO *number*

where *number* is the number of lines to include in the history file.

VERSION

dBASE III PLUS only

USAGE

The default value for SET HISTORY TO is 20. The allowable range of commands stored is from 0 to 16,000.

If HISTORY is set to a number that is less than the number of commands currently stored in HISTORY, all stored commands are erased. Otherwise, they are saved, and new commands are appended to the list.

TIPS

To calculate the amount of memory HISTORY consumes, add nine bytes to the number of bytes in each command.

SEE ALSO

SET HISTORY
DISPLAY HISTORY
LIST HISTORY
SET DOHISTORY

The SET INDEX Command

Activating or Deactivating Index Files

SET INDEX activates index files for the currently open database file.

SYNTAX

SET INDEX TO *[file names]*

where *file names* are all the index files to activate.

VERSION

dBASE III PLUS, dBASE III

USAGE

A maximum of seven index files can be opened at once for a given database.

The first-listed index file is the master index, which determines the sort order of the records in the database. The master index is the only index file that can be searched with a SEEK or FIND command. All listed index files are updated automatically when data are changed in the database file.

Specifying SET INDEX TO by itself closes all index files for the given database. It has the same effect as the CLOSE INDEX command.

EXAMPLES

The following command line causes both the NameOrd and ZipOrd index files to be updated automatically whenever information is added to, changed in, or deleted from the Mail database. The NameOrd index determines the sort order and is the only index file that can be searched with SEEK or FIND.

USE Mail INDEX NameOrd,ZipOrd

SEE ALSO

CLOSE
INDEX
REINDEX
SET ORDER
USE

The SET INTENSITY Command

Activating or Deactivating Reverse Video

SET INTENSITY determines whether the fields in a database are highlighted in reverse video for full-screen commands such as EDIT and APPEND.

SYNTAX

SET INTENSITY *[OFF][ON]*

where the default setting is ON (indicating that reverse video is normally in effect).

VERSION

dBASE III PLUS, dBASE III

USAGE

Normally, there are two types of screen attributes: standard and enhanced. When INTENSITY is set to ON, the enhanced attributes are displayed in reverse video for full-screen operations. When INTENSITY is set to OFF, the standard attribute is used for both standard and enhanced areas.

EXAMPLES

The following commands allow the user to enter records through a custom screen named CustScre. Entry fields are not displayed in reverse video, but instead are displayed with bracket delimiters.

```
USE AnyFile INDEX AnyIndex
SET FORMAT TO CustScre
```

SET DELIMITERS TO "[ ]"
SET DELIMITERS ON
SET INTENSITY OFF

APPEND

SEE ALSO

SET COLOR

The SET MARGIN Command
Setting the Left Margin Width

SET MARGIN adjusts the left margin for all printed output.

SYNTAX

SET MARGIN TO *number*

where *number* is the number of characters to leave blank in the left margin.

VERSION

dBASE III PLUS, dBASE III

USAGE

The default value for the printer margin is 0. The SET MARGIN command lets you reset this margin to any number of spaces. SET MARGIN has no effect on video display.

The following commands print all records in the Mail database, using a left margin of 10 characters.

USE Mail
SET MARGIN TO 10
LIST TO PRINT

When you print reports with the REPORT FORM *AnyFile* TO PRINT command, the left margin setting specified in MODIFY REPORT is added to the SET MARGIN setting.

MODIFY REPORT
SET PRINT

The SET MEMOWIDTH Command

Setting Memo Field Widths

SET MEMOWIDTH determines the column width of memo field output.

SET MEMOWIDTH TO *number*

where *number* is the width of the memo field display.

dBASE III PLUS only

The default width for memo field displays is 50 characters. The SET MEMOWIDTH command can be used to alter this width. Memo fields will be word-wrapped within the specified width. SET MEMOWIDTH affects only LIST, DISPLAY, and ? commands.

The following command displays fields from the Mail database, including the memo field named Notes. All entries in the memo field will be word-wrapped in a column 35 characters wide.

```
SET MEMOWIDTH TO 35
LIST LName, FName, Notes
```

MODIFY REPORT
LIST
DISPLAY

The SET MENU Command
Activating or Deactivating Menus

SET MENU determines whether a cursor-control-key menu appears with full-screen commands.

SYNTAX

SET MENU [OFF]/[ON]

where the default setting is ON.

VERSION

dBASE III PLUS, dBASE III

USAGE

With SET MENU in its default mode, full-screen commands such as APPEND and EDIT automatically display a menu of cursor-control keys at the top of the screen. With SET MENU OFF, this menu is not automatically displayed. Regardless of the SET MENU command, the F1 key turns the menu display off and on during a full-screen operation.

EXAMPLES

The following command suppresses the initial display of cursor-control-key menus in full-screen displays.

SET MENU OFF

SEE ALSO

SET HELP

The SET MESSAGE Command
Displaying a Status Bar Message

SET MESSAGE displays a message centered at the bottom of the screen.

SYNTAX

SET MESSAGE TO *[string]*

where *string* is the message to display.

VERSION

dBASE III PLUS only

USAGE

The message line will be displayed only if the SET STATUS parameter is set to ON. Messages cannot exceed one line, which is a maximum of 79 characters. The message must be enclosed in single or double quotation marks or brackets, unless it is stored in a memory variable.

The command SET MESSAGE TO with no message erases the message currently at the bottom of the screen.

EXAMPLES

The following commands display the message *Try again!* at the bottom of the screen.

SET STATUS ON
SET MESSAGE TO "Try again!"

SEE ALSO

SET STATUS
SET SCOREBOARD

The SET ODOMETER Command
Specifying the Odometer Update Frequency

SET ODOMETER determines how often the odometer is updated during commands that display their progress.

SYNTAX

SET ODOMETER TO *number*

where *number* is the increment that the odometer displays. The default value is 1.

VERSION

dBASE III PLUS version 1.1 only

USAGE

If the SET TALK parameter is on, commands such as COPY, PACK, and APPEND FROM display their progress on an "odometer" on the screen as they work. Usually, this odometer counts individual records as the command processes them. You can have the odometer display progress in other increments, such as groups of 10 or 100 records, by assigning the appropriate value with the SET ODOMETER command.

The following routine copies a large file named Biggie to a file named BigCopy. Because the process takes some time, the routine shows the user how many records need to be copied. Because SET TALK is on, COPY will automatically display an odometer of its progress as it copies the records. In this example, the odometer displays the progress in groups of 10 records.

```
USE Biggie
? "Copying " + LTRIM(STR(RECCOUNT())) + " records..."
SET TALK ON
SET ODOMETER TO 10
COPY TO BigCopy
```

SET TALK

The SET ORDER Command
Selecting an Index File

SET ORDER selects any open index file as the master index or removes control from all open index files.

SET ORDER TO *[number]*

where *number* is the number of the index file to be made into the master. The default number is 1.

VERSION

dBASE III PLUS only

USAGE

The master index controls the order in which records are displayed in the database and also determines the fields that SEEK and FIND can search. The SET ORDER command lets you change the controlling index to another index file in use so that a new order can be used to move within the database file.

Before using the SET ORDER command, you must have already opened a database file and its associated index files with a statement like the following:

USE My_file INDEX Ndx1,Ndx2,Ndx3...Ndx7

The order of the index files in this statement establishes the original order of what is formally called the *index list*. To select the third index file (Ndx3 in the example) as the new controlling index, you would type **SET ORDER TO 3**.

The dBASE III PLUS program limits the number of open index files to seven, so the numeric expression used in the SET ORDER command must be 7 or less.

If you type **SET ORDER TO 0**, none of the index files will be in control, and the record pointer can be moved through the database in physical (or nonindexed) order. Also, the order of the index list is not changed when you type **SET ORDER TO 0**, so the index files can be reactivated afterward with another SET ORDER TO 1 command.

EXAMPLES

The Mail database shown here is opened with NameOrd as the master index file.

USE Mail INDEX NameOrd,ZipOrd

To display records in zip code order or to seek a particular zip code, make ZipOrd the master index file using the command

SET ORDER TO 2

TIPS

After adding new records or packing the database file with the command SET ORDER TO 0, you should type **SET ORDER TO 1** and **REINDEX** to ensure that all index files are properly updated.

SET ORDER is slightly faster than SET INDEX, because it does not have to search the disk for the index files to open.

SEE ALSO

INDEX
SET INDEX
NDX( )

The SET PATH Command

Specifying a Path for File Searches

SET PATH defines the directory path that dBASE will follow to locate a file not found in the current directory.

SYNTAX

SET PATH TO *[path list]*

where *path list* is a list of path names separated by commas or semicolons.

VERSION

dBASE III PLUS, dBASE III

USAGE

A path directory is a list of directories separated by backslashes and listed in order from the top-level directory to subdirectory levels. A path list is a series of path directories separated by commas or semicolons.

If dBASE cannot find a file in the current directory, paths listed in the SET PATH command are searched one by one until the file is located.

EXAMPLES

In the following commands, dBASE attempts to locate the file named Program.prg in the current directory. If dBASE cannot find the file, it searches the \LETTERS\PERSONAL directory, then the \ROUTINES directory, and finally the EFFECTS directory.

SET PATH TO
\LETTERS\PERSONAL;\ROUTINES;\EFFECTS
DO Program

SEE ALSO

SET DEFAULT
DIR

The SET PRINT Command
Channeling Output to the Printer

SET PRINT directs all output, except @...SAY command displays, to the printer.

SYNTAX

SET PRINT /OFF/[ON]

where the default setting is OFF.

VERSION

dBASE III PLUS, dBASE III

USAGE

SET PRINT ON channels all output to the printer, except output displayed with @...SAY commands. To channel @...SAY displays to the printer, use the SET DEVICE TO PRINT command.

EXAMPLES

The following ? commands display their results on the printer.

SET PRINT ON
? 27 ^ (1/3)

? SQRT(88)

SET PRINT OFF

TIPS

Not all printers respond immediately to the screen output. Some printers respond to output only after a second line is printed. To ensure that all output is printed, issue an EJECT command after printing and setting PRINT to OFF to empty the print buffer and eject the page from the printer.

SEE ALSO

SET DEVICE
EJECT

The SET PRINTER Command

Selecting a Printer Port

SET PRINTER selects a DOS device for printer output.

SYNTAX

SET PRINTER TO *device*

where *device* is a valid DOS device name.

VERSION

dBASE III PLUS only

USAGE

The default printer device is the first parallel port, LPT1. Use SET PRINTER to redirect output to other output devices if available, including both serial and parallel printers. For parallel printers, use SET PRINTER TO LPT1 (or LPT2 or LPT3). For serial printing devices, use SET PRINTER TO COM1 (or COM2).

EXAMPLES

The following example shows how you might switch to an alternate serial printer to print a report.

```
SET PATH TO \DOS              && \DOS contains
                                 mode.com
RUN MODE COM1:9600,N,8,1,P    && Set the serial port
SET PRINTER TO COM1           && Select printer port
USE AnyFile
REPORT FORM AnyRep TO PRINT
```

TIPS

SET PRINTER behaves a little differently in network environments. See Chapter 19, "Commands for Networking," for further information.

SEE ALSO

SET PRINT   RUN
SET DEVICE

The SET PROCEDURE Command
Opening a Procedure File

SET PROCEDURE opens a designated procedure file. See Chapter 13, "Commands for Procedures and Parameters," for further information.

The SET RELATION Command
Defining a Relationship Between Files

SET RELATION links two open database files according to a key expression shared by both files. See Chapter 11, "Commands for Managing Multiple Database Files," for further information.

The SET SAFETY Command

*Activating or Deactivating the
File Overwrite Safety Feature*

SET SAFETY provides some protection against the overwriting or destruction of files.

SYNTAX

SET SAFETY [OFF][ON]

where the default setting is ON.

VERSION

dBASE III PLUS, dBASE III

USAGE

When SET SAFETY is on, warning messages such as the following occur before an existing file is overwritten or deleted:

file name **already exists, overwrite it? (Y/N)**

When SET SAFETY is off, files are deleted or overwritten without any warning.

EXAMPLES

In the following example, records from the Charges database are copied to a file named Temp. Even if the Temp file already exists, dBASE won't ask for permission before overwriting the file because the SAFETY parameter is set to OFF.

SET SAFETY OFF
USE Charges
COPY TO Temp FOR .NOT. Posted

SEE ALSO

COPY
ZAP

The SET SCOREBOARD Command
Activating or Deactivating Row 0 Messages

SET SCOREBOARD determines whether dBASE III PLUS key messages are displayed at the top of the screen.

SYNTAX

SET SCOREBOARD [OFF][ON]

where the default setting is ON.

VERSION

dBASE III PLUS, dBASE III

USAGE

When SCOREBOARD is on and STATUS is off, scoreboard messages appear in row 0 on the screen. Scoreboard messages include Del (indicating that a record is marked for deletion), Ins (indicating that insert mode is on), the state of the NumLock key, and errors caused by entries that fall outside an acceptable RANGE specification.

When STATUS is on, scoreboard messages appear in the status bar and error line (row 22), regardless of the SET SCOREBOARD status.

EXAMPLES

The following commands prevent scoreboard messages from being displayed the screen.

SET SCOREBOARD OFF
SET STATUS OFF

SEE ALSO

SET STATUS

The SET STATUS Command
Hiding or Displaying the Status Bar

SET STATUS determines whether the status bar is displayed at the bottom of the screen.

SYNTAX

SET STATUS *[OFF]/[ON]*

where the default setting is ON.

VERSION

dBASE III PLUS only

USAGE

When SET STATUS is on, the status bar is displayed in row 22 on the screen. The status bar displays information about the current working environment: the current command, current database in use, current record number, insert/overwrite mode status, and NumLock status. Scoreboard information is also shown in the status bar.

EXAMPLES

The following commands remove the status bar before displaying a bar graph with a procedure named BarGraph.

```
SET STATUS OFF
DO BarGraph WITH 0,100,9,"Sample Graph"
```

SEE ALSO

SET MESSAGE
SET SCOREBOARD

The SET STEP Command
Single-Stepping Through a Command File

SET STEP stops program execution after each line of instruction. See Chapter 15, "Debugging Commands," for further information.

The SET TALK Command
Hiding or Displaying Progress Messages

SET TALK determines whether certain commands display informative messages.

SYNTAX

SET TALK [OFF]/[ON]

where the default setting is ON.

VERSION

dBASE III PLUS, dBASE III

USAGE

SET TALK displays the progress of commands that do not otherwise display any data on the screen, such as the APPEND FROM, COPY, PACK, STORE, AVERAGE, and SUM commands.

EXAMPLES

The following commands pack the Charges database and show the progress along the way. When packing is complete, the TALK parameter is set to OFF.

SET TALK ON
PACK
SET TALK OFF

TIPS

Specifying SET TALK ON while running programs can be useful for debugging purposes, because this command shows some of the activity that occurs as the program runs.

SEE ALSO

SET ECHO
SET DEBUG
SET STEP

The SET TITLE Command

Activating or Deactivating
Catalog File Titles

SET TITLE determines whether catalog file titles are displayed.

SYNTAX

SET TITLE [ON]/[OFF]

where the default setting is ON.

VERSION

dBASE III PLUS only

USAGE

When adding a new file to a catalog, you are normally prompted for a catalog file title. When SET TITLE is off, this prompt is not shown.

EXAMPLES

The following commands open and activate a catalog file named ThisApp but prevent the catalog title prompts from being displayed.

```
SET CATALOG TO ThisApp
SET CATALOG ON
SET TITLE OFF
```

SEE ALSO

SET CATALOG
SET CATALOG TO

The SET TYPEAHEAD Command
Determining the Size of Typeahead Buffer

SET TYPEAHEAD establishes the number of characters that the typeahead buffer holds.

SYNTAX ════════════════════════════════

SET TYPEAHEAD TO *number*

where *number* is the number of keystrokes that the typeahead buffer will store. The default value is 20 keystrokes.

VERSION ════════════════════════════════

dBASE III PLUS only

USAGE ════════════════════════════════

A typeahead buffer stores keystrokes that are typed too fast to be processed instantaneously and then feeds these keystrokes to dBASE when the program is ready to accept them. The SET TYPEAHEAD command determines the number of keystrokes that this typeahead buffer holds. The acceptable range is 0 to 32,000 characters. SET TYPEAHEAD works only when ESCAPE is set to ON.

To disallow typeahead keystrokes, enter **SET TYPEAHEAD TO 0**. Any keystrokes typed faster than dBASE can process them will cause the bell to ring (assuming SET BELL is on). Extra keystrokes will be lost. Note that setting the typeahead buffer to 0 disables the ON KEY command and the INKEY() function.

TIPS ════════════════════════════════

In procedures called by an ON ERROR condition, you can enter **SET TYPEAHEAD TO 0** immediately to prevent further keystrokes from complicating the error condition. Before returning control to the calling program, issue a SET TYPEAHEAD command again to return to the default value of 20 or to set any other value.

SEE ALSO ════════════════════════════════

INKEY( )   SET ESCAPE
ON   CLEAR TYPEAHEAD
SET BELL

The SET UNIQUE Command
Hiding or Displaying Duplicate Records

SET UNIQUE determines whether all records or only records with unique key values are included in an index file.

SYNTAX

SET UNIQUE *[OFF]/[ON]*

where the default setting is OFF.

VERSION

dBASE III PLUS, dBASE III

USAGE

An index file created with SET UNIQUE ON will contain only unique values within the database. When the field being indexed contains duplicate values, only the first of the duplicate records will be included in the new index file.

Once the index file is created with SET UNIQUE ON, the file will keep its UNIQUE status (even after reindexing). To create a normal index file of the same name, issue a SET UNIQUE OFF command before reindexing.

If you add new records to a database file indexed using the UNIQUE status, the records will be stored in the database file as usual, but they will remain hidden from displays if they match the key indexing expression of an existing record.

EXAMPLES

To view a list of all unique zip codes in the Mail database, set UNIQUE to ON and index on the zip code field. Then list the field of interest, as follows:

```
USE Mail
SET UNIQUE ON
INDEX ON Zip TO UniqZips

* – – – View unique zip codes.
LIST Zip
```

SEE ALSO

INDEX
SET INDEX
REINDEX
USE

The SET VIEW Command

Opening a View File

SET VIEW opens a view (.vue) file created with the CREATE/MODIFY VIEW command.

SYNTAX

SET VIEW TO *file name*

where *file name* is the name of the view file, with the extension .vue.

VERSION

dBASE III PLUS only

USAGE

SET VIEW opens a view file, which in turn opens multiple database files and defines relationships between the files. The view file is created with the CREATE VIEW or MODIFY VIEW command. A single view file can replace a series of SELECT, USE, SET RELATION, SET FIELDS, SET FORMAT, and SET FILTER commands.

To access the SET VIEW command from the Assistant menu, highlight the Set Up option on the top menu and select View from the pull-down menu.

To close an existing view file, enter the command **CLOSE DATA-BASES**.

EXAMPLES

The following command opens a view file named BigPict.vue.

SET VIEW TO BigPict

SEE ALSO

MODIFY VIEW   SET FORMAT
SET FIELDS   SET RELATION
SET FILTER

18

Event Processing and Error Trapping

This chapter discusses the commands for incorporating *event processing* and *error trapping* into your dBASE command files. *Event processing* allows an application program to respond to a keystroke, regardless of the task the program is performing at the time. *Error trapping* allows an application program to respond to an error condition without simply returning to the dot prompt. With these commands, you can refine your applications to provide users with elegant and informed ways of interrupting long processes and responding to errors.

The ON command is used for both event processing and error trapping. ON KEY and ON ESCAPE provide event processing capabilities, and ON ERROR provides error trapping capabilities. The RETRY command, discussed in this chapter as well, is also useful in error trapping and recovery. These commands are used only in command files and are therefore not accessible from the Assistant menu.

The ON Command

Responding to an Event During Program Execution

ON takes a specific action in response to an error or event, regardless of the task dBASE is performing at the moment.

SYNTAX

ON KEY *command*
ON ESCAPE *command*
ON ERROR *command*

where *command* is the action to take when the event occurs.

VERSION

dBASE III PLUS only

USAGE

The three ON options each respond to a unique situation, as follows:

ON KEY	Responds to any keypress
ON ESCAPE	Responds to the Esc key
ON ERROR	Responds to a dBASE error

The three versions of the ON command can be active simultaneously within a given program or application.

ON KEY

ON KEY checks for a keystroke after executing each command in a command file. If a key was pressed while the command was being executed, dBASE performs the action specified in the ON KEY command line.

The keypress that triggers the ON KEY command stays in the keyboard buffer until it is explicitly removed by another command or stored in a memory variable. To remove the triggering keypress from the keyboard buffer, store it in a memory variable using the INKEY( ) function. In the example in the "Example" section, the command Dummy = INKEY( ) clears the buffer so that the triggering keypress does not interfere with the GET and READ commands later in the procedure.

The command ON KEY, without any additional instruction on the command line, deactivates any previous ON KEY command.

If an ON ESCAPE command is active at the same time that an ON KEY command is active and the SET ESCAPE parameter is on, ON KEY responds to any key *except* the Esc key.

ON ESCAPE

The ON ESCAPE command responds only to the Esc key, and only if the SET ESCAPE parameter is on. Unlike the ON KEY command, ON ESCAPE is executed immediately, even in the middle of a long process such as that triggered by REPORT FORM or LIST. As noted, the ON ESCAPE command takes precedence over the ON KEY command when both are active.

The command ON ESCAPE, with no additional instruction on the command line, deactivates any previous ON ESCAPE command.

ON ERROR

The ON ERROR command responds to any dBASE error by performing the instructions that follow it. For example, the command

ON ERROR DO ErrCheck

passes control to a program or procedure named ErrCheck as soon as a dBASE error occurs. The ERROR( ) function receives a numeric value representing the error, and the MESSAGE( ) function receives a character string describing the error. (Appendix D lists the dBASE error messages by number.) ON ERROR responds only to dBASE errors, not to DOS errors such as invalid disk drive or printer requests.

The command ON ERROR, without any additional command on the line, deactivates any previous ON ERROR command.

EXAMPLES

OnProcs.prg is a sample procedure file designed to respond to ON conditions. The KeyPress procedure responds to an ON KEY command, EscPress responds to an ON ESCAPE command, and ErrTrap responds to an ON ERROR condition.

```
********************************* OnProcs.PRG
*- Procedure file to responds to ON commands.

*- Responds to ON KEY to abort printing.
PROCEDURE KeyPress
Dummy = INKEY() && Clear out keypress.
Abort = .T.
a 23,1 SAY "Abort printing? (Y/N)" ;
GET Abort PICTURE "Y"
READ
*- If aborting, set everything back to normal.
IF Abort
   SET PRINT OFF
   SET CONSOLE ON
   EJECT  && this is optional.
   ON KEY
   RETURN TO MASTER
ENDIF
RETURN


*-- Respond to Escape key.
PROCEDURE EscPress
a 23,1 SAY "Print job aborted..."
EJECT  && this is optional.
ON ESCAPE
RETURN TO MASTER
RETURN
```

```
*----- Sample procedure to trap common errors.
PROCEDURE ErrTrap
ə 19,0 CLEAR
ə 19,0 TO 19,79 DOUBLE
? CHR(7)
DO CASE

   CASE ERROR() = 4  && EOF() encountered.
        ? "End of file encountered unexpectedly."
        ? "Will try to repair.  Please wait."
        *-- If index file open, may be corrupted.
        IF NDX() # " "
           REINDEX
        ENDIF
        RETRY

   CASE ERROR() = 114  && Damaged index file.
        ? "Damaged index file!"
        ? Please wait while rebuilding..."
        REINDEX

   CASE ERROR() = 6  && Too many files open.
        ? "Check the Config.DB file on your root"
        ? "directory, as disccussed in the manual."
        CANCEL
        CLOSE ALL
        ON ERROR

   CASE ERROR() = 29  && File inaccessible.
        ? "Disk directory is full, or an illegal"
        ? "character appears in file name!"
        ? "Check filename and directory, then try again."

   OTHERWISE   && Other error: display dBASE message.
        ? "Unexpected error in program..."
        ? MESSAGE(),"["+LTRIM(STR(ERROR()))+"]"
        WAIT "Press Esc to abort, any key to continue..."

ENDCASE
RETURN
```

The following sample routine interrupts a DO WHILE loop and calls the KeyPress procedure when the user presses any key

```
*--- Sample routine allowing the user to
*--- press any key to stop the printer.
SET PROCEDURE TO OnProcs
USE Master

*---------------- Display instructions.
CLEAR
ə 2,1 SAY "Press any key to stop printing..."
*-------------- Set console off, printer on.
```

```
SET CONSOLE OFF
SET PRINT ON

*-------------- Set up response to keypress.
ON KEY DO KeyPress
*-------------- Print the report.
DO WHILE .NOT. EOF()
   ? PartNo,PartName,Qty
   SKIP
ENDDO

*---- Disable previous ON KEY.
ON KEY
*--- Set console and printer back to normal.
SET CONSOLE ON
EJECT
SET PRINT OFF
RETURN
```

The next routine interrupts a REPORT FORM command and calls the EscPress procedure when the user presses Escape.

```
*--- Sample routine allowing the user to
*--- press Escape to stop the printer.
SET PROCEDURE TO OnProcs
USE Master

*---------------- Display instructions.
CLEAR
a 2,1 SAY "Press Escape to stop printing..."

*-------------- Set the console off.
SET CONSOLE OFF

*-------------- Set up response to keypress.
ON ESCAPE DO EscPress

*-------------- Print the report.
REPORT FORM MastRep TO PRINT

*---- Restore console and disable ON ESCAPE.
SET CONSOLE ON
ON ESCAPE
RETURN
```

The ErrTrap procedure, shown in the OnProcs procedure file, may be called from any point in a command file (or application) after the commands

SET PROCEDURE TO OnProcs
ON ERROR DO ErrTrap

You need only issue these commands once within an entire application. From that point on, any error will access the ErrTrap procedure.

TIPS ======================

See the INKEY( ) function in Chapter 16, "dBASE Functions," for another technique that can be used to interrupt processing.

When using ON ERROR to trap errors and a DO CASE clause to respond to errors, always include an OTHERWISE clause to display the number and message of any errors that do not match any of the errors included in the CASE statements. Otherwise, tracking and correcting program bugs that are not detected by the DO CASE clause will be very difficult. The ErrTrap procedure shows an OTHERWISE clause that uses the expression

? MESSAGE( ),"[" + LTRIM(STR(ERROR( ))) + "]"

to print the error message and number in the following format should an undetected error occur.

End-of-file encountered [4]

SEE ALSO ======================

INKEY( )
ERROR( )
MESSAGE( )

The RETRY Command
Retrying a Command That Caused an Error

RETRY returns control to the calling program and reexecutes the line that was active when the call took place.

SYNTAX

RETRY

VERSION

dBASE III PLUS only

USAGE

Unlike the RETURN command, which passes control to the *next* line in a calling program, RETRY returns control to the line that initiated the error and reexecutes that line. RETRY is generally used in conjunction with the ON ERROR command to attempt to reexecute the command that caused the error.

RETRY can be used in command files and procedure files. When used in a command file, it closes the called program when it returns control to the calling program. RETRY also resets the ERROR( ) value to 0.

EXAMPLES

The following commands call a procedure named FileErr if an error occurs while the user is trying to rename a file.

```
* – Allow user to rename file,
* – but watch for file name error.
ACCEPT "Enter new name for file " TO NewName
IF .NOT. "." $ NewName
    NewName = NewName + ".dbf"
ENDIF
ON ERROR DO FileErr
RENAME ThisFile.DBF TO &NewName
ON ERROR          &&Deactivate previous ON ERROR.
```

If the name stored in the NewName variable already exists, the ON KEY command passes control to the FileErr procedure with an ERROR( ) value of 7. The FileErr procedure responds by asking the

user to enter a new name for the file and attempting to process the
RENAME command again. The FileErr procedure is as follows:

```
* - - FileErr procedure: Respond to illegal file name.
IF ERROR( ) = 7
    ? "File name already exists!"
    ? "Reenter file name and try again."
    ACCEPT TO NewName
    RETRY
ENDIF
RETURN
```

TIPS

Use RETRY to respond to recoverable errors only after allowing the
user to take some action to correct the error. For unrecoverable errors
such as that indicated by the message *Too many files open*, use
RETURN to pass control to the command beneath the line that caused
the error, or use CANCEL to terminate processing altogether.

SEE ALSO

ERROR( )
RETURN

19

Commands for Networking

This chapter discusses commands and functions that are used only in network environments. It also discusses commands that behave differently in a network environment as opposed to a single-user environment. A network environment allows several users, at different terminals, to share hardware resources, such as printers and hard disks, as well as programs and data.

A complete understanding of network setup and programming techniques requires an in-depth understanding of your networking system, as well as security schemes that you can set up with the PROTECT.EXE program that comes with the dBASE III PLUS package. Both topics are beyond the scope of this book.

All aspects of networking are handled by the dBASE ADMINIS-TRATOR, which is actually the multiuser version of dBASE that comes with your dBASE package. For proper installation of the dBASE ADMINISTRATOR or your particular network, refer to your dBASE III PLUS manual.

Commands That Behave Differently in a Network

This section summarizes commands used in single-user environments that behave differently in network environments. For detailed information about the commands, see the appropriate reference in the single-user chapters.

CHANGE and EDIT in a Network

The CHANGE and EDIT commands use the same syntax in a network environment that they do in a single-user environment. There are only two differences in their behavior. In a network environment, the status bar displays the following file or record information, as is appropriate to the file or record being edited.

Exclusive
File locked
Read only
Record locked
Record unlocked

If the file currently being edited is in shared mode, the record must be locked before it can be edited.

The second unique feature of the CHANGE and EDIT commands in a network environment is that the user can type **Ctrl-O** to lock and unlock the record currently on the screen.

DISPLAY and LIST STATUS in a Network

When used in a network environment, the DISPLAY STATUS and LIST STATUS commands display the lock status of the currently open database file. In addition, the status of the SET ENCRYPTION and SET EXCLUSIVE parameters is displayed.

SET in a Network

The SET command, with no additional parameters, displays a full-screen menu-driven technique for viewing and altering SET parameters, just as it does in single-user mode. However, the screen also includes the current settings for the SET ENCRYPTION and SET EXCLUSIVE commands.

USE in a Network

In a network, you can use the EXCLUSIVE command at the end of a USE command to open a file for exclusive use. This is similar to a SET EXCLUSIVE ON command, but it specifies only the file currently being opened for exclusive use. For example, the following command opens the database file named Charges and the ChrgNo index file for exclusive use.

USE Charges INDEX ChrgNo EXCLUSIVE

SET PRINTER in a Network

SET PRINTER directs printer output to a specific device in the network. On an IBM PC network, the general syntax is

SET PRINTER TO *station name**printer name* = *destination*

On a Novell/86 network, the general syntax is

SET PRINTER TO **SPOOLER**

To send printed output to a local printer, use the syntax

SET PRINTER TO *destination*

To empty the network print spooler and reset the default printer destination, use the syntax

SET PRINTER TO *printer or device name*

In the preceding commands, *station name* is a network-assigned workstation name, *printer name* identifies an IBM network printer, \\SPOOLER identifies a Novell network printer, *printer name* is a network-assigned printer name, and *destination* specifies the installed printer name (such as LPT1, LPT2, or LPT3).

For example, the following command directs printed output to the network printer attached to the LPT2 port of the workstation assigned the name Station1.

SET PRINTER TO **Station1****PRINTER** = **LPT2**

The following commands set up a serial laser printer in the COM1 port of the current workstation and send output to that port.

RUN MODE COM1: 9600,N,8,1,P
SET PRINTER TO COM1

For additional information about naming printers on your own network system, see your network manual. For additional information about the MODE command for defining parameters for devices, consult your DOS manual.

The ACCESS( ) Function
Determining the User's Access Level

ACCESS( ) returns the access level (1-8) of the user, based on the user profile defined in the dBASE PROTECT program.

SYNTAX

ACCESS( )

VERSION

dBASE III PLUS only

USAGE

To build additional security beyond the basic file protection scheme, you can use the ACCESS( ) function to prevent users from accessing particular programs in the system.

EXAMPLES

The following procedure determines whether a user can access a program.

```
PROCEDURE TestFrst
PARAMETERS ProgName,Required
   IF ACCESS() <= Required
      DO &ProgName
   ELSE
      ? CHR(7)
      a 20,2 SAY "Access to this function denied."
      ?
      WAIT
   ENDIF
RETURN
```

The name of the program that the user requested to run, along with the minimum access level required to run the program, are passed to the procedure as parameters. For example, the following command, in conjunction with the TestFrst procedure, denies access to the AddNew.prg program to any user with an access level greater than 3.

DO TestFrst WITH "AddNew",3

TIPS

To encode command files to prevent unauthorized tampering (so that files cannot be viewed or modified at all), you can use the Runtime+ package, which comes with the dBASE III PLUS package, or one of the commercial compilers available: Clipper, from Nantucket, Inc., in Culver City, California; or Quicksilver, from WordTech Systems in Orinda, California.

SEE ALSO

LOGOUT

The DISPLAY USERS Command
Displaying a List of Logged-On Users

DISPLAY USERS identifies workstations on the network that are currently logged into dBASE.

SYNTAX

DISPLAY USERS

VERSION

dBASE III PLUS only

USAGE

DISPLAY USERS lists the network-assigned names of all workstations currently logged into dBASE and places an arrow (>) next to the currently logged user (the workstation that issued the DISPLAY USERS command).

EXAMPLES

The DISPLAY USERS command might display a list like the following:

Computer Name
>Station1
  Station4
  Station6
  Station8

In this example, the DISPLAY USERS command was issued from the workstation named Station1.

TIPS

Before uninstalling the dBASE ADMINISTRATOR from a hard disk, use the DISPLAY USERS command to make sure no one is still logged onto dBASE.

SEE ALSO

DISPLAY STATUS

The FLOCK( ) Function
Attempting to Lock a File

FLOCK( ) attempts to lock a database file so a single user can make changes and avoid collisions with other users.

SYNTAX

FLOCK( )

VERSION

dBASE III PLUS only

USAGE

The FLOCK( ) function acts partly as a function and partly as a command. FLOCK( ) attempts to lock the file for the current user. If it is successful, it returns the value .T. and locks the file. If it fails, it returns the value .F. and does not lock the file.

When a file is locked, other users on the network cannot access the file. Instead, they receive the error message *File is in use by another*. If an ON ERROR command is in effect, the ERROR( ) function returns the value 108. The lock remains in effect until an UNLOCK command, or another command that unlocks the file, is issued.

EXAMPLES

Procedure AccFile is a sample routine that attempts to lock a file for a specified period of time. If the attempted lock operation fails, the procedure suggests that the user try again later.

```
PROCEDURE AccFile
   a 24,1 SAY "Trying to access file..."

   *----- Try accessing for 100 loops.
   FCount = 1
   DO WHILE FCount <= 100 .AND. .NOT. FLOCK()
      FCount = FCount + 1
   ENDDO (fcount)
   *----- If still not available, present message.
   IF .NOT. FLOCK()
      a 24,1 SAY "File not available. Try again later!"
   ELSE
      a 24,1 CLEAR
   ENDIF (not flock())
RETURN
```

Procedure ErrTrap is an ON ERROR procedure that can respond to the error message *File is in use by another* (ERROR( ) number 108).

```
******************************** ErrTraps.PRG
*----- Sample procedure to trap common errors.
PROCEDURE ErrTrap
   a 19,0 CLEAR
   a 19,0 TO 19,79 DOUBLE
   ? CHR(7)

   DO CASE
      CASE ERROR = 108 .OR. ERROR = 109
         a 19,2 SAY "Trying to access data..."
            *---- Wait a few seconds.
```

```
Timer = 1
DO WHILE Timer <= 50
   Timer = Timer + 1
ENDDO
Attempts = Attempts + 1
IF Attempts <= 10
   RETRY
ELSE
   a 19,2 SAY "Still can't get access."
   a 21,2 SAY "Try again later..."
   RETURN
ENDIF

*---- Additional CASES for ON ERROR may follow...

   ENDCASE
RETURN
```

The following routine demonstrates the error-trapping procedure.

```
SET PROCEDURE TO ErrTRaps
Attempts = 0
USE AnyFile INDEX AnyFile
*-- If Attempts reached 10, file/record not accessed.
IF Attempts > = 10  WAIT
RETURN TO MASTER
ENDIF
```

TIPS

Use FLOCK( ) for operations that involve global editing, such as a REPLACE ALL command or a DO WHILE loop that automatically changes the values in a group of records. When editing a single record with the READ command, use the RLOCK( ) function instead.

SEE ALSO

RLOCK( )
UNLOCK

The LOCK( ) Function
Attempting to Lock a Record

See the RLOCK( ) function later in this chapter.

The LOGOUT Command
Logging the User Out of the Network

LOGOUT logs out the current user and allows a new user to log in.

SYNTAX

LOGOUT

VERSION

dBASE III PLUS only

USAGE

LOGOUT forces a user to log out of the system and then redisplays the initial dBASE ADMINISTRATOR login prompt for a new user to log in. The login prompt waits for the new login name, group name, and password, as defined in the dBASE PROTECT program.

LOGOUT closes all open database and related files at the current workstation.

In a single-user system or in a system where no security system has been created with the PROTECT program, the LOGOUT command is ignored.

EXAMPLES

When the user exits the following main menu program, the program automatically logs the current user out and brings up a login screen for a new user. (See the "Examples" section under ACCESS( ) for the TestFrst procedure accessed in this program.)

```
******************************************* MainMenu.prg.
SET TALK OFF
NewUser = .T.
DO WHILE NewUser
   Choice = 0
   DO WHILE Choice < 4
      CLEAR
      TEXT
                     Main Menu

               1. Add new records
               2. Edit records
               3. Print Reports
               4. Exit
      ENDTEXT
      a 20,1 SAY "Enter choice " GET Choice PICT "aZ 9"
      READ

      DO CASE

         CASE Choice = 1 .
            *--- Only users with access levels <= 3.
            Do TestFrst WITH "AddNew",3

         CASE Choice = 2
            *--- Only users with access levels <= 3.
            DO TestFrst WITH "EditDel",3

         CASE Choice = 3
            *--- Only users with access levels <= 6.
            DO TestFrst WITH "PrintRep",6
      ENDCASE
   ENDDO (Choice < 4)
   LOGOUT   &&--- Log out the current user,
            &&--- and wait for a new one.
ENDDO (newuser)
```

When the new login screen appears, the new user is given three attempts to log in correctly. If the user fails to do so within three attempts, the program ends. (Optionally, the user can press Esc to leave the login screen and terminate the program.)

TIPS

Including a LOGOUT command within a DO WHILE loop ensures that a new user is brought into the same program that the previous user left. To prevent a user from automatically accessing the program that was in effect when the previous user logged out, place the LOGOUT command outside of the loop that controls the main menu.

The RLOCK( ) and LOCK( ) Functions

Attempting to Lock a Record

RLOCK( ) attempts to lock a single database record for editing.

SYNTAX

RLOCK( )

or

LOCK( )

VERSION

dBASE III PLUS only

RLOCK( ) and LOCK( ) are identical functions, though RLOCK( ) is preferred because it is clearer in meaning and less likely to be confused with FLOCK( ) by other programmers who work on your programs.

Using RLOCK( ) is the most efficient way to lock a record for editing, because other users still have access to other records in the file while the record lock is in place.

Though RLOCK( ) is a function, it behaves as a command in some ways because it performs an action. When a user attempts to lock a record, the RLOCK( ) function returns .T. if the record is available for locking and immediately locks the record. If the record is already locked by another user, RLOCK( ) returns .F. and does not lock the record.

If the RLOCK( ) function is successful, no other user can access the record until the record is unlocked. Instead, other users attempting to access that record receive the error message *Record is in use by another*. If an ON ERROR condition is in effect, the ERROR( ) function returns the value 109.

EXAMPLES

AccRec is a sample procedure that attempts to lock a record for a specific period of time. If the locking operation fails for the duration of the attempt, the procedure suggests that the user try again later.

```
PROCEDURE AccRec
   a 24,1 SAY "Trying to access record..."

   *----- Try accessing for 50 loops.
   RCount = 1
   DO WHILE RCount <= 50 .AND. .NOT. RLOCK()
      RCount = RCount + 1
   ENDDO (rcount)
   *----- If still not available, present message.
   IF .NOT. RLOCK()
      a 24,1 SAY "Record not available. Try again later!"
   ELSE
      a 24,1 CLEAR
   ENDIF (not rlock())
RETURN
```

The examples for the FLOCK entry show an ON ERROR procedure that responds to error 109, *Record is in use by another*, and a sample routine for calling the procedure.

TIPS

Use the RLOCK( ) function to lock a single record during editing with @...SAY...GET and READ commands or with a REPLACE command that accesses a single record. Use FLOCK( ) to lock an entire file when global editing is required.

SEE ALSO

FLOCK( )
UNLOCK

The SET ENCRYPTION Command
Enabling or Disabling File Encryption

SET ENCRYPTION determines whether a newly created (or copied) database file is encrypted.

SYNTAX

SET ENCRYPTION ON/OFF

where the default value is ON in a protected network environment.

VERSION

dBASE III only

USAGE

After the PROTECT program has been used to set up a security scheme, all database and index files are automatically encrypted so that users who do not have appropriate access levels cannot view the data. Users who log in with an appropriate access level (via the login name, group name, and password) will have access to the file in decrypted form.

To create a decrypted copy of a file for a single-user system or for storage on a floppy disk as a backup file, use the SET ENCRYPTION OFF command before copying the file. Only users who have complete access to all database records and fields (as defined in the user profile through the PROTECT program) will be able to make exact copies of files in decrypted form. This limitation exists because the copy operation is limited to the files and fields that the particular user has access to. A user who has no access to certain fields cannot produce a decrypted file containing those fields.

EXAMPLES

The following routine makes a decrypted backup copy of a database file, assuming that the user has an access level of 1 or 2. The backup copy of the file is stored on the disk in drive A.

```
IF ACCESS( ) < = 2
    USE Master
    SET ENCRYPTION OFF
    COPY TO A:Master
    SET ENCRYPTION ON
ENDIF
```

Note that a MODIFY STRUCTURE command can be used only with a decrypted file. Therefore, to modify the structure of a database file, you must make a decrypted copy of the file and modify the copied file. Then you can rename the file with the new structure using the original file name, as follows:

```
SET ENCRYPTION OFF
USE Master EXCLUSIVE
COPY TO Temp
USE Temp EXCLUSIVE
MODIFY STRUCTURE
ERASE Master.dbf
RENAME Temp.dbf TO Master.dbf
```

TIPS

All files in a single group (as defined in the PROTECT program) share the same encryption key, whereas files of differing groups have different encryption keys. Therefore, you cannot decrypt a file that is not within the group that you are currently logged into.

To export encrypted files to other software systems, the SET ENCRYPTION OFF command can be used prior to a COPY command with the option DELIMITED, SDF, DIF, PSF, SYLK, or WKS.

The SET EXCLUSIVE Command
Opening a Database File for Exclusive Use

SET EXCLUSIVE establishes the file-open attribute for all succeeding USE commands.

SYNTAX

SET EXCLUSIVE ON/OFF

where ON is the default value.

VERSION

dBASE III PLUS only

USAGE

When SET EXCLUSIVE is on, all opened files can be used only by the user who opened the files. Other users will receive the error message *File is in use by another* if they attempt to access the same database file.

When SET EXCLUSIVE is off, the database file is opened in shared mode, and other users in the network will have access to the same database file. In this situation, the programmer needs to use file and record locking to avoid collisions among simultaneous users of the database.

The following commands require exclusive use of the database file: INSERT [BLANK], MODIFY STRUCTURE, PACK, REINDEX, ZAP.

EXAMPLES

The following commands open the Master database in work area A for shared access by all users and the Charges database in work area B for exclusive use by the current user.

```
SET EXCLUSIVE OFF
SELECT A
USE Master INDEX PartNo
SELECT B
SET EXCLUSIVE ON
USE Charges INDEX ChrgNo
```

TIPS

In a single-user environment, all files are opened in SET EXCLUSIVE ON mode. If a SET EXCLUSIVE OFF command is issued in a single-user environment, the command is ignored.

The UNLOCK Command

Releasing a File Lock

UNLOCK releases any currently active file or record lock on a shared file so that other users can have access to that file or record.

SYNTAX

UNLOCK *[ALL]*

where the optional ALL parameter releases all current locks in all work areas.

VERSION

dBASE III PLUS only

USAGE

When one user locks a record or a file to perform an update operation with a READ or REPLACE command, other users in the network lose access to that file or record. To return access to other users, an UNLOCK command must be issued. (Note, however, that the commands CLOSE, USE, CLEAR ALL, and QUIT will also unlock a file.)

EXAMPLES

The following commands attempt to replace data in a single record by first locking the record. If the REPLACE command is successful, the UNLOCK command immediately unlocks the record for use by others.

```
GOTO 21
IF RLOCK( )
    REPLACE Unit_Price WITH Unit_Price * 1.10
    UNLOCK
ELSE
    ? "Can't access record right now..."
ENDIF
```

TIPS

Use UNLOCK immediately after editing is completed to ensure that other users have quick access to a previously locked record or file.

SEE ALSO

FLOCK( )
RLOCK( )

20

Commands for Running External Programs

The dBASE program has the ability to call subroutines written in assembly language. This is useful if you want your program to do something that the dBASE language doesn't provide for or to perform some task at a much faster speed than dBASE can achieve on its own. Some examples of applications for assembly language subroutines include music or sound effects, data logging from special-purpose hardware, specialized mathematical calculations, animated color graphics, high-speed data communication, and control of laboratory experiments.

You can also run programs that are external to dBASE, such as word processors, spreadsheets, and DOS commands, by using the RUN or ! command. This chapter discusses the commands used to load and call assembly language subroutines and to run external programs from within dBASE.

The CALL Command

Executing an Assembly Language Subroutine

CALL executes an assembly language (binary) module that has already been loaded into RAM.

CALL *module name* **WITH** *parameter*

where *module name* is the name of the assembly language module, and *parameter* is a character string being passed to the module.

dBASE III PLUS only

The optional WITH portion of the CALL command passes the starting address of a character string memory variable stored in RAM. This starting address is stored in the DS:BX register.

The assembly language subroutine can change the contents of the string or shorten the string by replacing some of its characters with zeros, but it cannot increase the length of the string.

The following source code is an assembly language subroutine named Demo.asm.

```
; DEMO.ASM - simple assembly language demo for dBASE
; modifies a string passed by dBASE III PLUS

mdstrng        segment        byte
       assume  cs:mdstrng

modstring      proc    far
       mov     [bx+4], byte ptr 'B'    ; write "BOY" in string
       mov     [bx+5], byte ptr 'O'
       mov     [bx+6], byte ptr 'Y'
       ret

modstring      endp

mdstrng        ends
               end
```

After creating this subroutine with a standard text editor like the dBASE MODIFY COMMAND editor and converting it to a binary file using the DOS MASM, LINK, and EXE2BIN programs, you can call it with a routine, as follows:

LOAD Demo   **&& Assumes Demo.bin.**
String = "The cat went to the market."
CALL Demo WITH String
? String

After dBASE runs these commands, the screen displays the message *The BOY went to the market.* (The assembly language subroutine inserted the word BOY into the string through the [bx+4], [bx+5], and [bx+6] memory addresses using the assembly language mov command).

TIPS ═══════════════════════

The DISPLAY STATUS and LIST STATUS commands show the names of all assembly language modules currently loaded into RAM.

SEE ALSO ═══════════════════════

LOAD
RELEASE MODULE
RUN

The LOAD Command

Loading an Assembly Language Subroutine into RAM

LOAD copies an assembly language subroutine into RAM, where it can be executed with a CALL command.

SYNTAX

LOAD *file name*

where *file name* is the name of the assembly language module to load.

VERSION

dBASE III PLUS only

USAGE

LOAD assumes that the assembly language subroutine has been converted to a binary file with the DOS EXE2BIN program, which produces a file with the extension .bin. To create assembly language subroutines, you'll also need the IBM or Microsoft Macro Assembler (MASM), which does not come with your DOS package, and the LINK.EXE and EXE2BIN.EXE programs, which do come with DOS.

Up to five assembly language subroutines can be loaded into RAM at once, each with a maximum length of 32,000 bytes.

EXAMPLES

The following commands load two assembly language subroutines named MyMod1.bin and MyMod2.bin into RAM.

LOAD MyMod1
LOAD MyMod2

To execute the subroutines, use the commands CALL MyMod1 or CALL MyMod2.

TIPS

The DISPLAY STATUS and LIST STATUS commands show the names of all assembly language modules currently loaded in RAM.

SEE ALSO

CALL
RELEASE MODULE
RUN

The RELEASE MODULE Command

Clearing an Assembly Language Subroutine

RELEASE MODULE removes an assembly language subroutine from RAM.

SYNTAX

RELEASE MODULE *module name*

where *module name* is the name of an assembly language subroutine in RAM.

VERSION

dBASE III PLUS only

USAGE

If the named module has not already been loaded into RAM, the command simply displays the error message *File was not LOADed.* Unlike the RELEASE command used with memory variables, RELEASE MODULE does not support wild-card characters. For example, you cannot use the command RELEASE MODULE LIKE M★ to release all assembly language subroutines that begin with the letter M.

EXAMPLES

The following command removes an assembly language subroutine named MyMod1 from RAM.

RELEASE MODULE MyMod1

TIPS

If a particular application requires more than the maximum five assembly language subroutines, you can use RELEASE MODULE to delete from RAM a module that is not required at the moment. Then use LOAD to load another module in its place.

The DISPLAY STATUS and LIST STATUS commands show the names of all assembly language modules currently loaded into RAM.

SEE ALSO

LOAD
CALL
RUN

The RUN and ! Commands
Running an External Program

RUN executes an external command or program from within dBASE.

SYNTAX

RUN *command*
! *command*

where *command* is the DOS command or the name of the external program to run.

VERSION

dBASE III PLUS and dBASE III

USAGE

RUN and the equivalent ! command execute an external DOS command or an external program and then return control to the dBASE dot prompt when the external task is completed.

RUN requires additional memory beyond the minimum 256K required by dBASE. An additional 17K, plus whatever memory is required by the external program, is necessary. If there is insufficient memory to run the external program, RUN returns the error message *Insufficient memory* and redisplays the dot prompt.

The DOS Command.com file must be in the drive and directory stored in the DOS COMSPEC parameter. In most cases, this is automatic, and the programmer need not be concerned about it. However, if Command.com is not available, the DOS SET command can be used to define the location of Command.com. For example, the DOS command SET COMSPEC = C:\Command-.com informs DOS that the command processor is stored in the root directory of drive C under the usual file name Command.com.

You can also temporarily exit dBASE back to the DOS prompt if you know the location of the DOS Command.com program, or if you have included the drive for the Command.com program in your PATH command. (To determine the drive and directory location of Command.com, enter **? GETENV("COMMAND.COM")** at the dBASE dot prompt.)

To exit dBASE temporarily to DOS, enter the RUN or ! command with the drive, directory, and Command.com file name. For example, if Command.com is stored in the root directory of drive C (which has no directory name), enter **RUN C:\Command**. The DOS prompt will appear on your screen. From here, you can execute *any* DOS command or run any other program. Be forewarned, however, that if you load any memory-resident programs while in DOS, enough memory may not remain to return you to dBASE. If this occurs, you may lose some data. (To be safe, close all files in dBASE before issuing the RUN Command command.)

To return to dBASE from the DOS prompt, enter **EXIT** at the DOS prompt.

EXAMPLES

The following commands allow the user to reset the DOS system date and time from within dBASE.

RUN Date
RUN Time

| TIPS |

You can use RUN or ! to access an external word processor for editing command files without leaving dBASE.

Keep in mind that some DOS commands, such as PRINT and ASSIGN, remain in memory after being run. If only limited memory is available, enough memory may not be left for dBASE to resume processing. When this is the case, these DOS commands should be run before dBASE is used.

Configuring
and Starting
dBASE III PLUS

This appendix provides a general overview of dBASE III PLUS. It begins with some basic information about configuring DOS for dBASE and getting dBASE up and running. Then it discusses the various modes of operation within dBASE. From there, it focuses on the more technical details of dBASE.

Configuring DOS for dBASE III PLUS

Although dBASE allows a maximum of 15 files to be open simultaneously, DOS does not provide enough file handles for this in its default state. To remedy this situation, you need to alter or create the file named Config.sys on your startup disk. (On a floppy disk system, this would be the disk you use to boot your computer. On a hard disk system, this would be the root directory.)

To see the contents of the Config.sys file, issue the DOS TYPE command. Log onto the disk from which you usually boot your computer, and at the DOS A> or C> prompt enter **TYPE Config.sys** and press Return. If there is no Config.sys file, you'll need to create one. If there is one, it should specify at least 20 files and 15 buffers, as follows:

```
FILES = 20
BUFFERS = 15
```

You can use any word processor or text editor (including the dBASE MODIFY COMMAND editor discussed in Chapter 12, "Programming Commands") to alter or create the Config.sys file. Just be sure that you store the resulting file on the disk or directory you use to boot the system.

If there is no Config.sys file on your startup disk, you can quickly create it with the COPY command. At the DOS prompt, type **COPY CON Config.sys** and press Return. Type the lines

```
FILES = 20
BUFFERS = 15
```

pressing Return once after each line. Next press F6 (or Ctrl-Z, whichever displays ^ Z on the screen) and Return. When the DOS A> or C> prompt reappears, you're done. To verify that you've created the file, enter **TYPE Config.sys** once again at the A> or C> prompt. You should see the FILES and BUFFERS commands in the file exactly as you typed them. The Config.sys file settings will take effect *after* you reboot your computer and will remain in effect when you start your computer again.

Be forewarned that dBASE III PLUS will run even without the proper settings in the Config.sys file. However, if the FILES setting in the Config.sys file is less than 20, the error message *Too many files are open* will appear before you reach the dBASE maximum of 15 open files.

Initial Settings

The dBASE III PLUS System Disk #1 contains a file named Config.db, which you can modify to change the initial default settings in dBASE III PLUS. (When installed on a hard disk system, the Config.db file is on the same directory as dBASE itself.) Initially, the Config.db file contains only the commands

```
STATUS = ON
COMMAND = ASSIST
```

which ensure that dBASE begins with the status bar on and the Assistant menu showing. (If you were to remove these two commands, dBASE III PLUS would start with a dot prompt only, like earlier versions of dBASE.)

You can use any word processor in ASCII text mode or the dBASE MODIFY COMMAND editor to change the Config.db file to new settings.

Keywords Used in the Config.db File

Table A.1 lists the commands that Config.db recognizes (excluding the SET parameters, which are discussed later), along with a description of what each command does.

SET Parameters Used in Config.db

You can set most of the dBASE SET parameters in the Config.db file to establish their status before the dBASE dot prompt appears. The SET parameters recognized by Config.db, along with the values you can assign to them, are listed in Table A.2. (Chapter 17, "SET Commands," discusses each of these parameters in detail.) Note that the syntax used with SET parameters in the Config.db file is different from that used in dBASE commands. Whereas dBASE commands use the syntax SET *parameter* TO *setting*, Config.db uses the syntax *parameter* = *setting*. Hence, where dBASE uses the command SET TALK OFF, Config.db uses TALK = OFF.

A Sample Config.db File

The following sample Config.db file demonstrates the proper syntax for the various commands.

```
COLOR = GR+/B,W+/RB,BG+
DEFAULT = C
PATH = C:\DBFILES\FW
```

```
TEDIT = WORD
WP = WS
F9 = "DISPLAY STRUCTURE;"
F10 = "DISPLAY STATUS;"
PROMPT = Command:>
HELP = OFF
TALK = OFF
COMMAND = DO MyProg
```

KEYWORD	**EFFECTS**
COMMAND	Any command listed with this option is executed the moment dBASE III PLUS begins. Therefore, the COMMAND = ASSIST line in Config.db causes the Assistant menu to appear the moment dBASE III PLUS is started.
BUCKET	Specifies the amount of memory allocated for PICTURE and RANGE commands. The default setting is 2, which stands for 2 × 1024 bytes.
GETS	Specifies the number of @...SAY...GET statements that can be active at any one time. The default setting is 128.
MAXMEM	Specifies the amount of memory preserved when dBASE III PLUS executes an external program. The default value is 256K bytes.
MVARSIZ	Specifies the amount of space allocated for storing memory variables. The default value is 6000 bytes (approximately 6K).
PROMPT	Specifies the dBASE III PLUS prompt, which appears as a dot (.) by default.
TEDIT	Specifies an external word processor to be used in place of MODIFY COMMAND.
WP	Specifies an external word processor to be used with memo fields.

Table A.1: Commands Used in the Config.db File

SET KEYWORD	VALUES
ALTERNATE	*file name*
BELL	ON/OFF
CARRY	ON/OFF
CATALOG	*file name*
CENTURY	ON/OFF
COLOR	*color codes*
CONFIRM	ON/OFF
CONSOLE	ON/OFF
DEBUG	ON/OFF
DECIMALS	*0 to 14*
DEFAULT	*drive designator*
DELETED	ON/OFF
DELIMITER	ON/OFF
DELIMITER	*one or two characters*
DEVICE	SCREEN/PRINT
ECHO	ON/OFF
ESCAPE	ON/OFF
EXACT	ON/OFF
F<number>	*function-key commands*
HEADING	ON/OFF
HELP	ON/OFF
HISTORY	*0 to 16000*
INTENSITY	ON/OFF
MARGIN	*1 to 254*
MEMOWIDTH	*0 to 80*

Table A.2: SET Parameters Recognized by Config.db

SET KEYWORD	VALUES
MENU	ON/OFF
PATH	*path name*
PRINT	ON/OFF
SAFETY	ON/OFF
SCOREBOARD	ON/OFF
STATUS	ON/OFF
STEP	ON/OFF
TALK	ON/OFF
TYPEAHEAD	*0 to 32000*
UNIQUE	ON/OFF
VIEW	*file name*

***Table A.2: SET Parameters Recognized by Config.db
(continued)***

The sample Config.db file has the following effects:

1. The COLOR = GR+/B,W+/RB,BG+ command causes
   dBASE to start with yellow letters (GR+) on a blue background (B) for the standard screen, with white letters (W+) on
   a magenta background (RB) where reverse video is used. The
   screen border will be light blue (BG+).

2. DEFAULT = C specifies drive C as the default drive for storing and searching for files.

3. PATH = C:\DBFILES\FW tells dBASE to follow a route
   when looking for files. If dBASE cannot find a file on the current directory, it will search the DBFILES and FW directories
   for the file.

4. TEDIT = WORD causes dBASE to access Microsoft Word
   rather than the usual dBASE III PLUS MODIFY COMMAND
   editor. (This command requires more than 256K RAM.)

5. WP = WS causes dBASE to run WordStar when the user

enters Ctrl-PgDn to enter or edit a memo field. (This command requires more than 256K RAM.)

6. F9 = "DISPLAY STRUCTURE;" and F10 = "DISPLAY STATUS;" assign the commands DISPLAY STRUCTURE and DISPLAY STATUS to function keys F9 and F10, respectively. The semicolon in the commands tells dBASE to perform a carriage return after the command (the equivalent of the user pressing the Return key).

7. PROMPT = Command: > causes dBASE to display the prompt *Command:* > instead of the usual dot prompt.

8. HELP = OFF turns the SET HELP parameter to the OFF setting.

9. TALK = OFF turns the SET TALK parameter to the OFF setting.

10. COMMAND = DO MyProg causes dBASE to run a program named MyProg.prg, which presumably already exists on the disk.

Neither the status bar nor the Assistant menu appear when dBASE is first started, because the original STATUS = ON and COMMAND = ASSIST commands have been removed from the Config.db file.

Your Config.db file will not have any effect until dBASE is started from the DOS A > or C > prompt. Therefore, if you create a Config.db file using the MODIFY COMMAND editor, you'll have to quit dBASE and then start it again to see the effects of the file.

Installing dBASE III PLUS

Different versions of dBASE require different installation procedures. For example, the copy-protected version 1.0 of dBASE III PLUS uses a different installation procedure than the non-copy-protected version 1.1. Furthermore, networks require still other installation procedures.

For information about installing your particular version of dBASE, refer to the dBASE user's manual. That way, you'll be sure to get the proper information for your computer and your needs.

Starting dBASE

After installing dBASE on your computer, you can get it up and running with a single command. However, instructions for starting dBASE vary somewhat, depending on whether your computer has a hard disk.

Starting from a Hard Disk

Assuming you've already installed dBASE III PLUS on your computer and it is already booted up (the C> prompt is displayed), you first need to log onto the appropriate directory using the DOS CD\ command. Then enter **dBASE** at the DOS prompt. You'll see a copyright notice and instructions to press Return to continue. After pressing Return, you'll see the dBASE Assistant menu.

Starting from Floppy Disks

If you are using a computer with floppy disks and no hard disk, first boot up in the usual fashion (using your DOS disk or a copy of it). Be sure that the floppy disk that you boot up from has the appropriate Config.sys file on it, as discussed above.

After the A> prompt appears on your screen, place the dBASE System Disk #1 in drive A and type **dBASE**. Press Return. You'll see a copyright notice. Press Return to continue. You'll see a message telling you to place dBASE System Disk #2 in drive A. Remove the disk currently in drive A, insert System Disk #2, and press Return. You'll see the dBASE Assistant menu when dBASE is fully loaded and ready to run.

Leaving dBASE

Whenever you've finished a session with dBASE III PLUS, you should always exit dBASE back to the DOS prompt before turning off your computer. (Failure to do so may result in a loss of data.) To exit dBASE, simply enter **QUIT** at the dBASE dot prompt and press Return. To exit dBASE from the Assistant menu, highlight Set Up on the top menu and select Quit dBASE III PLUS from the pull-down menu. When the DOS prompt (usually A > or C >) reappears, all of your data are saved on disk, and you may safely remove any disks and turn off the computer.

DBASE Operating Modes

Because dBASE III PLUS is designed for a wide range of users, it offers three basic modes of user interaction: assist mode, interactive (or dot prompt) mode, and programming language mode.

Assist Mode

When run in its off-the-shelf configuration, dBASE always begins by displaying the Assistant menu at the top of the screen. The Assistant menu allows you to select major categories of commands (using the arrow keys and the Return key) and then build commands from the pull-down menus that appear beneath each menu item as it is highlighted. Chapter 1 discusses the Assistant menu and the associated ASSIST command in more detail.

Interactive Dot Prompt Mode

The dot prompt is the dBASE "ready-to-accept-commands" signal. At the dot prompt you can enter any valid dBASE command, and dBASE will attempt to interpret and execute the command immediately. To leave assist mode and work interactively with dBASE at the dot prompt, press the Esc key at any time while the menu is showing. To return to assist mode from the dot prompt, enter **ASSIST** and press Return.

The interactive dot prompt mode is valuable for programming: It lets you test procedures that you want to use in a program, develop screen and report formats, and perform other tasks that help in the overall development of custom applications.

When in dot prompt mode, you can remove the status bar from the bottom of the screen by entering **SET STATUS OFF** and pressing Return. To return the status bar to the screen, enter **SET STATUS ON**.

The status bar and assist mode can also be controlled through the Config.db file.

dBASE as a Programming Language

Beyond the dBASE assist and dot prompt modes is the dBASE III PLUS programming language. This programming language allows you to develop custom applications to perform specific jobs such as keeping payroll or accounts receivable records. To create custom applications (with dBASE *programs* or *command files*), you can use the dBASE MODIFY COMMAND editor or any other word processor, as discussed in Chapter 12, "Programming Commands."

dBASE III PLUS Basics

Table A.3 summarizes the technical specifications and limitations of dBASE III PLUS that you will want to keep in mind while using dBASE. The remainder of this introduction discusses general background information about dBASE III PLUS. (Specifications for dBASE III are the same.)

Data Types

When you store information in databases or memory variables, the data must be one of four data types: character, numeric, date, or logical. In addition, database files can store data in memo fields. The various data types are summarized here.

- The character data type is used to store nonnumeric types of information, such as names and addresses. The maximum length of a character string is 254 characters.

- The numeric data type can store numbers up to 19 digits long (including the plus or minus sign and decimal point). Numeric accuracy is to 15.9 digits, excluding the decimal point, which means that the 15 most significant digits in the number will be reliable. When comparing nonzero numbers (with operators such as $<$ and $>$), numeric accuracy is to 13 digits. Although dBASE cannot display numbers with more than 19 digits, you can store and manipulate much larger numbers in variables. The largest allowable number in dBASE III PLUS is 10^{308}. The smallest positive number is 10^{-307}.

DATABASE FILE LIMITATIONS

- 1 billion records per file maximum
- 128 fields or 4,000 bytes maximum record size (additional 512K in memo fields)
- Maximum length of field names: 10 characters
- 128 fields per record maximum
- 4,000 bytes per record maximum

DATA LIMITATIONS

- Character data: 0–254 characters
- Numeric data: 19 bytes maximum length
- Date data: always requires 8 bytes
- Logical data: always requires 1 byte in database, 2 bytes in memory
- Memo fields: 5,000 bytes or the capacity of external word processor

FILES OPEN SIMULTANEOUSLY

- All types: 15 files total, including database, index, command, procedure, format, and other files
- Database files: 10 maximum; database with memo fields counts as 2 open files
- Index files: 7 per open database file
- Format files: 1 per open database file

MEMORY VARIABLES

- 256 maximum memory variables active in RAM, or 6,000 bytes (modifiable through Config.db)

Table A.3: dBASE Technical Specifications

COMMAND FILES

- 254 characters maximum command line length
- 5,000 characters maximum command file length if created and edited with built-in MODIFY COMMAND editor; otherwise, limited only by word processor used

NUMERIC ACCURACY

- Computational accuracy: 15.9 digits
- Accuracy for nonzero comparisons: 13 digits
- Largest number: 10^{308}
- Smallest positive number: 10^{-307}

Table A.3: dBASE Technical Specifications (continued)

- The date data type stores dates in mm/dd/yy format (the format can be modified). In most cases, dates are checked automatically for validity without programmer intervention. Date arithmetic is also supported. The date data type consumes 8 bytes of disk space.

- The logical data type stores one of two conditions: true (.T.) or false (.F.). Though always stored as .T. or .F., the true condition can be entered as .T., .t., .Y., or .y., and the false condition can be entered as .F., .f., .N., or .n. dBASE automatically converts any valid entry to the .T. or .F. equivalent. Each logical data type entry consumes 1 byte of disk space.

- Memo fields are stored in files outside of the actual dBASE database file. Memo fields cannot be stored in variables in main memory (RAM). The maximum length of a memo field is 4,000 characters, or whatever limit is imposed by an external word processor.

dBASE Databases

Database files store data that most dBASE commands operate upon. The data in database files is organized into records and fields. Theoretically, a database can have a maximum of one billion records or two billion bytes, whichever occurs first. However, the practical limitation of the size of a dBASE database on today's microcomputers is probably under 100,000 records when the size and speed of disk drives is taken into consideration.

Each database field must have a name that can be a maximum of 10 characters long, with no spaces. The only punctuation allowed in a field name is the underscore (_) character. Each record in a database file can contain a maximum of 128 fields or 4,000 bytes, whichever comes first. (Including memo fields, the maximum number of bytes in a record is 512K.)

The dBASE III PLUS program allows a maximum of 10 simultaneously open database files. Keep in mind that an open database that contains memo fields counts as two files. The number of open database files should not be confused with the 15 *total* files (of all types) that dBASE allows to be open simultaneously.

Memory Variables

All databases are stored on disk. In addition, data can be stored in RAM in *memory variables.* Memory variables are used as a sort of scratch pad to store values temporarily during the current session with dBASE.

Memory variable names follow the same rules as field names: a maximum of 10 characters, no spaces, and no punctuation except the underscore character (_). The same data types used in fields are allowed in memory variables, except for the memo data type. Memo fields are allowed only in database files. For a complete discussion of memory variables, see Chapter 14, "Commands for Memory Variables."

dBASE Operators

An operator is a symbol that performs an arithmetic or other operation or is used for logical comparisons. For example, the + operator means *add.* Operators are used in many situations in dBASE. For example, the command

    ? 2 + 3

means *display the results of 2 plus 3.* Relational operators, such as < (less than), can be used to find information that compares to some value. For example, the command

LIST FOR Salary < 10000

displays all records in which the Salary field contains a number less than 10,000.

The three types of dBASE operators (mathematical, relational, and logical) are summarized here and in Tables A.4 through A.6.

- Mathematical operators generally perform basic arithmetic on numeric values, though the + and − operators can be used with character strings, as outlined in Table A.4.

- Relational operators compare two values and result in one of

OPERATOR	FUNCTION
+	Adds two numbers or concatenates two character strings. For example, **3 + 5** produces 8. **"Hello " + "there"** produces "Hello there".
−	Subtracts two numbers or concatenates two character strings without any trailing blank spaces. For example, **10 − 6** produces 4. **"Hello " − "there"** produces "Hellothere".
*	Multiplies two numbers. For example, **20*2** produces 40.
/	Divides two numbers. For example, **40/2** produces 20.
^ or **	Exponentiation. For example, **3 ^ 3** produces 27, and **27**(1/3)** produces 3.
( )	Used for grouping. For example, **2*3 + 4** evaluates to 10, because multiplication takes precedence over addition. However, the expression **2*(3 + 4)** results in 14, because the addition inside the parentheses takes precedence over (occurs before) the multiplication.

Table A.4: Mathematical Operators

two possible outcomes: true (.T.) or false (.F.). Relational operators can be used to compare numeric, character, or date data types. However, both sides of the equation must be of the same data type. For example, you cannot compare character data to numeric data, or date data to character data. (However, there are many functions, discussed in Chapter 16, "dBASE Functions," that can convert data types so that you can perform logical comparisons among different data types.) The relational operators are listed in Table A.5.

- Logical operators produce a true or false result after comparing two or more expressions that use the mathematical or relational operators. The logical operators are listed in Table A.6.

Operator Precedence

When dBASE calculates expressions, it follows the standard order of precedence (as opposed to strict left-to-right order). For example, the expression 3 + 4 * 2 evaluates to 11 because the multiplication occurs first. The expression (3 + 4) * 2 evaluates to 14 because the parentheses take precedence. The order of precedence for mathematical operators is as follows:

1. Unary + (positive) and − (negative) signs
2. Exponentiation
3. Multiplication and division
4. Addition and subtraction

The order of precedence for logical operators is as follows:

1. .NOT.
2. .AND.
3. .OR.

Relational operators and operators that work on character strings follow no order of precedence. They are performed from left to right.

When an expression includes many different kinds of expressions, the order of precedence is mathematical, then relational, then logical. All operations at the same level of precedence are performed from left to right.

OPERATOR	FUNCTION
<	Less than. For example, **1** < **10** is true, **"A"** < **"B"** is true, and **12/31/86** < **01/01/87** is true.
>	Greater than. For example, **1** > **10** is false, **"A"** > **"B"** is false, and **12/31/86** > **01/01/87** is false.
=	Equal. For example, **1 = 1** is true, **"Smith" = "Jones"** is false, and **12/01/86 = 12/01/87** is false.
< > or #	Not equal. For example, **1** < > **10** is true, **1** < > **1** is false. The command **LIST FOR City # "San Diego"** lists all records in a database file where the field named City does not contain "San Diego".
< =	Less than or equal to. For example, **9** < = **10** is true. **"Adams"** < = **"Bowers"** is also true, because "Adams" is alphabetically less than "Bowers". The date expression **01/01/87** < = **12/31/86** is false, and the expression **10** < = **10** is true.
> =	Greater than or equal to. For example, **10** > = **9** is true, **"Bowers"** > = **"Adams"** is true, **12/31/86** > = **01/01/87** is false, and **10** > = **10** is true.
$	Character for comparing whether one character string is embedded in another. For example, **"dog" $ "Hot dog and a Coke"** is true, because the characters "dog" appear within the character string "Hot dog and a Coke". (See the UPPER and LOWER functions in Chapter 16 for techniques for handling upper- and lowercase distinctions.)

Table A.5: Relational Operators

OPERATOR	FUNCTION
.AND.	States that two things must be true. For example, **LIST FOR LName = "Smith" .AND. State = "NY"** displays all Smiths in the state of New York.
.OR.	States that one or two things must be true. For example, **LIST FOR Past_Due > = 90 .OR. Notice2** displays all records with a number greater than or equal to 90 in the Past_Due field, in addition to all records with .T. in the logical field named Notice2.
.NOT.	States that one thing must not be true (works with a single expression). For example, **LIST FOR .NOT. "Apple" $ Address** displays all records except those with the word Apple in the field named Address.
( )	Parentheses used for grouping logical expressions. For example, **LIST FOR LName = "Smith" .AND. (State = "NY" .OR. State = "NJ")** displays all Smiths in the states of New York and New Jersey.

Table A.6: Logical Operators

Although the rules of operator precedence might seem complex, they are actually designed to make the syntax of expressions intuitively obvious. For example, the command

LIST FOR X + Y < 10 .OR. X + Y > 20

will locate all records where the sum of X and Y is less than 10 or greater than 20. When in doubt about how dBASE will interpret an expression, you can specify precedence with parentheses, as follows:

LName = "Miller" .AND. (State = "CA" .OR. State = "NY")

Here, the parentheses cause the .OR. expression to be processed before the .AND. expression. Hence, the parentheses ensure that only Millers in the states of New York or California will be accessed. On the other hand, if you wanted to access all the Millers in the state of California and everyone (regardless of last name) in the state of New York, you could move the parentheses, as follows:

(LName = "Miller" .AND. State = "CA") .OR. State = "NY"

dBASE Files   A summary of the types of files that dBASE creates and manipulates, along with their default file names, is shown in Table A.7. Generally speaking, you assign the initial file name (eight characters with no spaces and only the underscore character allowed) whenever you enter the CREATE or MODIFY command to create the file. The dBASE program automatically adds the file-name extension. It also assumes the extension when it tries to locate a file.

FILE-NAME EXTENSION	TYPE OF FILE
.cat	Catalog files, used to store the names of files used in a single application, created by SET CATALOG TO command
.db	File for configuring dBASE at startup; always uses the full name Config.db
.dbf	Database files created with the CREATE command
.dbt	Database text files used to store memo fields
.fmt	Format files used to display custom data entry and editing screens, created by the CREATE/MODIFY SCREEN command
.frm	Report format files used to display formatted reports, created by the CREATE/MODIFY REPORT command

Table A.7: Types of dBASE Files

FILE-NAME EXTENSION	TYPE OF FILE
.lbl	Mailing label format files created by the CREATE/MODIFY LABEL command
.mem	Memory variables stored on disk with a SAVE command
.ndx	Index files used to maintain sort orders, expedite searches, and link related database files; created by the INDEX ON command
.prg	Command (program) files created with the CREATE/MODIFY COMMAND editor or an external word processor
.qry	Query files created with the CREATE/MODIFY QUERY command
.scr	Intermediate files between the MODIFY SCREEN editor and the finished format (.fmt) file
.txt	Text files created by the SET ALTERNATE command
.vue	View files created by the CREATE/MODIFY VIEW command

Table A.7: Types of dBASE Files (continued)

INDEX

Command Index

&& (dBASE III PLUS only), 178–179

*, 178–179

@ ... SAY ... GET ... PICTURE ... RANGE, 35–46

@ *row, col* component of, 36, 39

CLEAR component of, 35, 39, 44

GET component of, 37–38, 39, 45, 46–47

PICTURE component of, 35, 36, 38–39, 40–43, 45

RANGE component of, 35, 39, 44

SAY component of, 36–37, 39, 44

TO component of, 39, 44

!, 447–449

?, 65–66

??, 65–66

ACCEPT, 179–181

APPEND, 22–25

APPEND BLANK, 25–26

APPEND FROM, 26–30

ASSIST, 1–7

AVERAGE, 127–128

BROWSE, 84–87

CALL, 442–443

CANCEL, 232–233

CHANGE, 87, 423

CLEAR, 135–137

CLEAR GETS, 46–48

CLOSE, 138–139

CLOSE PROCEDURE, 208

CONTINUE, 114–115

COPY, 139–143

COPY TO component, 140–141

COPY FILE component, 142

COPY STRUCTURE component, 142

COPY TYPE component, 141

COPY STRUCTURE EXTENDED component, 142–143

COUNT, 129–130

CREATE, 12–16

CREATE COMMAND, 181

CREATE LABEL. *See* MODIFY LABEL

CREATE QUERY (dBASE III PLUS only), 119–123

CREATE REPORT. *See* MODIFY REPORT

CREATE VIEW (dBASE III PLUS only), 162–167

DELETE, 88–89

DIR, 144–145

DISPLAY, 145–147

DISPLAY MEMORY, 218–220

DISPLAY STATUS, 233–236, 423

DISPLAY STRUCTURE, 236–237

DISPLAY USERS, 427–428

DO, 181–183

DO CASE ... ENDCASE, 183–185

DO WHILE ... ENDDO, 186–188

DO WITH, 209–210

EDIT, 89–92, 423

EJECT, 66–67

ENDTEXT, 81–82

ERASE, 147–149

EXIT, 189–190

EXPORT (dBASE III PLUS only), 149–150

FIND, 115–117

GO, 150–152

GOTO, 150–152

HELP, 8–10

IF ... ELSE ... ENDIF, 190–193

IMPORT (dBASE III PLUS only), 31–32

INDEX, 101–109

INPUT, 194–195

INSERT, 32–33

JOIN, 167–168

LABEL FORM, 67–69

LIST, 152–154

LOAD, 444–445

LOCATE, 117–118

LOGOUT, 431–433

LOOP, 195–197

MODIFY COMMAND, 197–202

MODIFY LABEL, 69–72
MODIFY QUERY (dBASE III
PLUS only), 119–123
MODIFY REPORT (dBASE III
PLUS only), 73–78
MODIFY SCREEN (dBASE III
PLUS only), 48–59
MODIFY STRUCTURE, 154–155
MODIFY VIEW (dBASE III PLUS
only), 162–167
NOTE, 178–179
ON, 414–419
  ON ERROR component of,
  415–416
  ON ESCAPE component of, 415
  ON KEY component of, 415
PACK, 93–94
PARAMETERS, 210–212
PRIVATE, 220–221
PROCEDURE, 213–214
PUBLIC, 222–223
QUIT, 437
READ, 59–61
RECALL, 94–95
REINDEX, 110
RELEASE, 224–225
RELEASE MODULE, 445–447
RENAME, 155–156
REPLACE, 96–97
REPORT FORM, 79–81
RESTORE, 225–227
RESUME, 238
RETRY, 419–421
RETURN, 202–204
RUN, 447–449
SAVE, 227–228
SEEK, 123–125
SELECT (dBASE III PLUS only),
  168–171
SET, 343–344, 423–424
SET ALTERNATE, 344–346
SET ALTERNATE TO, 346–347
SET BELL, 347–348
SET CARRY, 348–350
SET CATALOG, 350–351
SET CATALOG TO, 351–353
SET CENTURY, 353–354
SET COLOR, 354–355
SET COLOR TO, 355–357

SET CONFIRM, 357–358
SET CONSOLE, 359–360
SET DATE, 360–361
SET DEBUG, 239–240
SET DECIMALS, 362–363
SET DEFAULT, 363–364
SET DELETED, 365–366
SET DELIMITERS, 366–367
SET DELIMITERS TO, 367–368
SET DEVICE, 368–369
SET DOHISTORY, 241–242
SET ECHO, 242–243
SET ENCRYPTION, 435–437
SET ESCAPE, 370–372
SET EXACT, 372–373
SET EXCLUSIVE, 437–438
SET FIELDS, 373–374
SET FIELDS TO, 374–376
SET FILTER, 376–378
SET FIXED, 378–379
SET FORMAT, 61–63
SET FUNCTION, 380–381
SET HEADING, 381–382
SET HELP, 383
SET HISTORY, 384–385
SET HISTORY TO, 385–386
SET INDEX, 386–387
SET INTENSITY, 388–389
SET MARGIN, 389–390
SET MEMOWIDTH, 390–391
SET MENU, 391–392
SET MESSAGE, 393–394
SET ODOMETER, 394–395
SET ORDER, 395–397
SET PATH, 397–398
SET PRINT, 398–399
SET PRINTER, 400–401, 424–425
SET PROCEDURE, 215–216
SET RELATION, 171–173
SET SAFETY, 402–403
SET SCOREBOARD, 403–404
SET STATUS, 404–405
SET STEP, 244–245
SET TALK, 406–407
SET TITLE, 407–408
SET TYPEAHEAD, 408–409
SET UNIQUE, 410–411
SET VIEW, 411–412
SKIP, 157–158

SORT, 111–112
STORE, 229–230
SUM, 130–132
SUSPEND, 245–247
TEXT, 81–82
TOTAL, 132–134
TYPE, 158–159
UNLOCK, 439–440
UPDATE, 174–176
USE, 17–20, 424
   ALIAS component of, 18–19
   INDEX component of, 18
WAIT, 204–206
ZAP, 98–99

Function Index

&, 249
ABS( ), 250–251
ACCESS( ), 251, 425–426
ASC( ), 251–252
AT( ), 252–253
BOF( ), 254–255
CDOW( ), 255–256
CHR( ), 256–257
CMONTH( ), 257–258
COL( ), 258–259
CTOD( ), 260–261
DATE( ), 261–262
DAY( ), 262–263
DBF( ), 263–264
DELETED( ), 264–265
DISKSPACE( ), 265–266
DOW( ), 267
DTOC( ), 268–269
EOF( ), 269–270
ERROR( ), 270–272
EXP( ), 272–273
FIELD( ), 273–274
FILE( ), 275–276
FKLABEL( ), 276–277
FKMAX( ), 277–278
FLOCK( ), 279, 428–430
FOUND( ), 279–280
GETENV( ), 280–281
IIF( ), 281–282

INKEY( ), 284–285
INT( ), 285
ISALPHA( ), 286–287
ISCOLOR( ), 287–288
ISLOWER( ), 288–289
ISUPPER( ), 289–290
LEFT( ), 290–291
LEN( ), 291–292
LOCK( ), 293, 433–435
LOG( ), 293–294
LOWER( ), 294–295
LTRIM( ), 295–296
LUPDATE( ), 296–297
MAX( ), 297–298
MESSAGE( ), 298–299
MIN( ), 299–300
MOD( ), 301
MONTH( ), 302
NDX( ), 303–304
OS( ), 304–305
PCOL( ), 305–306
PROW( ), 306–307
READKEY( ), 308–313
RECCOUNT( ), 313–314
RECNO( ), 314–315
RECSIZE( ), 315–316
REPLICATE( ), 317–318
RIGHT( ), 318–319
RLOCK( ), 319, 433–435
ROUND( ), 319–320
ROW( ), 321–322
RTRIM( ), 322–323
SPACE( ), 323–324
SQRT( ), 324–325
STR( ), 325–327
STUFF( ), 327–328
SUBSTR( ), 329–330
TIME( ), 330–331
TRANSFORM( ), 331–333
TRIM( ), 334–335
TYPE( ), 335–336
UPPER( ), 336–337
VAL( ), 338–339
VERSION( ), 339–340
YEAR( ), 340–341

SYBEX Computer Books
are different.

Here is why . . .

At SYBEX, each book is designed with you in mind. Every manuscript is carefully selected and supervised by our editors, who are themselves computer experts. We publish the best authors, whose technical expertise is matched by an ability to write clearly and to communicate effectively. Programs are thoroughly tested for accuracy by our technical staff. Our computerized production department goes to great lengths to make sure that each book is well-designed.

In the pursuit of timeliness, SYBEX has achieved many publishing firsts. SYBEX was among the first to integrate personal computers used by authors and staff into the publishing process. SYBEX was the first to publish books on the CP/M operating system, microprocessor interfacing techniques, word processing, and many more topics.

Expertise in computers and dedication to the highest quality product have made SYBEX a world leader in computer book publishing. Translated into fourteen languages, SYBEX books have helped millions of people around the world to get the most from their computers. We hope we have helped you, too.

For a complete catalog of our publications:

SYBEX, Inc. 2021 Challenger Drive, #100, Alameda, CA 94501
Tel: (415) 523-8233/(800) 227-2346   Telex: 336311